The Story of the World

ALSO BY SUSAN WISE BAUER

The Story of the World: History for the Classical Child
(WELL-TRAINED MIND PRESS)

Volume 1: Ancient Times (2006)
(REVISED EDITION)
Volume 2: The Middle Ages (2007)
(REVISED EDITION)
Volume 4: The Modern Age (2005)

The History of the Ancient World:
From the Earliest Accounts to the Fall of Rome
(W.W. NORTON, 2007)

The History of the Medieval World:
From the Conversion of Constantine to the First Crusade
(W.W. NORTON, 2010)

The History of the Renaissance World:
From the Rediscovery of Aristotle to the
Conquest of Constantinople
(W.W. NORTON, 2013)

The Well-Educated Mind:
A Guide to the Classical Education You Never Had
(REVISED EDITION, W. W. NORTON, 2016)

WITH JESSIE WISE

The Well-Trained Mind:
A Guide to Classical Education at Home
(REVISED EDITION, W. W. NORTON, 2016)

www.susanwisebauer.com

The Story of the World
History for the Classical Child

Volume 3: Early Modern Times
From Elizabeth the First to the Forty-Niners

Susan Wise Bauer

illustrations by Sarah Park

WELL-
TRAINED
MIND
PRESS

CHARLES CITY, VIRGINIA

Manufacturing by BookMasters, Inc.
Cover design by Andrew J. Buffington
Cover painting by James L. Wise, Jr.

Publisher's Cataloging-in-Publication

Bauer, S. Wise.
    The story of the world : history for the classical
child. Volume 3, Early modern times / by Susan Wise
Bauer ; [illustrations by Sarah Park and J. Wise].
    p. cm.
    Includes index.
    SUMMARY: History of the world from 1600 to 1850.
    Audience: Ages 5-11.
    LCCN 2003106804
    ISBN 0-9714129-9-5 (paper)
    ISBN 0-9728603-0-4 (hardback)

    1. History, Modern.   I. Park, Sarah. II. Wise, J.
(James L.) III. Title.

D209.B27 2003   909.08
              QBI03-200435

Well-Trained Mind Press, 18021 The Glebe Lane, Charles City, VA 23030
www.welltrainedmind.com
info@welltrainedmind.com

Contents

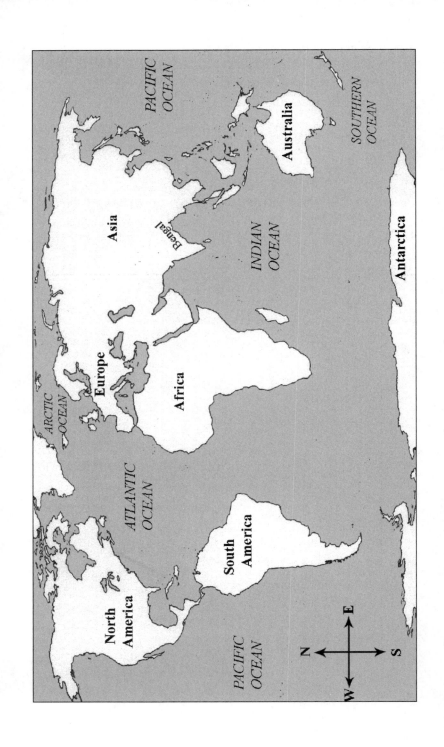

Introduction

Explorers discover treasure beneath mountain rocks. Pirates roam the seas. Kings huddle on their thrones, hoping that they will keep their crowns—and their heads. And adventurers sail around the world on tiny wooden ships, risking starvation and treacherous seas to find strange new lands.

Before you read these stories, you need to know a little bit about the world where they happened. The adventurers who sailed the sea in the year 1600 knew that huge oceans divided countries from each other—but they didn't know just how huge those oceans were. Today, we know that water covers almost three-quarters of the earth's surface. Geographers divide all this water into five oceans: Pacific, Atlantic, Indian, Southern, and Arctic. Here's a limerick to help you remember them:

The Pacific is largest of all,
The Indian starts at Bengal,
The Atlantic Ocean
Is always in motion,
The Arctic and Southern are small.

Between and around these oceans lie large *continents,* or masses of land. We divide the earth's dry land into seven continents: North America, South America, Africa, Europe, Asia, Australia, and Antarctica. You can remember them by memorizing this poem! Look at a globe while you read the poem, and move your finger along the path that the poem describes.

Start at Antarctica, way down south, a cold and icy spot,
Head north into Australia, where the sun shines bright and hot.
Keep going north, across the ocean, til you reach the land:
Now you're in Asia, where you'll find both ice and desert sand.
Turn west, and Europe's mountains soon will loom up into view,

In Europe you'll find Greeks and Germans, French and Spanish too!
 Go south from Europe, and you'll soon reach jungles and wide plains:
Zebras graze in Africa, and lions shake their manes.
Now follow the equator west, to South American shores,
You might see llamas here, along with jaguars and condors.
Go north across the central bridge of land beneath the sun,
You'll be in North America. Your continent trip is done!

The Empires of Ferdinand and Philip

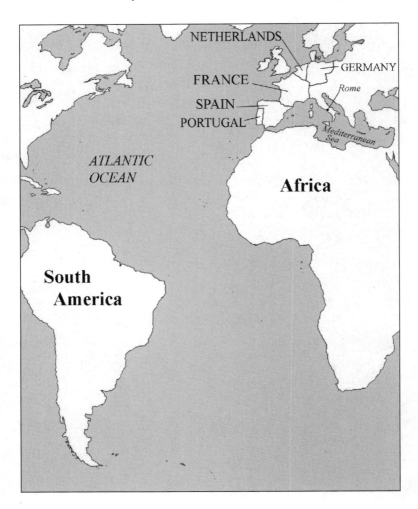

Chapter One
A World of Empires

The Holy Roman Empire

Imagine that you're a world traveler in the year 1600. You've spent the last twenty years journeying around the world. You've slept in Arabian tents, European palaces, and Native American longhouses. You've eaten fermented fish sauce in Rome, calf's-intestine pudding in England, sugar-coated beets in Wittenberg, and gilded boar's head in France. You only have two teeth left (the rest fell out because of scurvy and the sugared beets), and on your last journey to Iceland, you lost three toes to frostbite. You've been bitten by a camel in Asia, a cobra in India, and a water moccasin in North America.

In your travels around the world, you've seen two flags—one with a red cross on a white background, and the other bearing a two-headed eagle—all over the world. You've seen the red cross and the two-headed eagle in Spain and Portugal and all over Europe, from the Alps up to the soggy coast of the Netherlands. You've seen these flags flying over settlements in North America, South America, and even in the Philippines. No matter where you go, the red cross and the two-headed eagle are there!

The two kings who fly these flags, Philip II of Spain and Ferdinand I of the Holy Roman Empire, are nephew and uncle. And they rule over an enormous part of the world because of one very fortunate little boy.

A hundred years before our story begins, in the year 1500, this fortunate baby was born in a cold stone palace in northern Europe. His father was the king of the Netherlands. His grandfather ruled over lands in Germany. And his other grandfather was the king of Spain. This baby, who was named Charles, had three kings in his family!

When Charles was only six, his father died and Charles became king of the Netherlands. When he was sixteen, his Spanish grandfather died and left him the throne of Spain. When he was nineteen, his German grandfather died and he became king over the German lands. Charles was still a teenager—but he was a teenager with three thrones.

But Charles wanted even more. He wanted the title "Holy Roman Emperor."

Fifteen hundred years before Charles was born, the Roman Empire spread across Europe and down into Africa. Everyone who lived inside the empire's borders was expected to follow Rome's laws and to live in peace. This "Roman peace" lasted until barbarians invaded. Then the Roman empire collapsed.

For the next five hundred years, warring peoples fought with each other all over Europe—until a great king named Charlemagne came to the throne of France. Charlemagne conquered the nearby German lands and added them to his own territory. He passed laws to keep his kingdom peaceful. His empire became so large that the pope—the leader of the Christian church in the West, called the Catholic Church—held a special church service and proclaimed Charlemagne to be the Roman Emperor.

But the Roman empire had been destroyed centuries ago. So what did this mean?

It meant that Charlemagne's new empire would keep the peace over a large part of Europe, just as the Roman empire had done in ancient times. And since Charlemagne was a Christian, his new "Roman empire" could also spread Christianity through the world. That's why Charlemagne eventually became known as the *Holy* Roman Emperor.

Charles wanted to be known as the Holy Roman Emperor too. But first, he had to convince the pope to hold a special service proclaiming *him* Holy Roman Emperor! And the pope wasn't sure he wanted to give Charles this title—and the power that went along with it. Charles already ruled most of Europe. If Charles became even stronger, what would happen to the power of the pope?

The pope wasn't alone in his worries. The king of France was afraid that Charles might invade France. And the princes who ruled over Italy were also anxious to keep their independence from Charles. So the king of France, the pope, and the Italian princes all joined together to fight against Charles and his armies.

Charles wasn't discouraged. If he couldn't convince the pope to crown him emperor willingly, he would resort to force.

His strategy was simple—and shocking. For years, Charles had oppressed the Protestant Christians who lived in his territories. These Protestants believed that the Catholic church was corrupt and that the pope did not have the authority to tell all Christians how to worship and live. Charles had put Protestants in jail, taken away their land, and executed them. But Charles knew that these Protestants would be willing to fight against the Pope. So he hired an army of German Protestants and sent them, along with his own soldiers, to attack Rome!

Charles V

This angry army, called the "German Fury," marched down to Rome and surrounded it. The pope's soldiers were outnumbered. They fired a few shots from the walls with their old, battered cannons—but the invaders broke down the gates and streamed through the city. The pope and his soldiers retreated to a fortress inside the city and barred themselves in. For eight months, the pope remained a prisoner inside this fortress, while the German Fury stormed through Rome, burning, killing, and stealing treasure.

Meanwhile, Charles was still up in Spain, pretending that he knew nothing about the attack on Rome. He sent a

17

message to the pope, claiming that the German Fury had acted without his permission. "I'm outraged!" Charles exclaimed. "How could such a thing happen?"

Did the pope believe this message? We don't know. But we do know that the pope agreed to hold the special service which would crown Charles "Holy Roman Emperor." In return, Charles helped the pope to fend off the Fury.

Now Charles could describe himself as "King of the Romans; King of Spain, Sicily, Jerusalem, the Indies and the mainland on the far side of the Atlantic; Archduke of Austria; Duke of Burgundy and Athens; Count of Habsburg and Flanders; Lord of Asia and Africa." But despite his fancy titles, Charles had plenty of problems. He had spent years and years of his reign fighting, and wars cost money. He was growing poorer and poorer. Within his own kingdoms, Catholics and Protestants were constantly battling with each other. And his Protestant subjects no longer wanted to obey Charles's decrees.

Twenty-four years after the pope crowned him as emperor, Charles decided that he could no longer rule his empire. Dressed in black, leaning on the arm of one of his favorite noblemen, he rose from his throne and told his followers, "I have done my best to protect my country and my faith. But I am too weak and ill to continue the struggle. So I must resign my throne. I will give Spain, the Netherlands, and my Italian lands to my son, Philip." All of Charles's followers wept as the emperor sank back onto his throne.

One year later, Charles V gave the rest of his empire to his brother Ferdinand, who became the Holy Roman Emperor in his place. Charles went to live in a monastery, where he spent his days praying and reading. He died less than two years later.

The fortunate little boy had lost his kingdoms. But his brother, Ferdinand, and his son, Philip, now ruled over the richest kingdoms in the West. And their actions would change the world.

The Riches of Spain

A young boy stands in a dark cave. A heavy sack leans against his bare legs. Beneath his feet, he feels damp, slick clay and rough ridges of stone. Sweat runs down his face. Ahead of him, dim torchlight flickers in the blackness. The hollow sound of metal picks, hacking away at mountain rock, rings through the dark.

He turns around and sees a tunnel, sloping sharply up toward a far-away gleam of daylight. He bends down to lift the sack; needle-edged pieces of stone jut through its rough sides and scrape against his arms and back. He starts to struggle up the tunnel, bent almost double by the weight and gasping for breath. But the air is so warm and foul that he can barely pull it into his lungs.

He isn't much older than you. And he works in a South American mine, collecting gold for Philip II, the king of Spain.

The Spanish came to South America the very first time by accident. For hundreds of years, traders from Spain and other European countries had traveled east (*right* on your map) to India, where they bought cloves, nutmeg, and pepper. But the long and difficult road to India lay through dry deserts and over steep mountain ridges. So an adventurer named Christopher Columbus set sail from Europe and went west (*left* on your map), hoping to go all the way around the world and reach India from the other side. When he caught sight of land, he was sure that he had reached the islands near India. He named the people who came out to meet him Indians. And he claimed the land for Spain, because the queen of Spain had given him money to buy his ships.

After Columbus returned home, other Spanish adventurers, called *conquistadores,* followed his sea route to "India." They realized that Columbus hadn't reached India at all. He had found an entirely new land! And this new land held something more exciting than spices. The native people of South America wore gold jewelry. They offered the conquistadores gold and silver ornaments. And they told stories about a king called *El Dorado* (or, in English, the "Man of Gold"), who was so rich that he wallowed in gold dust every day.

When Philip II heard these stories, he decided that Spain needed this gold. So he granted Spanish conquistadores special contracts, called *encomiendas.* The encomiendas gave the conquistadores permission to sail to South America and take all its gold.

Of course, South America wasn't a big empty country filled with gold. Native South American tribes called Aztecs, Mayans, and Incas already lived there. But Philip II announced that Spain could claim South America because the tribes who lived there were not Christians. "God has given all of the world to the pope," one royal decree explained, "and the pope has given these new lands to the King of Spain."

Not everyone in Spain agreed that God wanted Spain to

A conquistador

have South America's gold. Many Christian priests preached sermons against Philip's encomiendas. But the conquistadores ignored these priests. At first, they took jewelry away from the native tribes. Then they learned that bits of gold were mixed into the sand of the cold mountain streams. So they began to pan gold out of these streams. They crouched over the icy water with metal pans and dipped the pans down into the sand beneath the stream's surface, filling them about half full. Then they held the pans in the current, letting water run over the sand while they shook the pans gently up and down. The rushing water washed the sand out, while the heavy gold sank to the bottom.

But panning for gold didn't make the conquistadores rich enough. So the Spanish began to dig mines into the ground, looking for a rock called *quartz* that often has little lines of gold running through it. Miners hacked quartz out of the mines with iron axes, carried the rocks up to the surface, crushed them into powder, and heated the powder over a fire. The gold melted and ran off into molds, where it hardened into coins or gold bars called *ingots*.

The mines started to pour out gold—and silver as well. In all, the Spanish took five hundred billion dollars' worth of gold and silver out of South America.

Think for a moment about the number five billion. If you could count day and night, it would take you a hundred and fifty years to count to five billion. And if you could lay five billion pennies side by side, you would have a line of pennies that wrapped all the way around the earth more than seven times! Now imagine a hundred times as many. It would take you fifteen thousand years to count to five hundred billion— counting day and night. And your line of five hundred billion pennies would wrap around the earth over seven hundred times. If you had five hundred billion dollars, you could buy a ten- speed bicycle for every single person in the world!

Spanish law declared that the king got a share of every load of gold brought from the New World. South American gold made Philip II the richest king in the world! And his people prospered too. Thousands and thousands of poor Spanish men and women traveled to South America and grew rich. "God has given me silver!" one Spanish settler wrote home from South America. "I am rich and honored here. Who would make me go back to Spain and live in poverty?" So many Spanish came to South America that parts of the continent became known as New Spain.

But while the Spanish prospered, the native South Americans suffered. The Spanish forced them to work long, miserable hours mining gold. Men spent months in the damp darkness of the mines. Women panned for gold and pounded quartz into powder. Even children spent their days gathering rocks and carrying them up to the surface of the mines. And the Spanish also brought slaves from Africa to work in the South American mines. Working hard, eating little, catching diseases from the conquistadores, thousands of Africans and native South Americans grew sick and died. "Dead slaves are buried every day in big piles," one Spanish onlooker wrote home. South American gold brought riches and power to Spain and to Philip—but it brought misery to South America.

Scotland and the Netherlands

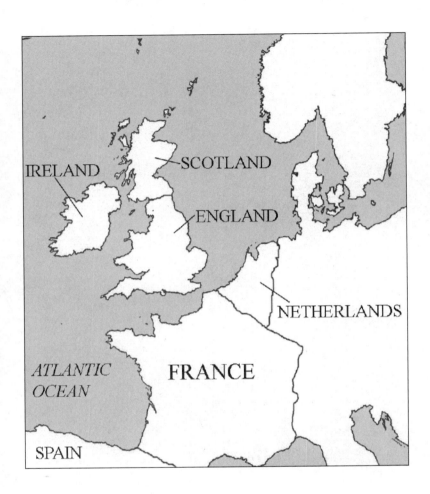

Chapter Two
Protestant Rebellions

The Dutch Revolt

If you were to go north along the coast of Spain and keep traveling north, along the coast of France, past the English Channel, you would come to a damp seaside country where the land slopes down to the ocean and water lies in pools all over the farmland. To the people who lived in the large cities of Spain and Italy, this country seemed to be in the far reaches or "nether parts" of Europe. So they called it the Netherlands, or "far-away lands."

When the Holy Roman Emperor Charles V gave Spain and the Netherlands to his son Philip, Philip also inherited a problem: a rebellious nobleman named William the Silent.

William was born when Philip was six years old. The two little boys were raised very differently. Philip lived in a palace in Spain and was brought up to be a faithful Catholic; William grew up in Germany and was taught by his parents to be a good Protestant.

When William was eleven, one of his cousins died and left him two large *provinces,* or areas of land, in Charles's empire: one in the south of France, and the other in the Netherlands. The emperor Charles realized that the eleven-year-old William would one day be a powerful nobleman. He didn't want William to grow up hostile to the Roman Catholic faith—and to the Holy Roman Emperor. So he ordered the young boy taken away from his mother and father and brought to live at the royal court. Charles hired tutors to teach William princely skills: how to speak French, how to plan battles and run a country, and (most important of all) how to be a good Catholic. Soon, little William became the emperor's favorite page. He grew into a strong, thoughtful young man, loyal to Charles and his family. And when Charles rose from his throne to tell his followers that he had decided to give up the title of Holy Roman Emperor, he leaned on William's arm.

Philip then became king of the Netherlands—and he gave William the job of governing a large part of the country for him. As William ruled, he discovered that the people of the Netherlands spent most of their time fighting, not against other countries, but against the sea. The Netherlands were also known as the Low Countries because they were below the level of the ocean. Whenever the tide came in or a storm drove waves toward the land, water washed all over the Low Countries. But Low Country people were determined to drive back the sea. They pulled hundreds of bucketfuls of wet mud from the bottom of shallow lakes and swamps and piled this mud into huge earthen walls called *dikes*. These dikes kept the sea away from land. If you were in the Netherlands, you could stand next to a dike, look up—and see the ocean on the other side, higher than your head! If a dike broke, the sea would flood in and cover the land where houses, farms, and cities stood.

William was determined to make the Netherlands prosperous and peaceful. But as time went on, he became unhappy with Philip's rule. Philip passed laws for the Netherlands without asking any of the leaders whether the laws would be good for their people. Many of those laws kept Protestants from preaching and from practicing their faith. And William always remembered that he had been born a Protestant. Even though he had been taught Catholicism at Philip's court, William was sympathetic to Protestants who wanted to worship God in their own way.

William tried to remain loyal to Philip. But three years after Philip became king, William heard a horrifying secret. He was visiting the court of the French king—who, like Philip, was Catholic. The French king didn't know that William had been born a Protestant. He told William that Philip intended to destroy Protestantism in the Netherlands—and to massacre Protestants. But William didn't show his dismay. He didn't even answer back. He simply listened and nodded. Because he held his tongue, he later became known, as "William the Silent."

When William returned to the Netherlands, he still seemed loyal to Philip. But he was already thinking about ways to protect his people from Philip's plans. When a group of his subjects banded together and declared that they would fight against Philip's authority, William agreed to meet with their leaders. He convinced them to send a petition to Philip's court, asking that the laws against Protestantism be lifted.

But when the petition arrived at the royal court, the noblemen standing around the throne laughed at the sight of it. "Why bother with such a rabble of beggars?" one of them sneered. Leaders of the rebellion took this title as a compliment.

William the Silent

They began to call themselves the Beggars—and to lead armed uprisings against Spanish rule. Mobs led by Beggars stormed through the countryside, burning Catholic churches and smashing statues of Catholic saints.

When Philip heard this news, he sent a Catholic soldier and nobleman, the Duke of Alba, to crush the revolt. The Duke of Alba invited William and two other leaders of the Netherlands to come and talk with him about his plans to restore peace. The two friends went—but William, suddenly uneasy, decided to take a trip to his family lands in Germany instead. When the two leaders arrived, the Duke of Alba arrested them and had them beheaded! He ordered William's lands in the Netherlands confiscated. William was now an enemy of the crown.

For the next ten years, the people of the Netherlands fought against the Spanish soldiers occupying their country.

The Duke executed over a thousand people—some simply because they were Protestants. He gave his soldiers permission to burn towns and kill their inhabitants.

Over in Germany, William raised an army and tried to march back into his country. The war went on and on. Two of William's brothers were killed in the fighting! But William and the Beggars continued to fight. The Beggars broke dikes, flooded the countryside, and sailed into cities besieged by Spanish soldiers, turning land battles into sea battles. Finally, seven provinces in the north of the Netherlands announced their independence from Spain—and made William the Silent their new king.

Philip was furious! He offered a large sum of money to anyone who would assassinate his one-time friend. A young man named Balthazar Gerard volunteered to carry out this terrible task. He traveled to William's court, pretending to be a Protestant whose family had been executed in the war. William welcomed him and gave him some small tasks to do around the court.

One evening, Balthazar wrapped himself in a long dark cloak and hid just outside William's dining room. After William finished eating, he rose and strolled out of the room. Balthazar sprang from the shadows and fired his pistol. "O my God, have mercy on this poor people!" William exclaimed, and collapsed. The great champion of the Netherlands was dead just a few minutes later.

But his country remained independent. Today, we call this country Holland and the people who live there the Dutch. And Queen Beatrix, who rules Holland today, is William's great-great-great-great-great-great-great-great-great-great-great-grandaughter.

The Queen Without a Country

Holland wasn't the only country where Catholics and Protestants disagreed. Catholics and Protestants were fighting with each other all through Philip II's kingdom, all through the Holy Roman Empire—and even over in Scotland.

Today, England and Scotland are part of the same country, the United Kingdom (or Great Britain). But at the beginning of the seventeenth century, Scotland was an independent country with its own royal court, its own laws, and its own queen.

Mary, Queen of Scots, inherited the throne when she was only five days old! Because she was so young, her mother, Mary of Guise, became her *regent*: Mary of Guise would rule Scotland until her daughter was old enough to take the throne.

Mary of Guise was a good regent. But she was Catholic, and many of the powerful Scottish noblemen, called Lords, were Protestants who didn't want a Catholic ruler. So they formed themselves into a Protestant Council and gave *themselves* the responsibility of governing Scotland until little Mary came of age.

Mary of Guise was afraid that this Council would try to make the baby queen into a good Protestant. So when small Mary was five years old, her mother sent her to France, where she could be raised as a good Catholic among other Catholics. Mary of Guise remained in Scotland. She died a few years later—without ever seeing her daughter again.

Little Mary lived in France for the next thirteen years. Meanwhile, the Protestant Lords of Scotland grew more powerful. A Protestant preacher named John Knox traveled all through Scotland, preaching that no woman—especially a Catholic woman—should sit on the throne. "It is a thing repugnant to the order of nature that any woman be exalted to rule over men!" Knox declared.

But Mary didn't agree! When she was eighteen, she decided to return to Scotland and take back her throne.

Some of the Catholics who lived in Scotland hoped that Mary would march into Scotland with a French army and throw out all of the Protestants. But Mary announced that she didn't want to kill Protestants or Catholics simply because of their faith. She wanted to rule in Scotland as a good Catholic queen, but she intended to let her Protestant subjects worship in their own way.

One hot August day, Mary set sail from France in a royal ship, headed for Scotland. The Protestant Council of Lords met together at this alarming news. What would they do when the rightful Queen landed? If they tried to drive her away, the Catholics of Scotland might take up swords to defend Mary against the Protestant Lords. A civil war could begin!

Mary, Queen of Scots

So when Mary's ship landed in Scotland, the Lords went out to meet her and told her that she was welcome. John Knox refused to go with them. On the morning of her arrival, a thick, dim fog had descended on the Scottish coast; Mary, Knox snapped, was already bringing "sorrow, dolour, and darkness" with her. But when the Lords met Mary, they were charmed. She was beautiful, intelligent, and sympathetic. They believed her when she said that she would never persecute the Protestants of Scotland. Mary even married a Protestant nobleman, Lord Darnley. For a little while, her reign went smoothly.

But then Lord Darnley decided that he wanted more power. He began to scheme with some of the Protestant Lords who still hated Mary's Catholicism. They planned to shut Mary up as a prisoner in her own house and put Lord Darnley on the throne, to rule in her place. Then Lord Darnley and the Protestant Lords would make Catholicism illegal!

When Mary found out about this plot, she crept out of the palace late at night through a tiny side door. She rode by horseback through the night to another castle, where soldiers loyal to her gathered into an army. When the Lords who were plotting against her found out about this army, they fled the country. And what about Lord Darnley? He decided to blame the whole scheme on the absent Lords.

When Elizabeth, queen of England, heard about Lord Darnley's treachery, she remarked, "Had I been Mary, I would have stabbed Darnley with his own dagger!" But Mary decided to pardon her husband. She was expecting a baby—and she wanted Lord Darnley by her side.

But she never truly forgave her husband.

One cold February night, after Mary's baby was born, Lord Darnley and his valet were staying in a small house in the Scottish city of Edinburgh. Mary, her new baby son, and the rest of the royal court were staying at a larger house in the same city. At two o'clock in the morning, Edinburgh was still and dark—until an enormous explosion shattered the quiet. Bits of stone and brick rained down on Edinburgh's streets. Lord Darnley's house had blown up! When Mary and her attendants rushed over to see what had happened, they found Lord Darnley's body in the garden. He had been strangled.

Who had arranged for Lord Darnley to die? No one knew. But plenty of people suggested that Mary herself had planned the murder.

Mary became less and less popular. And as she lost influence, the Protestant Lords tried again to take control of Scotland. They announced that her baby son, James, should become king of Scotland in Mary's place.

Mary tried to assemble another army to fight against the rebels. But when most of her soldiers deserted her, she had to walk out on foot and surrender to the Lords.

The Lords took Mary to a far-away castle in a wild and lonely spot. They visited her every day, telling her that she had to sign a paper that would make little James king in her place. Finally, with one of the Lords holding her arm to force her to write, Mary, Queen of Scots signed the papers. Her baby James was crowned King of Scotland—at thirteen months of age. John Knox preached at the ceremony!

Mary fled to England, hoping that her cousin, Queen Elizabeth, would help her. But Elizabeth, who had no children, knew that Mary was her closest relation—and the next heir to the English throne. She was afraid that Mary might arrange to have her assassinated and claim the crown of England.

So she sent a band of soldiers to meet Mary and had Mary taken to a comfortable house in the north of England. Mary remained a prisoner of the Queen of England for the next nineteen years.

Poor Mary! She had very little to do. She kept dozens of little dogs and birds as pets. She did a lot of needlework and even sent some to Elizabeth as presents—along with indignant letters.

As time went on, she began to plot her escape. Elizabeth's spies kept track of every letter she wrote—and every message she sent. Finally, the spies brought Elizabeth letters that Mary had written to a group of English Catholics. In these letters, she spoke of becoming Queen of England if they could set her free. This could only mean that she was planning Elizabeth's death. Mary insisted that she would never harm Elizabeth. But Elizabeth, afraid for her life, signed Mary's death warrant for treason.

On a cold February morning, Mary walked to the scaffold. She knelt down at the execution block—and was beheaded. When the executioner held up her head, everyone could see that beneath her cap, her hair had turned pure white. Mary, Queen of Scots, was dead, and a Protestant king ruled in Scotland.

England and Its First Colony

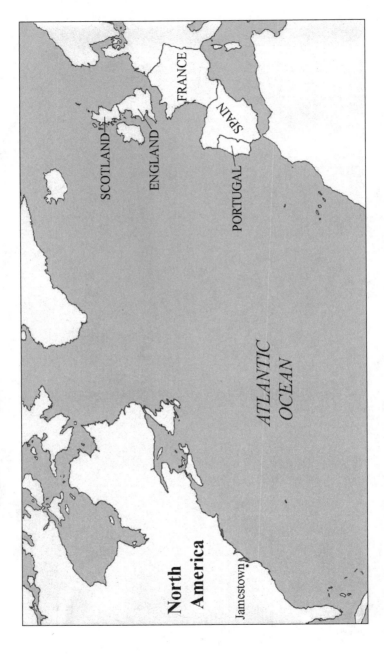

SCOTLAND

ENGLAND

FRANCE

SPAIN

PORTUGAL

North America

Jamestown

ATLANTIC OCEAN

Chapter Three
James, King of Two Countries

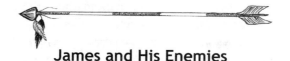

James and His Enemies

Mary's son, James VI, didn't even remember his mother. As long as he could remember, he had lived in Scotland, looked after by his tutor. James's tutor, a stern Scottish schoolmaster named George Buchanan, taught James Greek, Latin, philosophy, and Protestant theology. He also taught the young king that a ruler's right to sit on a throne was given to him by his people—and that the king had a duty to listen to the opinions of his subjects.

But as soon as James grew old enough to rule by himself, he rejected Buchanan's ideas. A king, James insisted, rules by *divine right*: His power doesn't come from the people he rules. It comes directly from God, so the will of the king is the same thing as God's will! James wrote a little booklet, called *The True Law of Free Monarchies,* about his divine right to rule. In it he announced, "The King is overlord of the whole land...He [is] master over every person that inhabiteth the same, having power over the life and death of every one of them."

For twenty years, James exercised his "divine" power in Scotland. Meanwhile, down in England, Queen Elizabeth was growing older. She had no children of her own; her closest relative was James, because Mary, his mother, had been Elizabeth's cousin. So when Elizabeth died in 1603, James became King of England. He was given a new name: James I of England. Now he was the king of two different countries! From this time on, he was known as James VI of Scotland and James I of England.

James traveled south into England for his English coronation. He was welcomed to London by five hundred leading citizens, all wearing velvet and golden chains. A parade was planned in his honor—a parade that included the famous playwright William Shakespeare! James was amazed by the wealth and luxury of this country to the south. In comparison, the Scottish court seemed poor and shabby.

But even while James was planning his spectacular coronation ceremony, a terrible sickness called the Black Death was spreading throughout the city. Over a thousand people were dying each week. Londoners were too terrified to gather into big crowds, where disease might spread even faster. So James had to cancel his coronation ceremony and his huge celebrations. Instead, he and his wife Anne walked quietly to Westminster Abbey and were crowned King and Queen of England.

The disappointing coronation was just a foretaste of troubles to come! During his reign, James would make enemies of Catholics, Protestants—and Parliament itself. (Parliament was the group of Englishmen who helped rule England.)

James's disagreements with Catholics and Protestants came first. When James was crowned king, there were three groups of Christians in England. Catholics hoped that James would give them special privileges, since his mother Mary had been Catholic. English Protestants, called Anglicans, hoped that James would stick to the Protestant beliefs he had learned in Scotland. And a third group of Protestant Christians hoped that James would make the Anglican church even *more* Protestant. They believed that the Anglicans had borrowed too many church traditions from Catholicism. These reformers were called Puritans, because they wanted to "purify" the Anglican church of all Catholic influences.

As soon as James arrived in England, the Puritans brought him a petition, signed by a thousand English Puritans, begging him to make the English church more Protestant. James agreed to meet with the Puritans to discuss their demands. But at this meeting, he rejected all of the Puritan ideas. When the Puritans continued to insist that God wanted James to change the English church, James grew furious. He told the Puritans that he would "harry them out of the Kingdom"—and he made Puritan worship services illegal.

Next, James made the English Catholics angry. Under James's laws, Catholics who refused to go to Anglican church services on Sundays had to pay a fine. And the year after his coronation, James ordered all Catholic priests to leave the country.

At this, two Catholics, Robert Catesby and Guy Fawkes, came up with a plan to get rid of James and the Protestant leaders of Parliament, all in one day. They bought a house next to the huge stone building where Parliament met. Along with eleven friends, they started to dig a tunnel from the basement of their house, through the nine-foot stone wall that surrounded the foundation of Parliament House. They planned to pack this tunnel full of gunpowder. As soon as James and the Parliamentary leaders were gathered together for the new session of Parliament, Catesby and his companions would blow the whole building up!

They dug for months—but as they got closer to Parliament House, the tunnel began to fill with water. So instead they smuggled barrels full of gunpowder into Parliament House itself. Soon, thirty-six barrels of gunpowder were hidden beneath firewood in the cellar. But just hours before the explosion was to take place, Guy Fawkes was discovered in the cellar, holding a match. He was arrested and tortured until he confessed—and was put to death. Today, English children still celebrate the day that Guy Fawkes was arrested by setting off fireworks.

After this Gunpowder Plot was discovered, James passed even more laws forbidding Catholic worship in England. Now Catholics and Puritans were both angry with James.

And soon Parliament was angry with James as well. James insisted that, because he ruled by the will of God, he could do exactly as he pleased. "The King is above the law," he announced. When Parliament refused to do exactly what James ordered, James told them, "Monarchy is the greatest thing on earth. Kings are rightly called gods since just like God they have power of life and death over all their subjects in all things. They are accountable to God only... so it is a crime for anyone to argue about what a king can do." And then James sent all of the members of Parliament home—and ruled England without their help!

James had made Catholics, Puritans, and Parliament all angry. But today, he is most famous for something he did *right*. During his reign, James I agreed to make a brand new English translation of the Bible, so that everyone in his country—Catholic, Puritan, and Anglican—could use the same Bible. He appointed 54 scholars to make this new translation. It was finished in 1611, eight years after James became king. Today, this Bible, called the King James Version, is still used by many people around the world!

King James's Town

While Spain hauled boatloads of gold out of South America and brought it to King Philip II, James looked on in envy. He wanted his share of the gold too!

So he gave a group of wealthy Englishmen royal permission to look for gold in *North* America. These wealthy men joined together to buy three ships: the *Susan Constant,* the *Godspeed,* and the *Discovery*. They filled the ships with food and tools and offered free land in the New World to men who would sail the ships to North America and search for gold. The new settlement, or *colony,* would belong to King James, and each wealthy man would get a share of the gold. "Instead of milk and honey," one wrote to a friend, "we will find pearls and riches!"

The three ships set out from England one cold December day, filled with bricklayers, blacksmiths, sail makers—and goldsmiths. But as soon as the ships turned west, a strong wind blew them back. The ships struggled for six weeks against the wind before they got out of sight of shore! The hopeful colonists, crammed into tiny cabins beneath the decks, began to get seasick and argue with each other.

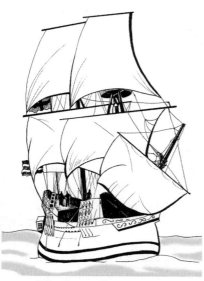

The *Susan Constant*

At last the wind changed, and the ships began the long journey across the ocean. For five miserable months, the colonists lived on biscuits baked as hard as iron and meat pickled in salt. Their fresh water, stored in barrels on board, was green with algae. They had barely enough to drink—and no one took a bath for the entire voyage!

Finally, the North American coast came into view. On May 13th, 1607, the three ships landed. The colonists staggered to shore and found shady green woods, streams of water, and tall thick grass. The spring weather was warm and sunny. The forests were filled with wild geese, deer, and rabbits; the river nearby teemed with fish, crab, and oysters. The "Indians" (Native Americans) who lived nearby seemed friendly. The colonists, sure that they had found the perfect place for their new home, built a few huts and named their colony Jamestown, in honor of King James.

The settlers didn't spend very much time building, though. They spent their days searching for gold! One of Jamestown's leaders, John Smith, soon grew exasperated. "There is no talk, no hope, no work, but dig gold, wash gold, refine gold, load gold!" John Smith complained. He knew that the colony's grain supplies, brought from England, would soon run out. He was afraid that the Indians might grow hostile. He wanted the colonists to grow their own crops and to build walls to protect themselves.

Meanwhile, the Indians near Jamestown were watching the English explore further and further into their country. They were worried! How much land did these newcomers want? One day, Indian warriors attacked a little group of colonists who were out searching for gold. The colonists, frightened by the attack, finally listened to John Smith's advice. They built a fort with thick log walls to protect them. And they began to clear fields for crops.

But it was too late.

The English had arrived in Jamestown during a terrible drought. There was no rain. The fields were dry, and the crops didn't grow. Water grew scarce—and dirty. The grain from England was almost gone. The colonists began to grow ill from disease and starvation. One colonist, George Percy, wrote, "There were never Englishmen in such misery as we. Five men had to divide a small can of barley soaked in water. Our water was filled with slime and filth. Sometimes three or four men died in a single night!"

By fall, half the colonists were dead. And then winter came. The men who were still alive huddled in their icy wooden huts. Their feet froze; their joints were swollen from cold and hunger.

But John Smith was determined to make Jamestown a success. Just before Christmas, he rounded up a few healthy men to go looking for food—and perhaps for a better place to settle. Smith and his companions paddled their way slowly up the river that ran deep into the woods. The water grew shallower—and narrower. Overgrown banks rose up on either side. Briars reached down into the canoe. Finally, they came to a fallen tree, collapsed across the water, and could go no further.

John Smith pushed the canoe to shore and got out. "Go up on the bank and cook our food," he told his companions. "I'll see if I can figure out where we are."

He walked away along the muddy edge of the water. The river turned and twisted. Soon, he lost sight of his men. He paused, looking around. Suddenly he heard a faint rustle ahead of him. An arrow struck him in the thigh and bounced off his heavy leather breeches! John Smith drew his gun, shouting a warning. He could see two Indians, half hidden by the undergrowth, notching arrows to their strings. He backed away from them—and stumbled into the shallow river. More Indians appeared from the brush around him. Smith, floundering in the

40

river mud, shot all the bullets out of his gun. By the time he ran out of ammunition, he was stuck to his waist in muck.

Smith laid down his empty weapon and held up his hands in surrender. The Indians pulled him out of the mud and marched him through the thick woods. Finally, they arrived at the edge of a large clearing filled with Indian houses. Children played nearby; women were cooking and carrying water. A large hut stood at the village's center. It was the palace of Powhatan, the great Indian chief.

Inside, Powhatan was lying on thick mats, wearing strings of pearls and a rich garment of raccoon skins, surrounded by his chief warriors. He stared at the muddy, disheveled Englishman for a long time.

Of course, the two men did not speak the same language. But John Smith had learned a few words of the Indian language, and some of the Indians knew a little bit of English. With the help of these translators, Powhatan and John Smith managed to talk to each other. Put into English, their conversation might have sounded something like this:

"Why have your people come to our land?" Powhatan asked.

"We had a fight with the Spanish," John Smith lied, "and they drove our ship onto your coast. Now the ship has sprung a leak. We have to stay here."

"Why have you and your companions wandered so far into my territory?" Powhatan demanded.

John Smith had to think fast. "Great Chief," he said, "we intended only to attack your enemies, who live up the river and who fight against you."

"If that is true," Powhatan said, "we can live in peace together."

So John Smith promised that the colonists would not attack Powhatan's people—and Powhatan let him return to Jamestown unharmed. Eventually another Jamestown leader, John Rolfe, married Powhatan's daughter, Pocahontas. Now there was truly peace between Jamestown and Powhatan's tribe! The Jamestown colony grew stronger and stronger. The English were in North America to stay.

French and English Settlements in the New World

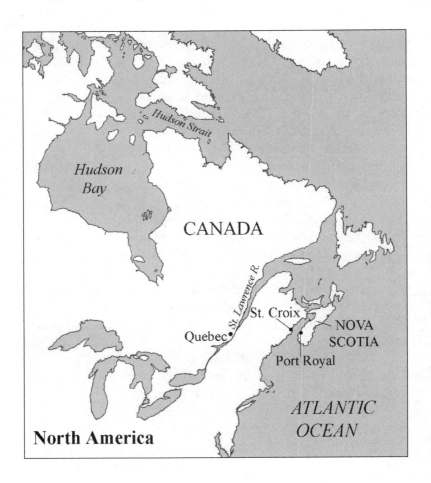

Chapter Four
Searching for the Northwest Passage

The French in the New World

Although some adventurers came to North America looking for gold, others came with a different purpose. They hoped to find a *Northwest Passage*—a river that would run all the way through North America, out into the Pacific Ocean on the other side. If merchants could sail through a Northwest Passage and get to the eastern ports of China and India, they could grow wealthy trading for silks and spices.

Explorer after explorer tried to find the Northwest Passage—and failed. But in the same year that James VI of Scotland inherited the English throne, the king of France, Henry IV, hired a tough, determined ex-soldier named Samuel Champlain and told him to make one more attempt to find the Northwest Passage for France.

Samuel Champlain sailed across the Atlantic with his crew and landed far, far north of Jamestown, in the country that we now call Canada. He could see a huge river, the St. Lawrence River, winding away into the land in front of him. The land was green with trees and rich grass; geese soared overhead, and herds of moose grazed along the shores. There was plenty of fresh water and fertile land for crops. Friendly native people came out to meet Champlain. They offered to exchange beaver and wolf skins for French metal pots and knives, and they treated the French explorers to an enormous feast of cooked moose, bear, seal, and beaver.

Champlain was amazed by the beauty of this new land! Unlike earlier explorers, Champlain realized that Canada was more than a big piece of land blocking the way to India and China. Canada was the perfect place for a new French settlement. "No one could hope to find a more beautiful country!" he announced.

He returned to France with armloads of furs and a vivid description of this splendid new land. King Henry IV listened to Champlain's enthusiastic descriptions—and agreed that Champlain should return to Canada and start a French colony there.

So Champlain and a group of adventurous colonists boarded a wooden ship and headed back across the Atlantic. They sailed down the St. Croix River until they saw a tiny island in a wide, calm bend of the river. The colonists thought that the island would be a warm and sheltered place for their new home. They named it St. Croix Island, built a cluster of little wood huts, and settled in.

But the soil of St. Croix was so salty that crops wouldn't grow. The water on the island was too foul to drink. And winter was on its way. Soon, icy winds howled down the river and blasted St. Croix Island, covering it with ice and snow. Huge cakes of ice filled the water between St. Croix and the mainland. The colonists were trapped, unable to get to the shore! They grew ill with scurvy because they had no fresh food. Their teeth

Samuel Champlain navigates the St. Croix River

fell out and their arms and legs became swollen with disease. Before spring came, almost half of the colony was dead. Finally, supply ships arrived from France with more colonists, tools, and seeds. The colony was saved!

Champlain decided to move the settlement to Port Royal, a protected harbor on the west side of Nova Scotia (a peninsula that stretches down from the mainland). So the French colonists took down their St. Croix houses, piece by piece, moved their colony to Port Royal, and rebuilt it. They added new strong log buildings and planted fields full of crops. They hunted for fresh meat and fresh fish, and stored away food for the winter.

When winter came again, the colony was ready. Snow fell, and icy winds blew down from the north, but the colonists were warm and dry. They had plenty of wine, meat, and firewood. And Champlain encouraged them to put on musical plays and fancy dinners to entertain themselves on those long, dark winter evenings.

But just as Port Royal began to prosper, the French king decided that France had spent enough money on a North American colony. He ordered the colonists to abandon their settlement and come home! Sadly, Champlain loaded the settlers and their goods onto his ships, and sailed back to France. But he didn't give up. He spent months at the French court, begging the king for another chance to establish a French colony in Canada.

Finally, the king agreed to one last attempt. So Champlain collected twenty-eight adventurous men and headed to a larger river called the St. Lawrence River. This time, Champlain took his ship ashore near a narrow channel in the river. The Indians who lived nearby called this place *Kebec,* which in their language meant "Place where the River Narrows." Here, Champlain built yet another French town.

But another icy winter, the coldest yet, threatened the tiny settlement of Kebec. Despite their careful preparations, the twenty-eight men ran out of fresh food. They began to die once again of scurvy. The colony's doctor died. Champlain himself grew sick. The winter was so fierce that even the nearby native tribe, the Montagnis, began to run out of food. Some of the Montagnis had to go to Kebec and beg for dried peas and bread!

Champlain shared his food with them. By summer, when a French ship arrived with supplies and food, Kebec had only eight settlers left alive. But Champlain was one of those eight. And Champlain had made fast friends of the Montagnis people, who were now ready to help the settlers of Kebec.

For years, Champlain worked to make Kebec prosperous and permanent. He wrote books about the "New France" in Canada, filling them with beautiful sketches of Canada's plants and animals. He made the long journey from Kebec back to France twenty-three times, trying to convince more French settlers to come to his new colony! But Kebec grew very, very slowly. Colonists who settled in Kebec risked frostbite and starvation every winter. Many of the people who came to this cold little settlement were beggars or convicted criminals with nowhere else to go.

But Champlain didn't give up. He cleared land. He ordered new buildings built. He encouraged the French and the Indians to marry each other so that they would always remain friends. And he refused to give up on the idea of a French settlement in the New World.

Thirty-two years after his first arrival in Canada, Samuel Champlain died on Christmas Day. After all his work, Kebec still only had a hundred French settlers living in it. But although Kebec was small, it survived—and went on growing. Today, the city of Kebec, which we now spell *Quebec,* is the capital of a whole Canadian province, also called Quebec. And the people of Quebec still speak French. Samuel Champlain's persistence had brought France to the New World, and earned him the nickname "Father of New France."

Henry Hudson's Quest

While the colonies of Quebec and Jamestown struggled to survive, French and English explorers kept right on looking for a northwest shortcut to the ports of China and India. They wanted eastern spices and silk, not North American wheat and fur! One of the most determined explorers was an Englishman named Henry Hudson. Hudson wrote to a friend, "He who finds...the sure sea path to the Indies...will be remembered for all time....I would that my name be carved on the tablets of the sea."

But Henry Hudson's attempts to find the sea path to India would lead to his death.

Hudson knew that dozens of sailors had already searched in vain for the Northwest Passage. But Hudson had a brand new idea. Instead of sailing west to North America and searching for a passageway through the continent, he wanted to sail straight up over the top of the globe and then down to Asia. He knew that in the summer, the sun shines on the North Pole all day and all night; Hudson was certain that all the sunlight would melt the ice so that his ship could get through.

Hudson set out north on a tiny wooden ship, the *Hopewell*. For six weeks, the crew fought through rough, frosty seas. Dense, icy fogs settled around them. Rain froze into sheets of ice on the decks and sails. The men's hands were criss-crossed with sores from pulling on the ice-coated ropes. Huge fields of floating ice-cakes forced Hudson off his planned course. Soon, Hudson was forced to turn his ship and head back for England.

Back home, Hudson decided to try a new course for his second attempt. Perhaps he could sail *northeast,* traveling along the northern coast of Russia, and then around the great land mass of China toward India!

Another English adventurer, Sebastian Cabot, had already tried this route. *His* ships had been driven to shore by ice and frozen in. When fishermen found the ships a year later, no one was left alive. They were "all frozen," reported one of the discoverers, "some of them seated in the act of writing, pen still in hand and the paper before them, others at tables, plate in hand and spoon in mouth." But Henry Hudson was convinced that he would be more successful. He hired a new crew and started off in the spring, when the northern waters would be free of ice.

But after three months of sailing, Hudson's ship came up against a long, thin barrier of land. Hudson sailed along it, looking for a way through. But the weather was beginning to grow colder. Ice was forming in the water. The crew begged their captain to turn back. Hudson agreed and turned the ship around. But he didn't head back toward England. He headed across the Atlantic, toward North America!

When his crew and his first mate, Robert Juet, realized that they weren't headed home, they threatened to mutiny. Once again, Hudson was forced to give up his journey and go back to England. A third attempt also failed!

Hudson refused to give up. This time, he planned to go across to North America and sail into a narrow channel called Furious Overfall. Some English sailors thought that Furious Overfall might lead to the Northwest Passage. But no ship had ever managed to sail very far into Furious Overfall. Treacherous rocks, swirling, sucking whirlpools, and floating cakes of ice made the channel almost impassable.

But Hudson wasn't discouraged. He found a ship, the *Discovery*. He collected a crew and appointed his young son John to be cabin boy. And once again he hired Robert Juet, the first mate who had joined in the mutiny on his second voyage.

That was a mistake.

Hudson, Robert Juet, and the crew sailed back across the Atlantic and into Furious Overfall. As the *Discovery* made its way through the channel, the tide began to pour away with alarming speed. Sharp rocks which had been under the water's surface suddenly jutted above the waves, and threatened to tear at the *Discovery*'s hull. Violent currents pushed the tiny ship back and forth. Enormous cakes of ice floated toward them, threatening to cave in the *Discovery's* fragile wooden sides.

Hudson set adrift

The sailors begged to turn back, but Hudson would not listen. For six weeks, they struggled to keep the ship away from the rocks as the water rose and fell. Finally the strait began to grow wider. The *Discovery* came out into a wide, salt expanse of water, free of ice. At last, the crew thought, they had reached the Pacific Ocean! They sailed into this new stretch of water filled with hope.

But suddenly a shore loomed up in front of them, cutting off their way. For weeks, Hudson sailed along this land, looking for a passage through. The weather began to grow colder and colder. The crew began to mutter and complain. And when some of them told First Mate Juet about their worries, he told them, "Keep your muskets charged and your swords ready. We'll need to use them before the voyage is over." Juet was suggesting mutiny—for the second time!

As the water grew icier, Hudson's men were forced to haul the *Discovery* up onto the shore. Soon, ice had frozen it into place. Snow began to fall. The crew grew so hungry that they foraged along the shore, eating frogs!

By the time the warm spring winds began to melt the ice, the crew of the *Discovery* was ready to go home. But Hudson ordered the crew to head west once more.

One early summer morning, Hudson got up out of his bed in his private cabin and opened his door to check on the weather. Immediately, three men leaped out from behind the door, wrestled him to the ground, and tied his hands and feet. They dragged Henry, his son John, and six of the sickest sailors to the ship's tiny lifeboat and forced them in. They shoved the lifeboat into the bay, leaving Hudson and the sick men to die without food or water, and headed for home.

But without its captain, the *Discovery* had a hard time finding the way back. The journey grew longer and longer. The crew ran out of food. They grew so hungry that they ate bird bones and the ship's candles, sprinkled with salt and vinegar. Robert Juet died of starvation. By the time the *Discovery* reached England in the fall, only five men were still alive.

Henry Hudson was never heard from again. But in his memory, Furious Overfall was renamed Hudson Strait. The huge body of water Hudson had discovered was called Hudson Bay. Later explorers discovered that Hudson Bay didn't go through to the Pacific at all. Hudson had been sailing along the shore of a huge landlocked body of water. Some people say that his ghost still wanders along its edge, looking for the way to India!

Japan, Korea, and China

Chapter Five
Warlords of Japan

Hideyoshi, Japan's Great Leader

Imagine that you could do what no English or French adventurer ever did: find that imaginary Northwest Passage! You steer your ship through North America, past mountains and meadows and deep pine forests—and come right out the other side, into the Pacific Ocean. Your ship catches a breeze and sails away from the western coast of North America, leaving it far behind. After weeks at sea, you finally see land: a long chain of islands, rising out of the ocean in front of you. The morning sun, coming up behind your back, throws golden light on the volcanic peaks and white sand beaches of these islands. You've reached Japan, the "Land of the Rising Sun."

During the years that sea captains searched for the Northwest Passage, Japan was at war with itself. The emperor had retreated to his palace, powerless. Warlike noblemen called *daimyo* ruled over different sections of Japan, each fighting against his neighbor for more power. Roving bands of Japanese knights, named *samurai,* wandered over the countryside, fighting for whatever daimyo could offer the most money or land.

But then a great leader named Toyotomi Hideyoshi helped to end Japan's long civil war.

Hideyoshi wasn't a prince or a rich nobleman. He was a peddler who made his living walking from place to place, selling goods. He had no money, no important family, and no good looks. As a matter of fact, his wife's nickname for him was "The Bald Rat"!

But Hideyoshi didn't intend to remain a peddler for the rest of his life. Instead, he joined the army of a Japanese nobleman named Oda Nobunaga. Nobunaga wanted to unify all the warring parts of Japan, under his rule. He convinced strong samurai to join his army. He attacked and killed anyone who opposed him! And Hideyoshi served faithfully in battle after battle.

Nobunaga's attention was attracted by this energetic, loyal young man. Soon he gave Hideyoshi the special position of his Sandal-Bearer. Hideyoshi carried out his tasks well and was promoted time after time. Eventually, Hideyoshi became Nobunaga's favorite general, famous for his brilliant strategies in battle. Once, Hideyoshi was given the task of capturing a castle where an enemy of Nobunaga was hiding. The castle seemed invincible—until Hideyoshi noticed that it sat in the middle of a valley with a river on the far side. Hideyoshi ordered his men to dam the river. The river spilled over its banks, ran into the valley, and flooded it! Stranded in the middle of this brand-new lake, the castle's owner surrendered.

Nobunaga spread his rule over more than half of Japan. But before he could continue his conquests, he was killed in battle. Immediately, four different samurai declared that they would help Nobunaga's baby grandson, the heir to his power, rule over Japan. The truth was that each samurai wanted the baby's title for himself!

Hideyoshi was far away from the capital city of Japan. But as soon as he heard of Nobunaga's death, he gathered over two hundred thousand soldiers and marched toward the palace. The ambitious samurai came out to meet him, but Hideyoshi and his army crushed their forces. Hideyoshi himself defeated the strongest of the samurai, cut off his head, and attended Nobunaga's funeral, setting the head of the rebellious samurai down on Nobunaga's grave.

Hideyoshi was even more powerful than Nobunaga. But his method of ruling was different. Nobunaga's people had said, "Our leader's motto is, 'If the cuckoo doesn't sing, I'll kill him!'" But of Hideyoshi they said, "His motto is, 'If the cuckoo doesn't sing, I'll make him!'" Nobunaga had killed his enemies, but Hideyoshi preferred to force his enemies to take oaths of loyalty to him. He didn't want armed revolt to break out, so he ordered that every Japanese man who refused to swear loyalty to him must give up his sword. He sent his soldiers on a sword hunt throughout Japan, taking weapons away from anyone who might possibly rebel against his rule.

Once Hideyoshi had established his rule in Japan, he planned to expand his boundaries. He wanted to make Japan the

biggest empire in the world—an empire that stretched far beyond the Japanese islands. So he gathered his army together and told them, "Look across the water. The land you see there will be ours!" The land across the water was China—a country with sixty-five million people in it. Could Japan, so much smaller, really defeat this massive and powerful country?

Hideyoshi

Hideyoshi was confident. He planned to ferry his soldiers across the water to the ports of Korea, land there, and then march through Korea into China. When his soldiers were ready to sail, he sent a message to Korea: "Make way. We are coming!"

Hideyoshi thought he was the most powerful man in the world and that the Koreans would immediately bow to his will. But the Koreans disagreed. They ignored Hideyoshi's demands! So Hideyoshi turned his landing party into an attack force. He sailed across the water, landed his army on Korea's southern shores, and ordered them to move toward China.

The Japanese soldiers rampaged forward, killing thousands of Koreans. But Chinese troops marched down into

Korea to help drive back this Japanese threat. Against the combined Chinese and Korean forces, Hideyoshi's army began to falter. And Hideyoshi soon found that the Korean navy was much stronger than his own. Whenever he sent supplies across to his army, the Koreans attacked his ships with their famous "tortoise boats." These boats were covered with iron plates, so that they looked like turtle shells. Rather than firing guns, they rammed the Japanese supply ships with sharp iron spikes!

Outnumbered, Hideyoshi announced that he would make peace on one condition: the daughter of the Chinese emperor must come to Japan and marry the Japanese emperor. If a Chinese princess married the Japanese emperor, their sons could claim the right to the Chinese throne. But the Chinese simply laughed at this sneaky attempt to make China part of Japan. In response, they told Hideyoshi, "Your emperor only holds his throne because *we* allow him to. He should ask *Chinese* permission to rule in *Japan*!"

Hideyoshi was infuriated. He gathered his forces together for yet another assault on Korea. But the soldiers had barely set foot on Korean land when Hideyoshi became ill. Soon, he was too sick to direct the attack. The soldiers retreated, and Hideyoshi died not long afterward. He had gained power over Japan—but he had failed to conquer China.

The First Tokugawa Ruler

Hideyoshi was dead. Now it was time for Tokugawa Ieyasu to step into the spotlight.

Like Hideyoshi, Tokugawa Ieyasu had been Nobunaga's second-in-command. When Nobunaga died and Hideyoshi seized power, Ieyasu made the best of it. He swore to be loyal to Hideyoshi. As a matter of fact, Hideyoshi trusted Ieyasu so much that he made him one of five guardians who would watch over his young son Hideyori.

But while Hideyoshi ruled, Ieyasu waited. He spent years in the east of Japan, in an area called the Kanto plain, ruling as Hideyoshi's helper—and building loyalty to himself. He became richer and richer; he used his money to build an army.

And then Hideyoshi died.

Hideyoshi left his power to his five-year-old son Hideyori. He appointed Hideyori's five guardians, including Ieyasu, to rule as regents on his son's behalf. But the five guardians didn't want to help Hideyori rule. They began to fight among themselves, each one hoping to become Japan's ruler.

Ieyasu was determined to win the fight.

Eventually, the five guardians and the daimyo (noblemen) who fought for them divided into two separate armies—the Western Army, which pledged loyalty to the five-year-old Hideyori, and the Eastern Army, which followed Ieyasu. But Ieyasu sent secret messages to the daimyo in the Western Army, promising them land and money if they would pretend loyalty to Hideyori while actually fighting for Ieyasu. His plan worked! Only two years after Hideyoshi's death, Ieyasu met the Western Army in an enormous battle, called the Battle of Sekigahara. His Eastern Army advanced forward. Suddenly, the daimyo of the Western Army refused to fight against Ieyasu's Eastern Army. Some of these treacherous daimyo even turned and attacked their own samurai! When the battle was over, Ieyasu had triumphed.

Three years later, Ieyasu took the title of *shogun,* or military ruler of Japan. His patience had paid off! Soon his people were saying of him, "Ieyasu's motto is, 'If the cuckoo doesn't sing, I'll wait until he does!'"

Ieyasu moved the capital of Japan to the city of Edo, where a strong castle fortress already stood. He made this castle stronger, so that he could defend himself against any uprising. Today, we call the city of Edo "Tokyo."

Now Ieyasu had power and his own capital city. But he had a greater goal: to establish his family as the rightful shoguns of Japan. He hoped that his sons and grandsons and great-grandsons would inherit the title of shogun without having to fight for it.

His dream of a Tokugawa Shogunate still had one flaw in it, though: Hideyoshi's son and heir was still alive.

After Ieyasu's victory at Sekigahara, Hideyori and the daimyo still loyal to him fled to a fortress in another Japanese city called Osaka. For fifteen years, Hideyori stayed in this castle. He grew up. He got married and had a son! All the time he remained in Osaka, afraid of the man his father had trusted.

Ieyasu wasn't yet ready to make a final attack on Hideyori. Instead, Ieyasu continued to build his own family's power. He gave the title shogun to his son, and together they planned ways of keeping the daimyo loyal. They ordered that every daimyo must destroy each castle in his territory except for the one where he actually lived. That way, no daimyo could build up a secret army in a hidden fortress. Ieyasu and his son forced the daimyo to swear oaths of loyalty to the Tokugawa family. And they made every daimyo bring his family to live in Edo, the Tokugawa capital. Any daimyo who might consider rebellion would remember that his wife and children were living in the shogun's city—and could be held as hostages!

Ieyasu didn't forget the samurai either. Japan was filled with samurai warriors—several hundred thousand—who had fought for their daimyo during Japan's civil wars. All these armed and skilful fighters could be a threat to Tokugawa rule!

So Ieyasu and his son gave the samurai new jobs. They were appointed to be tax collectors, bookkeepers, and policemen. Ieyasu ordered the samurai to spend their time studying literature, art, music, and poetry, not just the art of war. And he encouraged them to wrestle, rather than to fight with swords. Japanese warriors became famous for their skills in poetry, music, and wrestling. Today, we call this style of wrestling *sumo wrestling.*

But Ieyasu had one thorn left in his side. Hideyori still lived.

In 1614, fourteen years after the Battle of Sekigahara, Ieyasu finally collected his forces and besieged Hideyori's castle in Osaka. The samurai in both armies fought for months. The siege lasted for almost a year. Slowly, Hideyori began to lose hope. He began to plan for defeat. Rather than surrender, he would kill himself; for a Japanese warrior, suicide was more honorable than capture by an enemy.

Finally, in June of 1615, Ieyasu's armies broke into the castle. When Hideyori saw his enemy's soldiers climbing over his walls, he killed himself, as he had planned. Perhaps he hoped that Ieyasu would spare his family. But Ieyasu had no mercy. When he entered the castle, he ordered Hideyori's son and heir put to death. The family of Hideyoshi was gone at last; Ieyasu's family, the Tokugawa Shogunate, was firmly in charge of Japan.

English and Dutch Colonies in the New World

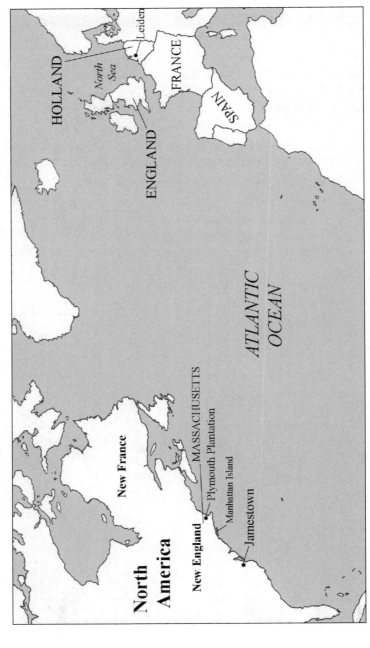

Chapter Six
New Colonies in the New World

Strangers and Saints in Plymouth

While Ieyasu Tokugawa was establishing his Shogunate in Japan, Henry Hudson was searching for the Northwest Passage in Canada, and the Jamestown colonists were struggling for survival in Virginia. And in England, a young man named William Bradford was making a difficult decision: to leave his home country forever.

William Bradford was a Puritan, an English Protestant who wanted the Church of England "purified" of everything borrowed from the Catholic church—including candles, incense, altars, priests, and prayer-books. But unlike other Puritans, Bradford and his friends had given up hope that the Church of England would ever be "purified." So they "separated" from the English church and held their own services. Other Englishmen called them Separatists.

King James forced Separatists to pay high taxes. He told Separatists that they could not use church buildings; William and his friends had to meet in barns and stables! And William knew that the king's soldiers would take any opportunity to arrest him and throw him into jail. So he and the other Separatists decided to leave England and go to a country where they could worship God in their own way—and in freedom.

Where would they go? Holland! The homeland of the Dutch welcomed Protestants, and since Holland was so close to England, the journey would not be long.

William Bradford and the other Separatists packed their belongings and families into a tiny wooden ship and sailed across the North Sea to Holland. They settled down in a small Dutch town called Leiden. Here, the Separatists were free to meet together in churches. They didn't have to pay extra taxes—or worry about being arrested. William Bradford soon married another English Separatist, a young woman named Dorothy. Together they had a son named John.

But in Leiden, little John Bradford and the other Separatist children learned to speak Dutch. They played with Dutch friends, and learned to wear wooden shoes and to skate on the icy canals. They began to forget English—and their Separatist beliefs as well. "Some of the children were drawn away from their parents," William Bradford later wrote. "Some became soldiers, others ran away to sea. Others took even worse courses, further from the ways of their fathers."

William Bradford and the other Separatist fathers wanted to take their families to a country where they could raise their children as good English Separatists. But they couldn't go back to England. So where could they go?

"What about North America?" they said to each other. "The English who settled in Jamestown are free to do as they please. If we travel to North America, we too could establish our own colony—a place where every citizen obeys God!"

The journey to North America was long and dangerous, but fifty of the Separatists were willing to go. Their leaders traveled back to England and went to visit rich English merchants. "Supply us money to buy a boat and food," the Separatists promised, "and we'll share with you all the gold and jewels we find in our new homeland!"

Several merchants agreed to pay for the ship and supplies—on one condition. The fifty Separatists had to take along sixty other settlers. Fifty men, women, and children couldn't establish a colony all alone!

The Separatists met the other settlers for the first time as they all boarded their new ship, the *Mayflower*. They called these new colonists "Strangers" and called themselves "Saints." But William Bradford used another name. He called the whole group of settlers "pilgrims"—Christians on a holy quest to build a colony where God would be worshipped. Today, we often borrow Bradford's name and call the whole group of settlers, Strangers and Saints alike, the Pilgrims.

The *Mayflower* sailed from England in 1620. William and Dorothy were aboard, but they left little John in Holland, where he would be safe. They knew that the new colony would be a perilous place to live.

After many cold, miserable days at sea, the *Mayflower* sighted land ahead. The Pilgrims had arrived at their new home. But before leaving the ship, the Pilgrims sat down together and drew up a set of laws for their new colony. They wanted to be sure that both Strangers and Saints would follow the same rules. This Mayflower Compact, said that all colonists must agree together before a law could be passed—and that once laws were passed, each colonist would obey with "all due submission and obedience." Almost every man on the Mayflower signed this compact. And then, together, the Saints and the Strangers elected a Separatist, John Carver, to be their governor.

At first, the women and children stayed on the *Mayflower* while Bradford and others went out exploring. Finally, the explorers found the perfect place for the new colony. Cornfields were already planted there. A freshwater stream flowed nearby. They even found the remains of a few houses, made of saplings bent into arches and thrust into the ground and then covered with thick mats made of reeds. It was an Indian village, deserted several years before.

They returned to the Mayflower, shouting out the news of their great find. But the women who came running to meet them were weeping. While the men were exploring, Dorothy Bradford had fallen overboard and drowned!

William Bradford had little time for grief. Winter was coming, and the Pilgrims had to build log houses for their families. The work was hard and slow. The food they had brought with them from England—dried biscuits, beans, pork soaked in salt water—began to run out. They began to die from fever, scurvy, and starvation. "Sometimes two or three died in one day," William Bradford wrote of these times.

But then the Native Americans who lived nearby took pity on these newcomers. Massasoit, chief of the Wampanoag tribe, was willing to be friendly. One of his warriors, Squanto, could speak English. So Squanto helped Massasoit and the

Englishmen make a treaty, in which they swore not to hurt each other. Squanto himself showed the Pilgrims how to grow crops in their new fields. William Bradford wrote, "He showed them how to set the corn in the ground, and how to tend it when it came up. Also he told them if they did not put a fish in the ground with the seed for fertilizer, in these long-used fields it would come to nothing."

Starvation was averted. But the young colony, which the English named Plymouth Plantation, was still a risky place to live. One hot day, governor John Carver was laboring in the cornfields when his head began to hurt. When he came in, he lay down to rest—and soon slipped into unconsciousness. Only a few days later, John Carver died.

The colonists elected William Bradford to be their new leader. Bradford worked hard to make the colony successful. He planted crops, bought food from English fishing boats that sailed by, and treated the Native Americans with friendship. By the fall of Bradford's first year as governor, the colony finally was beginning to prosper. Their crops, watched over by Squanto, had grown well and the harvest was plentiful. The Pilgrims built fires, cooked a huge feast of corn, wild turkey, fish, and deer, and invited Massasoit and ninety other Wampanoag Indians to be their guests. At this first Thanksgiving Feast, the Pilgrims gave thanks to God for their survival!

Soon, more Puritans would come to the New World, seeking the freedom to worship God in their own way. North of Plymouth Plantation, over two thousand Puritans formed a second Puritan settlement, called the Massachusetts Bay Colony. Today, Plymouth Plantation and the Massachusetts Bay Colony are both part of the state of Massachusetts.

The Dutch in the New World

More English settlers soon came to the New World. So many English colonies sprang up around Plymouth Plantation and the Massachusetts Bay Colony that the whole area became known as New England. Up in Canada, French colonists were living in New France. Down in South America, the Spanish had settled New Spain.

The Dutch weren't far behind!

After William the Silent freed Holland from Spanish rule, the Dutch became known for sailing their swift cargo ships all over the world. Groups of rich Dutch merchants joined together to build small settlements, called trading posts, in the distant lands of Asia. They hired Dutch captains who sailed to these trading posts, bought silks, spices, tea and coffee, and brought them back to European buyers. Then the merchants split the profits among themselves.

Soon the Dutch government organized all of these merchant groups into one big group, called the Dutch East India Company. The Dutch East India Company made the Netherlands very rich. Amsterdam, Holland's largest city, became the busiest port in Europe! Dutch schools and universities were filled with eager students. Dutch merchants built themselves huge homes, filled with beautiful handmade furniture and lovely paintings done by famous Dutch artists like Rembrandt and Vermeer. The Dutch became the greatest sea traders in the world.

Meanwhile, Henry Hudson was searching for that mysterious Northwest Passage. He convinced Dutch merchants to pay for one of his attempts. The attempt failed, but Hudson brought back tales of "Indians" (Native Americans) who were willing to trade beaver pelts, bearskins, and other rich furs. Dutch ships began to travel to the river which Hudson had explored, now called the Hudson River, offering to trade metal pots, pans, knives and arrow points to the native tribes in exchange for beaver, mink, and bearskins. So many Dutch merchants visited the shores of the Hudson River that the area around the water became known as New Netherland.

The government of Holland formed a new company, the Dutch *West* India Company. This company sent thirty families, along with cows, sheep, corn and wheat seeds, plows and harvesters, to settle on the banks of the Hudson River and live year round. Soon, other settlements followed.

In 1624, four years after the Pilgrims arrived at Plymouth Plantation, the Dutch West India Company decided to build a town called New Amsterdam on an island called Manhattan Island. New Amsterdam would become the main port and the capital city of New Netherland.

But a Native American tribe called the Lenape already lived on the island. So the Dutch offered the Lenape gifts in exchange for Manhattan Island. The Lenape took the gifts. According to stories told later, these goods were glass beads, pots and kettles, knives and axes, and a few rolls of cloth, worth around twenty-four dollars!

Of course, the island of Manhattan was worth far, far more. But the Lenape never intended to "sell" the land. They believed that land, like air, was something that everyone shared. The Lenape would settle down in a place, build houses of trees and bark, grow corn and squash, hunt deer and bear, and gather clams and crabs along the shores. After a few years, when the deer had grown scarce and the crabs were harder to find, the Lenape would gather up their belongings and move on.

The Lenape thought that the Dutch would live on Manhattan Island for a few years and then move on. But the colonists of New Amsterdam had no intention of leaving—ever. They built a large fort right at the end of the island and a wide road called the Broad Way that ran from the fort right across the island. Ships could dock easily at the island, allowing the Dutch to load furs and receive goods.

The town of New Amsterdam grew quickly. Ships brought sugar, rum, salt, and spices from India and Africa. Indians traded furs for these goods; colonists from Jamestown and New England came to New Amsterdam to buy. People from all over the world came to New Amsterdam on merchant ships. More and more houses were built, along with inns where travelers stayed, and public houses, or "pubs," where they could drink beer in the evenings. These pubs were so popular that, eventually, almost one-fourth of the buildings in New Amsterdam were pubs!

Although trade prospered, the town itself began to fall apart. When boards fell off houses, no one bothered to nail them back on. The dirt-packed Broad Way was full of holes. Pigs and cows wandered through the streets, eating garbage that the colonists threw out of their doors. Traders got drunk in the public houses and raced wagons at top speed through the narrow streets. New Amsterdam's one church fell apart from disuse. The fort at the town's center was collapsing. The Dutch West India Company kept sending new governors to New Amsterdam. But none of these governors could keep control of the rowdy trading center!

In 1647, the Dutch West India Company tried one more new governor. Peter Stuyvesant, a tall, grim ex-soldier, arrived from Holland on a bright, chilly May morning. When he strode down the gangplank of his ship, the gathered onlookers heard an odd sound...step, *thump,* step, *thump,* step, *thump.* Peter Stuyvesant's right leg had been shot off by a cannonball three years before. In its place, he wore a wooden peg leg, held together with silver nails and wrapped around by silver bands!

Stuyvesant was appalled at what he saw. He wrote, "New Amsterdam is now...greatly decayed, and the walls...more and more trodden underfoot by men and cattle." Immediately he began to make new laws. Colonists who wanted to drink would have to pay extra money for their wine and beer; the extra money would be used to repair buildings. All pigs and goats had to be kept in fences. Pubs had to close early in the evenings and stay closed on Sundays. Peter Stuyvesant even ordered ministers to preach more sermons on Sundays! When one colonist complained, Stuyvesant retorted, "I'll cut off your head and send the pieces to Holland, so they can complain there!"

The colonists didn't like the new laws. They called their new governor rude nicknames like "Old Silvernails" and "Stubborn Pete." But unhappy colonists were the least of Stuyvesant's worries. His colony was surrounded by English colonies, and the English were constantly trying to settle down on Dutch land and claim it as their own. Stuyvesant met with

Peter Stuyvesant

the leaders of the New England colonies, and together they agreed on a boundary line between English and Dutch lands. But Stuyvesant was sure that the English planned to invade New Amsterdam. He wrote to the Dutch West India Company, begging for soldiers and weapons. The Company, seeing no danger, refused.

Stuyvesant ordered a new, higher wall built around New Amsterdam. He put a guard around the wall, both day and night. But when the English did arrive to take over New Amsterdam, the wall was useless.

Over in England, King James had died and Charles II had become King. Charles II declared that the Dutch land in New Netherland was his—and gave it to his brother, the Duke of York, as a present. Immediately, the Duke of York sent English warships over to North America. The ships sailed into the harbor of Manhattan Island and surrounded it. No one could get into or out of New Amsterdam! Without soldiers, without weapons, running out of food, the people of New Amsterdam were terrified. They begged Stuyvesant to surrender peacefully, without fighting back. Reluctantly, Stuyvesant did.

Pleased by their victory, the English marched into New Amsterdam and renamed it New York, in honor of the Duke of York. The new English governor announced that all Dutch could keep their land and houses, and go on speaking Dutch—but that they would become English citizens. "Anyone who doesn't wish to become an English citizen," he proclaimed, "may return to Holland in peace."

Peter Stuyvesant didn't want to return to Holland. He now thought of New Amsterdam as home. Sadly, he gathered his family together and retired to his farm on Manhattan Island. He had worked for seventeen years to rule New Amsterdam, but now the Dutch empire in the New World was gone. From New England down to Jamestown, North America was all English.

But some remnants of New Amsterdam remain. In the modern city of New York, you can still walk down Wall Street—the path that once ran along the wall Stuyvesant built to protect New Amsterdam. You can eat dinner at a restaurant on Broadway, the Broad Way where Dutch public houses once served traders from all over the world. And you can still visit Peter Stuyvesant's grave. When he died, he was buried in the chapel on his farm. Today, that chapel is St. Mark's Church in Manhattan, New York—and the street that runs past it is called Stuyvesant Street.

The Triangular Trade Route

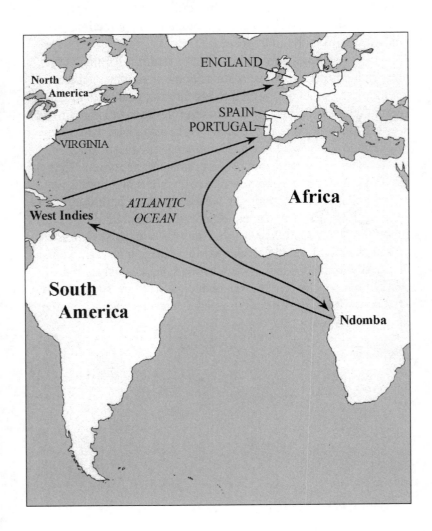

Chapter Seven
The Spread of Slavery

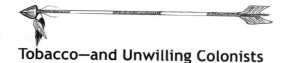

Tobacco—and Unwilling Colonists

The English wanted New Amsterdam (now New York) because the rich fur trade could make money for England. So far, the other English settlements in America hadn't produced much wealth! King James had hoped that the Jamestown colonists would find gold, but the rich soil of Virginia held no jewels or precious metals.

But soon Virginia's ground brought England another kind of gold—"green gold." And like the gold of South America, this "green gold" would bring riches to some and misery to others.

The story of Virginia's green gold began when a young Englishman named John Rolfe arrived at the Jamestown colony. Jamestown had been founded two years before, but the colonists were starving. They were ragged, poor, and wretched, struggling through long days of farming and huddling, still hungry, over their small fires at night. John Rolfe was sure that the colony would fail and that he would have to return to England. In the meantime, he had little food—and nothing fun to do after a hard day of labor in the hot Virginia sun.

But John Rolfe did have a few tobacco seeds. And like many Englishmen, he loved to smoke.

Rolfe had already noticed that the native Americans who lived near the colony grew a kind of tobacco of their own. They planted it, weeded it carefully, picked it by hand, hung the leaves up to dry over the smoke of a wood fire, and then rolled the leaves up and smoked them. Other colonists had tried this native Virginia tobacco, but they didn't like the way it tasted. "Poore and weake, and of a byting taste," one colonist complained.

But John Rolfe's seeds were *Spanish* tobacco—a rich kind of leaf that most Englishmen preferred. Rolfe found a fertile patch of land and planted his seeds. He copied the native American methods of raising the plants, picking the leaves, and hanging them up to dry. When he rolled up his leaves and smoked them, he was delighted. He thought that the Virginia-grown Spanish leaves tasted wonderful!

John Rolfe shared his tobacco with a few other colonists. They agreed: the leaf tasted wonderful. Together, the colonists grew a few more plants and sent some of the tobacco to London.

London was full of tobacco-users! All the most fashionable young men of England smoked. They blew so much smoke out of their mouths and noses that they were called "reeking gallants." Often, they had servants who did nothing but follow them around to taverns, balls, and theatres, carrying their tobacco equipment. A German visitor to England marveled, "Everywhere...the English are constantly smoking....They draw the smoke into their mouths [and] puff out again through their nostrils, like funnels, along with...plenty of phlegm from the head." But until now, the English had been forced to buy tobacco from the Spanish—and Spain and England were continually at war. If the English could buy Virginia tobacco instead, they wouldn't have to pay money to their enemies!

London smokers purchased all the tobacco that the Jamestown colonists sent—and exclaimed over the new leaf. "No country under the Sunne may, or doth affoord more pleasant, sweet, and strong Tobacco," one Englishman marveled. Merchants begged for more. The Jamestown colonists realized that although they had no gold, they might have something better. Only six years after Rolfe first planted his seeds, the Jamestown colonists were planting tobacco everywhere—even in the streets of their town! By the following year, England was buying more tobacco from Virginia than from Spain.

Not everyone was pleased with English smoking habits. King James wrote an essay called *Counterblaste to Tobacco*, in which he announced, "[Smoking is] a custom loathsome to the eye, hateful to the nose, harmful to the brain, dangerous to the lungs, and in the black, stinking fume thereof, nearest resembling the horrible Stygian smoke of the pit that is bottomless." Englishmen kept right on smoking. By 1630, Virginia was sending over a half million pounds of tobacco to England every year!

But raising tobacco took an enormous amount of work. The seeds had to be hand-planted, hand-weeded, and hand-pruned. Caterpillars and worms had to be picked off one at a time. When the tobacco plants were ready, the leaves had to be taken off one at a time and hung on pegs to dry for six weeks. Then the stems had to be taken off and the leaves packed, one at a time, into barrels. One farm worker could only take care of two or three acres of tobacco.

At first, tobacco farmers hired *indentured servants*— poor Englishmen and women who agreed to work for a colonist who paid for their journey to the New World and gave them food and a place to live. After six or seven years, the colonist would give the servant a new suit of clothes and enough money to get started. The servant was now a member of the colony. Many Americans who began as indentured servants later became wealthy, important citizens.

But as the tobacco fields grew larger, farmers needed even more help.

In 1619, a Dutch trading ship threw down its anchor in the Chesapeake Bay and offered to sell African slaves to the Jamestown colonists. The colonists bought twenty slaves and put *them* to work in the tobacco fields.

Although these Africans were the first North American slaves, slavery itself was nothing new. For at least a hundred years, European traders had brought slaves to the plantations of Central and South America. They would load their ships with metal knives, pots and pans, cloth, and rum, and would sail down to the west coast of Africa. There, they would dock their ships and meet with African war leaders who had taken members of other African tribes as prisoners of war. The war leaders would trade these prisoners for the European goods.

Then the European ships would sail across the Atlantic to the West Indies, the islands of Central America, trade the slaves for sugar, molasses, and cotton, and sail back to Europe. This became known as the "Triangular Trade" because the ships followed a triangular pattern.

But now slaves came, not just to the Portuguese and Spanish colonies in Central and South America, but to North America as well. At first, Virginia bought only a few hundred slaves per year. But the tobacco fields grew larger and larger. Other colonies, south of Virginia, began to plant not only tobacco but also rice and cotton. These fields also needed thousands of laborers to tend them, water them, and harvest them. More and more slaves came to North America— thousands, and then tens of thousands per year.

A hundred years after the first slaves came to Jamestown, almost half of the colonists in Virginia were slaves. The Virginia tobacco plantations prospered, but only because of slavery. And these unwilling colonists could never earn their freedom—or return home.

Queen Nzinga of Angola

The first slaves brought to Jamestown came from the west coast of Africa on a Dutch ship. But the Dutch weren't the first European nation to trade in West African slaves. The Portuguese, who lived in a small seagoing nation on the coast of the Spanish peninsula, had made a fortune selling African slaves to other European countries. Portuguese slave traders thought of the huge African continent as an inexhaustible source of slaves—and wealth.

But one woman made it her life's work to fight against the Portuguese invaders.

The princess Nzinga was born into the royal family of Ndomba, a kingdom on the western coast of Africa. As long as she could remember, Portuguese traders had been landing on the shores of her homeland, offering cloth, jewelry, and rum in exchange for prisoners. Nzinga didn't know what happened to these prisoners—but she knew that once they boarded the slave ships, they were never seen again.

Nzinga's father, the ruler of Ndomba, was wary of the Portuguese ships. They brought fascinating European goods, and they treated him with respect, as a king should be treated. But he had also heard rumors that they might attack him and capture some of his land.

The rumors were true. For many years, the Portuguese had been careful to make friends with the kings of African kingdoms near the coast: Ndomba, Kongo (to the north), and Matamba (a little to the northeast). The Portuguese king wrote letters to the king of Kongo, calling him "most powerful and excellent king," and sent experts in farming to West Africa to serve the African people. In exchange for this friendliness, the Portuguese expected to receive as many prisoners of war as these kingdoms could provide.

But as Nzinga grew to be a woman, the slave trade itself began to change. The colonies in North and South America demanded more slaves than the African kingdoms could willingly provide. And other European nations—the English, Dutch, and French—were beginning to send slave ships to West Africa. The Portuguese wanted to keep part of Africa for their very own—an African kingdom of slaves which no English or Dutch trader could use.

So the Portuguese king decided to attack and conquer Ndomba. He sent an army to invade Nzinga's homeland. After Ndomba was captured, the Portuguese planned to settle a hundred families there and rename it the Kingdom of Sebastiao.

But the conquest of Ndomba didn't go as planned. Nzinga's father led his people against the Portuguese invaders in battle after battle. By the time Nzinga had grown to be a woman, Ndomba and Portugal had been fighting for almost thirty years! Nzinga joined in the fighting. She led a trained band of women warriors against the Portuguese again and again. She gained a reputation for bravery—and cruelty.

When Nzinga was thirty-four, her brother Mbandi became king in her father's place. Nzinga loved her two sisters, who fought beside her in her warrior band. But she thought her brother was a weak, cowardly whiner, more interested in food than in leadership. Mbandi was afraid of his sister! He knew she was stronger than he was—and he suspected that she would be a better ruler. So when he took over the throne, he drove her out of the kingdom.

But after a few years of war, Mbandi realized that he would never be able to defeat the Portuguese. He decided that he would try to make a treaty with them instead. The Portuguese, tired of the unending battles, were willing to meet for peace talks—but Mbandi was too frightened to travel to their headquarters. Instead, he sent a message to his sister Nzinga. "Go and meet with the Portuguese for me," he said. "Convince them to leave us in peace, and I will allow you to return to your homeland."

Nzinga agreed to go. She knew that the people of Ndomba had not been able to outfight the Portuguese. Perhaps she could outwit them instead! So she dressed in her royal robes, collected a retinue of servants, and journeyed to the town where the Portuguese leaders had set up their headquarters. The Portuguese gave her a comfortable and luxurious house to stay in and sent missionaries to talk to her. Nzinga listened carefully. When she realized that the Portuguese would treat her with more respect if she were a Christian, she allowed herself to be baptized and to be given a Christian name, Anna de Sousa. She also ordered her sisters, Kifunji and Mukumbu, to be baptized. The Portuguese gave them the names Lady Grace and Lady Barbara.

And then the day to settle the terms of the treaty arrived. When Nzinga walked into the hall where she would meet with the Portuguese leader, she looked around and saw only one chair! The Portuguese leader sat on a jeweled, carved chair of state. But he had tossed a cushion on the floor for Nzinga.

Nzinga turned to the servant behind her and raised her eyebrows. At once, the woman came forward and fell down on her hands and knees. Nzinga tossed her robe out behind her and seated herself royally on her human throne. Now she could look the Portuguese in the eye!

When the treaty talks were over, the Portuguese had agreed to treat Ndomba as an independent African kingdom, as long as all of the Portuguese captives taken in the long war were sent home. Nzinga rose and started from the room. Her servant remained on her hands and knees. The governor stood as well.

Queen Nzinga

"Your...throne!" he pointed out.

Nzinga threw him a royal glance.

"Great queens," she said, "do not use the same throne twice." She stalked out—and returned home to Ndomba.

But the peace treaty Nzinga had negotiated didn't last. The Portuguese, once again running low on slaves, invaded Ndomba again, kidnapping its people and packing them on board the slave ships. Nzinga begged her brother to fight back, but he refused. Perhaps he was afraid to lead warriors armed with spears against the guns of the Portuguese.

Nzinga was furious with her brother's cowardice. Then, unexpectedly, Mbandi died. Many people whispered that Nzinga had poisoned him, afraid that he would lose the kingdom to Portugal forever. No one knows for sure.

But we do know that Nzinga declared herself queen and began a lifelong war against the Portuguese. The Portuguese captured her capital city and drove her from her palace. Nzinga simply invaded the nearby kingdom of Matamba and took its throne instead. Whenever the Portuguese tried to bring parties of slaves from other West African nations to the coast, Nzinga would send her soldiers to attack them.

After years and years of struggling against Nzinga's fighters, the Portuguese finally gave up. They told Nzinga that she could return to her throne in Ndomba and rule it in peace— as long as she allowed them to pass through her kingdom with slaves, on the way to the coast. Nzinga, now in her seventies, agreed. In great ceremony, she returned to the palace she had left years before. When she died, at the age of eighty-one, she was buried with a bow and arrow in her hands, ready for battle.

But after Nzinga's death, the Portuguese took over Kongo, Matamba, *and* Ndomba. Because Nzinga's people had called her *ngola,* or "war chief," the Portuguese thought that *ngola* was the proper name of her country. So they called their new colony Angola. And Angola remained under Portuguese rule until November 11th, 1975—three hundred years later.

The Ottoman Empire

Chapter Eight
The Middle of the East

The Persian Puzzle

Imagine that you're putting together a huge puzzle-map of the world. Each country is a different color. On the far right-hand side of the puzzle you fit together the white islands of Japan, just off the deep purple coast of China. You build India's orange shores and then decide to go up above the Mediterranean Sea and assemble Europe. Europe is full of different colors: England is scarlet, France pink, Spain golden, Holland grey.

You piece together the Atlantic Ocean and go to work on the continents of North and South America. But instead of the forest-green you expect, North and South American are rainbowed with the colors of Europe! French pink, English scarlet, and Dutch grey line the coast of North America. The whole western coast of South America is golden, like Spain; the east part of the continent is the lime-green of Portugal. You move back across the ocean to assemble Africa. But what happened to Africa's sapphire blue? Africa is patched over with Portuguese lime, Dutch grey, and English scarlet. The colors of Europe have bled over into three other continents!

Now it's time to assemble the blank area between Europe and China. You look around, wondering what color this part of the world will be, and notice something odd. A pile of pieces are splattered with patches of a dozen different colors: silver, olive, maroon, copper, primrose, saffron, emerald, indigo, violet, jade, with a top layer of thin chestnut brown.

These aren't European colors. They're the colors of the Middle East. You fit them together and see a country that has been ruled by empire after empire after empire: the country of Persia, lying between the Tigris River and the edge of China.

The bottom layer on that puzzle piece is silver. It represents the Assyrian empire, which ruled this part of the world

81

long ago. But then Assyria was conquered by the Babylonians (the olive layer), who were in turn defeated by the Persians. The Persians (the maroon color) gave this land their name—but they didn't keep their empire. They were conquered by Alexander the Great.

When Alexander died, his empire (copper, on your puzzle piece) was divided into three parts. His general Seleucus claimed Persia. But Seleucus and his descendents, called Seleucids (their empire is primrose-yellow), couldn't keep control of Persia. One part of Persia, called Parthia, broke away from the Seleucids and set up a kingdom of their own.

The Parthians (the saffron layer on those Persian pieces) grew larger as the Seleucids lost power. They even managed to keep off the Roman invaders who came from the west. For a short time, Parthia became the strongest empire in the Middle East.

Then the Parthian kings began to quarrel with their noblemen—and the empire shrank until one of those noblemen threw the Parthian ruler from his throne and took over. His descendents, the Sassanid dynasty of Persia, ruled in the central part of Persia for many years. (Their empire is emerald.)

But a wave of indigo was creeping across the map of the East. Down in the Arabian peninsula, a prophet named Muhammad was gathering Arab followers around him. These *Muslims* spread Muhammad's message all across the medieval world—and built the Islamic empire. The Sassanid dynasty fell to Muslim invaders, and Persia became an Islamic nation.

Meanwhile, nomads from Asia, called Turks, were wandering into Muslim Persia and settling down. They were fierce fighters. Many of them became soldiers in the army of the Islamic empire. As time went on, the Turkish soldiers became just as powerful as their Arab masters! One group of Turks, the Ghaznavids, rejected Islamic rule and took over the land of Persia. (The violet color, splattered overtop the indigo, represents the Ghaznavids.)

The Ghaznavids didn't have long to rule, though. Soon, Mongols invaded from the east, destroying Persian cities and leveling crops. Mongol *khans*, or warrior-chiefs, took over the rule of Persia; their conquest adds a layer of jade to your puzzle.

Finally, a man named Ismail decided that the time had come to throw off the Mongol yoke. He gathered his kinsmen, who were called the Safavids, around him in an army, and attacked the Mongol khan. Ismail won! He crowned himself *shah,* or ruler of Iran. Finally, you've arrived at that top layer of color: the Safavid color, chestnut brown. Ten empires—ten layers of color—have ruled in this Middle Eastern country!

The greatest Safavid shah, Abbas I, was Ismail's great-grandson. Abbas almost didn't survive to be Shah. When he was still a very young man, his uncle seized the Persian throne and ordered all other heirs to the throne executed! But before this ruthless command could be carried out, Abbas's uncle had a huge party to celebrate his new power—and drank himself to death.

Abbas came to the throne, determined to bring strength to a country almost destroyed by war. His first step was to make peace with another Turkish kingdom, the Ottomans. These warlike Turks lived to the west of Persia and kept trying to invade it. Abbas knew that the Persian army was too weak to fight off the Ottomans. So he told the Ottomans that he would give them part of Persia, as long as they would leave the rest in peace.

The Ottoman Turks thought that Abbas was afraid to fight. But Abbas had a plan. He hired an English soldier, Sir Robert Sherley, to train the disorganized Persian army. Sherley taught Abbas's soldiers to use muskets and other European weapons. He organized them into divisions: infantrymen, musketeers, artillerymen. He trained them to fight in formation. After several years of this training, the Persian army faced the Ottoman Turks—and crushed them in battle. Abbas reclaimed all of his territory and even took some Turkish land for his own!

Now, Abbas turned to another project: making Persia into a great trading nation. The best port in Persia, an island in the Persian Gulf, had been claimed by the Portuguese. Abbas drove the Portuguese out and built his own trading post on the island. Then he brought Chinese craftsmen into Persia to rebuild the trades of silk-making and carpet-weaving. He built new roads and bridges, so that goods could be carried through his empire. His new port, Bandar Abbas, became one of the busiest in the east! Today, we call Persia *Iran*. Bandar Abbas is still an important Iranian port.

But as Abbas labored hard to make Persia secure, he became more and more fearful. He thought that his noblemen were plotting against him. He was afraid of his own brothers. He even suspected his own son of treachery and ordered him executed! When he died at the age of seventy, Shah Abbas left behind him a strong and prosperous Persia—but he died overcome by grief and guilt.

The Ottoman Turks

As Persia grew stronger, the Ottoman Turks, who lived to the west of Persia, grew weaker. But like Persia, the Ottoman empire was rescued by a great and cruel ruler: the Sultan Murad.

When Murad was born, into a royal Ottoman family, Shah Abbas was already an old man, famous for his might.

As the young Murad grew, he learned the history of the empire he would someday rule. He learned that a single Turkish tribe, the Seljuk tribe, had wandered from central Asia into the Middle East, back in the days when the Islamic empire still ruled over Persian land. Just as the Ghaznavid Turks had rebelled against their Islamic rulers and taken control of the land of Persia, so the Seljuk tribe had rebelled and taken control of *their* own little piece of the Muslim empire.

The Seljuk Turks were fearless, savage fighters and soon expanded their kingdom. They took part of Persia for their own. They took land away from the Byzantine Empire. They captured Syria and Palestine.

But the Turks had always been nomads. Although they could conquer an empire, they didn't do a very good job of collecting taxes, fixing roads, and passing laws. Their empire began to fall apart. As it collapsed, one Turkish leader, a warrior named Osman, gathered his followers around himself and determined to save what he could. Osman and his followers lived just above the northwest corner of the Mediterranean Sea, in the country which we now call Turkey. Turkey soon became the center of the new Turkish empire: the Ottoman empire. Now the two great empires of the Middle East—the Persian and the Ottoman—were both ruled by Turks.

Under Osman's leadership, the Ottoman Turks captured a much larger kingdom than the Seljuks had ever ruled. They fought their way east, across the Tigris and the Euphrates, all the way to the borders of Persia. They captured most of Arabia—including the city of Baghdad. They took the Byzantine capital, Constantinople, and renamed it Istanbul. They claimed Egypt and North Africa, just as the Muslim empire had before them. And then they did something that frightened the rest of the world. They crossed over the Bosporus Strait—the water that divided Asia from Europe. Now the Turks were invading European land!

The kings of Europe began to get nervous. How far would the Ottoman empire spread? While they watched, the Ottoman Turks conquered Greece, fought their way up into Russia, and kept on coming west! The sultan of the Ottomans now called himself "Sovereign of the Two Lands and of the Two Seas," because he ruled a kingdom that stretched over two continents: Asia *and* Europe!

But like the ancient Roman empire, the Ottoman empire grew too large. The sultans began to spend too much money on feasts, palaces, and silks. So much Spanish gold had flooded into Europe from South America that no one wanted the silver coins of the Ottomans any more. One Ottoman writer remarked, "[The coins have become] as worthless as drops of

An Ottoman coin

dew." The Ottoman officials became corrupt and stole as much food and money as they wanted. "The Empire," wrote an Englishman who lived during the days of the Ottomans, "has become like an old body, crazed through many vices." The Ottomans even lost control of Baghdad, their prized city!

But then Murad inherited the throne of the Ottomans.

No one expected great things of Murad. He was only eleven years old, plain, quiet, and fat. His mother insisted on helping him rule—for ten whole years! While she commanded Murad's armies, the Ottoman empire went on shrinking. So many Ottoman soldiers were captured in battle and sold as slaves that you could buy an Ottoman soldier in the Russian slave markets for the price of a drink of fermented grain juice!

Murad waited. He exercised, training with a bow until he could shoot an arrow through a metal sheet four inches thick. He threw spears until he could kill a raven sitting on the top of a mosque a mile away. He wrestled until he could pick up two grown men, one in each hand, and fling them in different directions.

Finally, Murad's time came.

When he was twenty-three years old, the Ottoman army revolted. They marched on the sultan's palace, announcing that *they* planned to run the empire from now on! "Hand over your Grand Vizier to us!" they demanded. "You should listen to us—not to him!"

Murad didn't want to hand over the Grand Vizier, who was his friend. But then the Vizier himself came forward. "Sultan," he said to Murad, "let a thousand slaves like me perish for the safety of your throne. I will die a martyr—and the guilt for my blood will be on their heads." He drew his sword and sprang forward, aiming a blow at the rebel leader. But the mob swarmed around him, stabbing him and then cutting off his head.

Murad realized that the soldiers would attack him next. So he pretended to agree to their demands. Finally they let Murad return to his own quarters, thinking that the young sultan would now do exactly as the army suggested.

86

But Murad quietly sent out his own household spies to find out who had started the riot. Soon, he discovered the ringleader: one of his own officials, Rejeb Pasha. Murad had already made Rejeb his new Grand Vizier! But now he realized that Rejeb hoped to rule the empire through telling Murad what to do.

One morning, Rejeb was just leaving a meeting when a household servant approached him and bowed low. "Please," he said, "come to the palace. The sultan wishes to speak with you."

Rejeb agreed and followed along. The servant escorted him to a door and opened it. Rejeb walked through—and found himself surrounded by the Sultan's personal force of assassins. He heard Murad's voice command, "Cut off the head of the traitor!" And immediately it was done.

Murad then ordered Rejeb's body flung from the palace gates—right out into a group of army leaders! Terrified, the leaders ran away. Then Murad sent his own spies out through the city, telling them to find—and kill on the spot—anyone involved in the rebellion. Knowing that rebels often formed their plans while drinking together in taverns, late at night, he closed all the taverns—permanently! Anyone found drinking wine was instantly put to death. Soon the word spread: Murad was no longer a weak child. He would not tolerate rebellion!

Murad's power grew—and so did his ruthlessness. When his chief musician began to play him a Persian song, he beheaded the man instantly. When one of his doctors didn't cure him quickly enough, he forced the doctor to drink a dose of poison! Soon, whenever he approached, everyone would freeze completely, afraid to move or speak in case they might accidentally sound rebellious!

But Murad's cruelty stopped the decay of the Ottoman empire. With his army and his advisors too frightened to disobey him, he set out on a quest to recapture Ottoman land. He took back land that the Persians had claimed. He recaptured the city of Baghdad. He spread the empire back toward its old borders once more. The decline of the Ottoman Empire had been halted.

Shortly afterward, Murad fell ill. He lay in bed for two weeks, growing steadily worse. At the age of twenty-eight, he died—leaving behind him an empire rescued.

The Countries of the Thirty Years' War

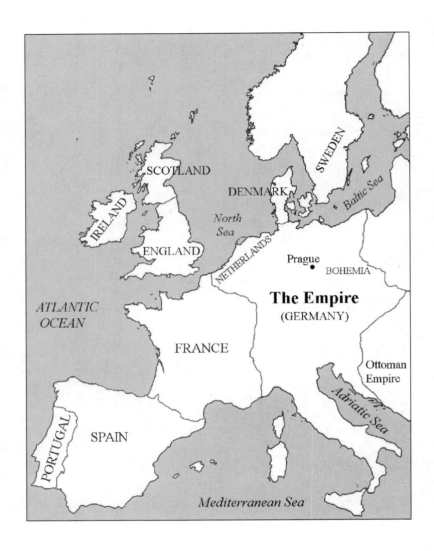

Chapter Nine
The Western War

The Thirty Years' War, 1618-1648

While Sultan Murad was battling his way across the Middle East, claiming land for the Ottoman Turks, Europe was fighting its own war—with itself. This European war started when a handful of unhappy Germans threw two German noblemen out of a window. Thirty years later, soldiers from every European nation lay dead across hundreds of battlefields.

The story of this "Thirty Years' War" begins all the way back with Charles V, the Holy Roman Emperor. We read about Charles in the very first chapter of this book. Charles divided his empire between his brother Ferdinand and his son, Philip II. Philip II inherited Spain and the Netherlands (although William of Silent then helped the Netherlands break free). Ferdinand got Charles's German lands—and eventually became Holy Roman Emperor in his brother's place.

When Ferdinand died, he left his German lands to his son Maximilian, who then passed them on to *his* son Matthias. When Matthias died without children, those German lands went to his cousin, Ferdinand II.

At once, trouble began.

In those days, Germany was a collection of small territories, each ruled by a powerful prince who owed allegiance to the German king. Each prince had the right to say whether *his* small territory would be Catholic or Protestant. Many of the German princes (and their territories) were Protestants. But like his great-great-uncle, Charles V, Ferdinand II was a devout Catholic. He hated Protestantism—and at once began passing laws to stamp out Protestant worship in his new kingdom.

The Protestant princes in one particular part of Germany, called Bohemia, were furious. So were their

Protestant subjects! They gathered together in the Bohemian city of Prague, ready to protest Ferdinand's Catholic laws.

But Ferdinand wasn't even in Germany. He had gone traveling and left two of his officials in charge of his kingdom while he was gone.

The two officials didn't know what to do with this huge angry crowd of Protestants. First, they tried to reason with the crowd. Then, they nervously ordered the crowd to disperse. "No!" the mob shouted. And then one of the leaders suggested, "Let's kill these two and form a new Protestant government, here and now!"

At that, the two officials beat a quick retreat. They ran to the royal castle of Prague and locked themselves in. The mob followed them, broke through the gates, and overran the castle's halls and chambers. Finally they found the two officials, hiding in an upper room, fifty feet above the castle's courtyard. The officials pushed a huge wooden table between themselves and the crowd, but it was no use. The rioters overturned the table, grabbed the two—and threw them out of the nearest window!

The two officials weren't even injured. They got to their feet and ran away. Catholics loyal to Ferdinand later said, "The Virgin Mary protected them!" But German Protestants remarked, "No wonder. They landed on a nice soft manure heap." This event was the beginning of over thirty years of fighting. Later, it became known as the Defenestration of Prague; *fenestra* is the Latin word for window, so *defenestration* is a fancy way to say "throwing someone out of a window."

The rebellious Protestants now declared themselves free from Ferdinand's rule. Perhaps they didn't think Ferdinand would fight back. Many Germans didn't take Ferdinand very seriously. He was a stout little man, red-haired and blue-eyed, cheerful and shortsighted. He bustled around his palace, looking more like a servant than a king! He gave money to the poor, went to church daily, and spent his free time hunting.

But Ferdinand was not as harmless as he looked. He was determined that Germany would remain Catholic. Ferdinand also had great ambitions; he was king of Germany, but he intended to become Holy Roman Emperor as well. And over the last century or so, a tradition had evolved: in order to become Holy Roman Emperor, a king had to convince seven German princes to elect him to the position in a special meeting called a *diet*. Three of those princes, or *electors,* were Protestants—and part of the rebellion!

To get the title Holy Roman Emperor, Ferdinand had to get his Protestant territories and their princes back under his control. So he convinced his allies in Austria and Spain to assemble two huge armies of tough, experienced soldiers. These armies marched into Bohemia, faced the rebels—and defeated them almost immediately. Ferdinand returned to Bohemia, hanged the leaders of the mob, and stuck their heads on the railings of Prague's largest bridge. Then he took away all the land that belonged to Protestant rebels and gave it to his faithful Catholic subjects. Finally, he forced the electors to make him Holy Roman Emperor.

But instead of crushing the rebellion, Ferdinand's actions produced more unrest. Other Protestant princes in the north of Germany hadn't been part of the rebellion—but they certainly didn't like seeing Protestant lands given away to Catholics. Would their territories disappear next? And the Protestant kings of England, the Netherlands, and Denmark (north of the Netherlands) were just as unhappy. When they looked over to Germany, they saw a Holy Roman Emperor who had just joined together with two other countries to wipe out Protestants. What if this three-country alliance decided to attack England or Denmark next?

So the king of Denmark, Christian IV, gathered up his army of thirty thousand soldiers and began his march into Germany, intending to put an end to Ferdinand's growing power. Christian IV was a skilled general and a smart man. (He and the king of England, James I, used to write letters back and forth in Latin.) He was filled with energy; according to popular rumor, he only stopped drinking to exercise, and only stopped exercising to drink some more. And although he wanted to defend Protestantism, he also hoped to claim some German land for himself.

As Christian IV advanced, his army grew larger; James I sent English soldiers to join his forces, and German Protestants came also to march with the Protestant Danish king. Faced with this huge army, advancing across his kingdom toward his capital city, Ferdinand hired a new general, Albert of Wallenstein. Wallenstein loved war. He was very tall and skeletally thin, usually dressed in sinister black, with a single streak of red. "[He is] unmerciful," wrote the astronomer Johannes Kepler, describing Wallenstein, "devoted only to himself and his desires...covetous, deceitful...usually silent, often violent." Wallenstein even frightened Ferdinand.

So when Wallenstein took command of Ferdinand's forces and met Christian IV's army full on, the Danish, English, and Protestant German soldiers were crushed. The soldiers were scattered; Christian IV himself was forced to flee for his life. Ferdinand's army marched right into Denmark and took it over!

The Protestant king of Sweden, Gustavus II, watched in horror. Sweden lies just across a narrow sea from Denmark; now the armies of the Holy Roman Emperor were camped only a few miles from his own country. Next, Ferdinand might decide to invade his land, take his throne, and force *his* people to become Catholics.

He met together with his advisors and noblemen. All agreed that it would be wiser to attack Ferdinand's army, before Wallenstein decided to turn and attack Sweden. "It is better," the Swedish noblemen announced, "that we tether our horses to the enemy's fence, than he to ours." So the Swedish army gathered itself for war.

Gustavus was better prepared than Christian IV had been. He trained his soldiers carefully, and he paid them well so that they would remain loyal. He outfitted them in the best and warmest clothes: fur cloaks, gloves, and waterproof leather boots. He taught them to fight in small groups which could move quickly and attack the enemy from any side, rather than marching in one long massive line, as most other armies did. And he was the first European commander to put all of his soldiers in the same uniform! Even when scattered across a battlefield, the Swedish soldiers could recognize each other by their bright blue and yellow coats.

Gustavus himself—a huge yellow-haired man, broad-shouldered and strong—led his soldiers into battle. The Swedish army drove Ferdinand's men back out of Denmark and

away from the coast, back toward Germany. Thousands of German soldiers were killed. Soon, Gustavus was marching into Germany itself, with Ferdinand's army in retreat ahead of him! Once in Germany, Gustavus convinced the Protestant princes to join with him against Ferdinand. Together, the Swedes and Germans formed a Protestant Union and stormed into the heart of Germany, headed

Gustavus II of Sweden

toward Ferdinand's capital city of Vienna. Victory seemed certain.

But Ferdinand wasn't ready to give up. He ordered Albert of Wallenstein assassinated and re-organized his army under another general. And as the Protestant Union advanced, Gustavus himself was killed in battle. Without his leadership, the Protestant Union began to fall apart. The Swedish soldiers became disorganized. One by one, the German Protestants began to approach Ferdinand, willing to discuss peace. The war had been dragging on for sixteen years, and they were ready to stop fighting.

Slowly, Ferdinand made peace with his enemies. A year later, the German princes and Ferdinand signed a treaty that said every Protestant prince could decide what religion his territory would follow—the very same agreement that had been in place before the war even started! Seventeen years of fighting had accomplished nothing at all. Thousands of Germans had died of wounds or disease. Many of those who lived had no homes; three-quarters of the villages in Bohemia had been destroyed. Ferdinand ruled a ruined land.

And the war wasn't over yet.

The ambitious prime minister of France, Cardinal Richelieu, saw that Ferdinand had been weakened by the war. He wanted the title Holy Roman Emperor to belong to the king of France, not the king of Germany. Just weeks after the new treaty was signed, France declared war on Ferdinand.

The fighting continued. Spain, Sweden, and the Netherlands joined back in. As battle followed battle, more Germans died. In some places, half the population was killed. The countryside was littered with unburied bodies. Soldiers roamed through the country, searching for food and robbing the starving populace. The poor began to eat grass in a desperate attempt to survive.

But then Ferdinand, aging and weary with battle, became ill, and died shortly afterward. The Germans fought on—until Cardinal Richelieu also died. With both the Holy Roman Emperor and the minister of France dead, the other countries of Europe began, cautiously, to try to arrange a peace.

But it took four years for peace to be arranged. Many of the leaders involved weren't even sure what they were fighting about any more! Finally, thirty years after the Defenestration of Prague, the countries of Europe agreed to sign the Peace of Westphalia. This treaty gave some German land to Sweden and some to France. The other German territories were allowed to govern themselves. The kingdom of Germany was so splintered that it no longer existed!

Even after the Peace of Westphalia, France and Spain went on fighting with each other for eleven more years. The Thirty Years' War didn't actually end until the year 1659, forty-one years after it began.

Japan and China During the Rise of the Manchu

Chapter Ten
Far East of Europe

Japan's Isolation:
Closed Doors in the East

While the Thirty Years' War between Catholics and Protestants destroyed villages all across Europe, the shoguns of Japan were watching from a distance.

The shoguns, like most of the Japanese people, were Buddhists. Catholic missionaries called Jesuits had come to Japan years before the Thirty Years' War began; although some Japanese listened, others were suspicious. The Jesuit missionary Francis Xavier wrote to his companions that one daimyo had driven him away, afraid "that if he allowed his people to embrace the Christian religion, his whole dominion would be destroyed, and the ancestral gods of the country...would come to be despised by the natives."

But other daimyo accepted Christianity. More missionaries came to Japan, and more Japanese became Christians. When Ieyasu, the first shogun of the Tokugawa dynasty, took power, he became worried about this foreign religion—and about the foreigners who were entering Japan to spread its beliefs.

So Ieyasu turned to his Western advisor, William Adams, and asked, "What do you think of these Jesuit missionaries?"

He was asking the wrong man! William Adams was a loyal Protestant. He had arrived in Japan as a crewman on a Dutch merchant ship, and Ieyasu had asked him to stay and help the Japanese government deal properly with the Europeans who came to Japan to trade. Adams hated Catholicism. So he warned Ieyasu to beware of all Catholic missionaries! When a Spanish ship came to Japan and its crew began to make maps and measurements of Japanese ports, Adams told Ieyasu to watch out for invasion. "First come merchants," he told Ieyasu. "Then they will send missionaries and Jesuits, and then their army will follow. This is how Spain conquers other countries."

Ieyasu believed Adams. He was afraid that if Catholic Spanish soldiers did invade, Japanese who had become Catholics would be unwilling to fight against them. So as Ieyasu's power grew, he slowly made Christianity more and more unwelcome in Japan. Twelve years after his first triumph in battle, he announced that Japanese could no longer become Catholic Christians. Two years later, he passed a law ordering that all foreign missionaries be driven from the country.

When Ieyasu died, his son Hidetada, the next Tokugawa shogun, made even more laws against Christianity. By now, the Thirty Years' War had started. Over in Europe, the Catholic Holy Roman Emperor was taking over other countries in the name of Catholicism! Hidetada had no intention of allowing this to happen in *his* country too. He ordered Japanese Christians executed. Catholic priests who wouldn't leave the country were thrown in jail.

When Hidetada's son Iemitsu began to rule alongside of him, an even more extreme law was passed. Iemitsu didn't want the Japanese to travel to other countries, learn about Christianity, and bring this religion (and the unrest it was causing over in Europe) back to Japan. So he decreed that the Japanese could not travel any further west than the country of Korea, just across the water. And he executed many Christians who lived in Nagasaki, the southern port city where most foreign merchants docked their ships.

Yet Christianity continued to spread. As a matter of fact, in the large, important city of Nagasaki, there were more Christians than Buddhists!

So the shogun Iemitsu took the most drastic step of all. He closed Japan.

Iemitsu declared that no ships could come in or out of Japanese ports. Shipbuilders were forbidden, on pain of death, to make any ship large enough to travel on the ocean! Any Japanese citizen trying to return to Japan from another country would be put to death, to prevent him from bringing foreign ideas into the country. And any Japanese man or woman trying to leave the country would be executed.

Iemitsu's severe laws caused a revolt! Christians at Shimabara, near Nagasaki, where thousands of Japanese had already been executed, banded together to fight against the shogun's edicts. But the Shimabara Uprising was doomed. The Christians were driven into a nearby castle, where they ran out of food, water, and weapons. When the Shimabara rebels finally surrendered, they were put to death.

Iemitsu

Iemitsu wasn't finished making laws. Now he passed a new set of restrictions. No European traders except for the Protestant Dutch were allowed to trade with Japan. Even the Dutch were only allowed to send one ship per year— and they weren't able to land on Japan's shores. Instead, they had to dock their ships at a tiny artificial island in the Nagasaki harbor, built specifically for them. They could never set foot on Japanese land.

For the next century, the Japanese were cut off from Western ideas and Catholic missionaries. Instead of Christianity, Buddhism flourished. A kind of Buddhism called *Zen* became particularly powerful. Zen Buddhists believed that wisdom came from the inside, not from outside teaching or travel to foreign lands. So Zen Buddhists didn't make pilgrimages or listen to preaching. Instead, they meditated, waiting for wisdom to be revealed in their own souls. Because Zen Buddhists believed that truth could be found in the smallest, simplest places, the Japanese became experts at small and beautiful arts; they made tiny miniature landscapes of sand and pebbles, grew tiny dwarf trees called *bonsai,* and built beautiful, simple gardens for meditation.

For the next century, Japan and Zen Buddhism continued to flourish—far away from Europe. Japan had closed its doors to the outside and had turned inward instead.

The "Foreign Conquest" of China: The Rise of the Manchu

Just west of Japan, the huge country of China was also struggling with foreign ideas and foreign invaders. But *these* "foreign invaders" didn't come from the West. They came from China itself!

For centuries, China had been ruled by a family of emperors called the Ming dynasty. The Ming family came from the south of China, where the people were known as Han Chinese. The Ming emperors and the people they ruled were both Han Chinese. They spoke the same language, ate the same foods, wrote in the same alphabet, wore the same clothes.

But in the northern part of China, in an area called Manchuria, a warlike group of people had come to hate the Ming dynasty. The leader of these *Manchu people* complained that Han Chinese soldiers came into Manchuria, stole food, and drove farmers from their land. He grew so angry that he took a battle oath, called "The Seven Hatreds for the Ming Dynasty," and set out to attack the borders of the Ming empire.

The Ming empire braced itself for the "foreign invasion" of the Manchu. But another threat was rising within China itself. For years, Ming China had been growing poorer and hungrier. The emperors had spent a tremendous amount of money fighting off Hideyoshi of Japan. And while they were spending money, China was growing. There were now 160 million people in China, and there was not enough farm land to grow enough food for them all. The weather had grown colder; unexpected frosts killed orange trees and young crops. Grain was scarce—and expensive. Soon the army ran out of money to pay or feed its troops. Soldiers began to desert. They joined up with bands of hungry peasants and roamed through China, robbing and destroying cities. Meanwhile, the Manchu launched attacks on cities in the north of China. The Han Chinese complained, "We are surrounded by battle, unsafe in our own homes—and the emperor does nothing to help us!"

One Chinese government official, a postman named Li Tzu-ch'eng, decided to set up his own government in place of the Ming. He gathered hungry and discontented men around him and marched his army toward the capital city of Peking. He was ready to fight for the throne, but when he reached Peking, no soldiers appeared on the city's walls. Li Tzu-ch'eng's army approached, cautiously. They pushed open the city gates. No Ming army stood ready to fight! The Ming soldiers, hungry and ragged, had been struck by plague. They were dead—or had fled the city.

Li Tzu-ch'eng marched toward the palace in triumph. As he approached, the last Ming emperor hung himself in his royal chambers. The Ming dynasty had ended.

But Li Tzu-ch'eng would not be the new emperor of China.

Down in the south of China, the remains of the Ming family and army gathered together, hoping to take the throne back. One of the Ming generals sent a message to the Manchu, who were still rampaging through the north of China. "We were once enemies," the general wrote, "but now we can join together and defeat this rebel peasant and his army."

That was a mistake!

The Manchu were happy to help out. They swept down from the north and drove Li Tzu-ch'eng out of Peking. And then, instead of putting the Ming back on the throne, they claimed the throne of China and began a new ruling dynasty of their own—a Manchu dynasty. Now China was ruled by a people who were not Han Chinese. The peasant emperor had been defeated, but a foreign emperor sat on China's throne.

Now the Manchu ruled over an entire country full of Han Chinese. The Manchu thought of themselves as superior to the Han Chinese. They called themselves the *Qing*—a word which means "pure." They refused to live in the same neighborhoods as their Han Chinese subjects. Manchu and Han Chinese boys and girls didn't play together—and they weren't allowed to marry each other when they grew up.

And as a sign of their control over the Han Chinese, the Manchu forced their subjects to cut their hair in the Manchu style. Han Chinese men believed that hair was a gift from family ancestors, so they grew their hair very long. But Manchu men shaved the fronts of their heads and braided the hair in the back into a long *queue,* or pigtail.

The Han Chinese thought that shaving your forehead was a barbaric, uncivilized practice, showing disrespect for ancestors. When the Manchu ordered them to start wearing pigtails, the Chinese revolted. They gathered to oppose their Manchu overlords, shouting, "Keep your hair, even if you lose your head!"

The Manchu were ruthless. They crushed the rebellions, executed the ringleaders, and forced their subjects to shave. The first Manchu emperor treated the Han Chinese like slaves. He put his Manchu countrymen into positions of authority and made the Han Chinese officials serve them.

But the second Manchu emperor, K'ang-hsi, changed all that.

K'ang-hsi inherited the throne when he was only seven. His regents had served the first Manchu emperor. Like the first emperor, they looked down on the Han Chinese and treated them like servants and slaves. But even as a child, K'ang-hsi realized that the Manchus were outnumbered by the Han Chinese—and that they would not be able to keep control of this huge empire if they treated their subjects with scorn. And although K'ang -hsi was loyal to his Manchu countrymen, he also loved the country of China.

At the age of thirteen, K'ang-hsi took power for himself. He fired his regents and set about gaining the support of the Han Chinese. He announced that all Chinese subjects, whether Manchu or Han Chinese, could gain favor and promotion at his court. He told the Han Chinese, "We have not conquered you. We have freed you! No longer will you have to worry about Ming soldiers stealing your crops—or the Ming emperors demanding high taxes." And so that the Han Chinese would feel liberated instead of enslaved, he reduced taxes. Soon, the Han Chinese peasants were paying less taxes than ever before.

K'ang-hsi's strategies worked. Hatred for the Manchu rulers began to diminish as the people of China grew richer. Under K'ang-hsi, China became stronger and bigger, as his army conquered other nations nearby and added them to the Manchu empire. For fifty years, this "foreign invader" ruled over his adopted country—and made it one of the largest and wealthiest nations in the world.

India During the Time of the Three Emperors

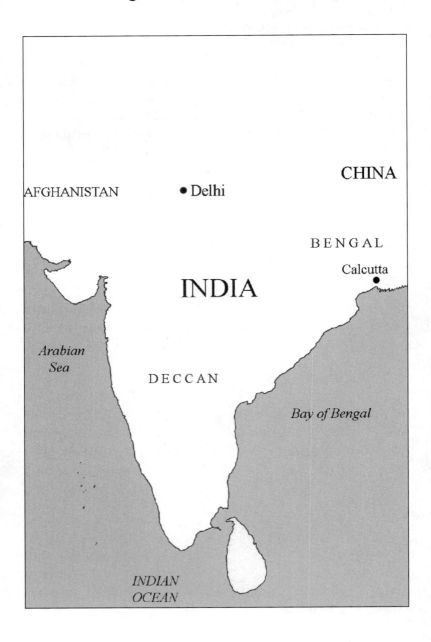

Chapter Eleven
The Moghul Emperors of India

World Seizer, King of the World, and Conqueror of the World

The Manchu emperors who ruled China believed that they had conquered the most important country on earth. The battling kings of Europe who fought the Thirty Years' War believed that *their* kingdoms were the center of all civilization. But the kings of India knew that *India* was the center of the world! During the years that we've been reading about, three emperors ruled in India. The first was named World Seizer. When World Seizer's son inherited his father's throne, he named himself King of the World. And when King of the World's son became king, *he* gave himself the proudest name of all: Conqueror of the World.

The first emperor, World Seizer, was a descendent of the great Mongol warrior Genghis Khan. Many years before, one of Genghis Khan's relatives, a prince named Babur, had wandered south, down into India. Here, he found a number of different little Indian kingdoms, each governed by a nobleman. Babur conquered these little kingdoms and united them all together into one Indian empire. For many years, India was ruled by Babur's sons, grandsons, great-grandsons, and great-great-great-great grandsons. This family of kings was called the *Moghul dynasty* because its kings were descended from the Mongols.

World Seizer, whose Indian name was Jahangir, was just as ruthless as his great ancestor Genghis Khan. When he suspected that his father's best friend was plotting against him, he ordered the man murdered. Every Tuesday, he held court at his palace and sentenced anyone who had broken his laws to be crushed by elephants or beheaded. And he put the heads of the condemned on special towers along the main roads of his empire as a warning to others.

But although Jahangir was cruel, he was also a clever and thoughtful king. He knew that India would grow richer if it could encourage more and more English traders to sail to its ports and trade for silks and spices. So he signed a *trade treaty* with James I, the king of England, allowing Englishmen to enter all Indian ports in safety. And Jahangir was the first Indian emperor to invite an English *ambassador* (a special state official, sent by one country to another in order to help the two countries be friends) to India.

The English ambassador was amazed by the riches in Jahangir's court. He wrote back to James I, describing the gold, jewels, silver, and exquisite paintings found in the palace. He described in amazement the enormous celebration held on the birthday of Khurram, the emperor's favorite son. On this day, Khurram was dressed in gold and jewels and was seated on one side of an enormous pair of golden scales. Courtiers heaped bags of gold, jewels, spices, corn, and butter on the other side of the scales, until they had measured out the weight of the prince in goods. Then the goods were all given away to the poor!

When Jahangir died, Khurram became emperor. As emperor, he was given a new name; just as his father Jahangir had been known as World Seizer, Khurram would now be called Shah Jahan, or King of the World.

As soon as Shah Jahan became king, he made sure that everyone knew he was just as powerful as his father. He ordered all rivals to the throne—including his own brothers—put to death. When he learned that some of the towns at the far edges of India were preparing to rebel against his rule, he set off himself to fight against the rebels. He spent years strengthening his control over India.

This King of the World didn't reign alone. His wife, Mumtaz Mahal, had already borne him thirteen children. Now, she traveled with him everywhere, helped him govern his kingdom, and worked with him to plan out his military campaigns. She kept his *seal*—the sign of his authority—and every decree that he made went to her to be approved.

But only three years after Shah Jahan became king, tragedy struck him! He was traveling to a battle with Mumtaz and his army when Mumtaz grew ill and died. Shah Jahan's hair turned white from grief. He cried so much that he ruined his eyesight and had to wear glasses for the rest of his life. He spent two years mourning his wife; during this time, he refused to hear any music, wear beautiful clothes, or eat any rich food.

When the two years was over, Shah Jahan decided to build Mumtaz Mahal a tomb, or *mausoleum*, that would show the whole world how much he loved her. Shah Jahan quarried the finest transparent marble and the reddest sandstone for this tomb. He gathered precious stones for its walls—shining green jade, sparkling diamonds, sky-blue turquoise. He chose a beautiful spot on the banks of the Yamuna River, where the tomb would overlook the clear running waters. Twenty thousand craftsmen labored over the building for over twenty years! They built a huge marble dome, surrounded by smaller domes, on a red sandstone foundation. A huge garden in front of the tomb was planted with tulips and daffodils. A red mosque was built on either side of the mausoleum, so that the Muslims of India could worship there. All of the buildings were covered with intricate carvings of vines, fruit, leaves, and flowing lines of Arabic writing from the Muslim holy book, the Koran. The flowers and vines were inlaid with jewels—sometimes as many as fifty jewels in a single flower!

Taj Mahal

Shah Jahan had built the most beautiful building in India. This mausoleum, the Taj Mahal, became known as the eighth wonder of the world.

While Shah Jahan supervised his building projects, he left much of the actual work of ruling the kingdom to his four sons. Each son was a general in Shah Jahan's army and ruled over one fourth of the empire. Shah Jahan's son Aurangzeb was one of his best generals and rulers, and Shah Jahan sent him out over and over again to fight for his father's empire.

But although Aurangzeb conquered cities and led his father's army to victory, Shah Jahan didn't reward him. Instead, he criticized Aurangzeb and reduced his rank! Meanwhile, Shah Jahan's favorite son, Dara, lounged around the court—and grew more and more popular with his father.

When Shah Jahan announced that Dara would be his heir, Aurangzeb rebelled. He collected his army together, marched into his father's capital city, and defeated Dara's soldiers. Dara ran away! And Shah Jahan himself had to surrender to his son.

Aurangzeb ordered his father imprisoned inside his own fortress. He made sure that the old emperor had food, water, servants, and doctors—but he never allowed Shah Jahan to leave the fortress again. After Shah Jahan wrote him letters complaining about his treatment, Aurangzeb even ordered that all of Shah Jahan's paper and pens be taken away!

Now Aurangzeb was the ruler of India. He gave himself the title Conqueror of the World. He kept Shah Jahan imprisoned until the old man died. Shah Jahan was buried next to Mumtaz Mahal in the Taj Mahal, and Aurangzeb, Conqueror of the World, was the undisputed emperor of all India.

Aurangzeb's Three Decisions

The Moghul emperor Aurangzeb, Conqueror of the World, was now the ruler of India. Like his father, King of the

World, and his grandfather, World Seizer, he was determined to be a strong and powerful ruler. And he succeeded. He ruled over a strong and powerful India for almost fifty years.

But when Aurangzeb died, fifty years later, India was doomed. Three of Aurangzeb's own decisions helped to pave the way for foreign invaders who would take away India's independence.

Aurangzeb's first decision had to do with religion. Aurangzeb, like all the Moghul emperors, was a Muslim—a follower of the teachings of Muhammad. But most of the people of India were Hindu. For many years, the Moghul emperors allowed their Hindu subjects to worship in their own way. The emperor Akbar, one of the greatest Moghul rulers of all (and Aurangzeb's great-grandfather), had even appointed a Hindu advisor to be his Minister of State.

But Aurangzeb was different. He wanted India to become a Muslim country, and he believed that his duty as emperor was to spread the Muslim faith.

After long hours of reading the Koran and discussing its teachings with the Muslim theologians who came to his court, Aurangzeb decided that the law of the Muslim faith, called *Shari'ah,* should also be the law for all of India. And he also decided that only Muslims should have power in India. So he refused to give Hindus positions at court and only promoted Muslims. He forced all Indian Hindus to pay extra taxes. When new Hindu temples were built, Aurangzeb had them destroyed. Because the Koran forbids Muslims to drink wine, the emperor made wine illegal throughout all of India. And because he believed that the Koran banned all kinds of art and parties, he put an end to all music at his court and made festivals illegal.

Muslim Indians welcomed Aurangzeb's laws. But Hindu Indians hated the emperor! Aurangzeb's decrees meant that Muslims and Hindus in India began to quarrel with each other. And when Aurangzeb made his *second* decision, the hostility between Hindus and Muslims in India grew even stronger.

Aurangzeb's second decision was to spend years and years trying to conquer the southern parts of India. During the reigns of his father and grandfather, the Indian army had conquered the northern parts of India all the way up to the high mountains dividing India from Asia. And because India is a peninsula, Aurangzeb couldn't expand his empire to the east or the west. But he was still determined to make India larger, so he turned his army south.

The southern lands of India, called the Deccan, were covered with jagged hills, rough country, and thick brush. The kingdoms in the Deccan were not yet under Aurangzeb's control. And although most of the Deccan leaders were Muslim, they didn't want to come under the rule of the Moghul emperor. So the kingdoms of the Deccan made alliances with Hindu tribes who lived in the southwest parts of India. These Hindu tribes, called the Marathas, resented the way that Aurangzeb treated the Hindu people who lived under his reign. They were happy to help the people of the Deccan fight Aurangzeb!

After years of fighting, Aurangzeb managed to add the kingdoms of the Deccan to his empire. But the Deccan was never loyal to Aurangzeb's rule. The people continued to mount little rebellions against him. And the Marathas kept right on sending little bands of *guerrilla warriors* (soldiers who fight in sneak attacks and from under cover, rather than in an organized army) to harass the Moghul officials and soldiers. Aurangzeb spent twenty-six years in the Deccan, fighting off Hindu guerrilla warriors and trying to keep the cities of the Deccan peaceful! Meanwhile, he ignored the rest of his empire. He didn't visit his capital city, Delhi, for a quarter of a century!

Aurangzeb had decided to treat Muslims better than Hindus—and made enemies of part of his empire. He had decided to conquer the south of India—and ignored the rest of his kingdom. And then he made a third decision that would change India forever. While he was busy fighting against the kingdoms of the Deccan, he allowed Englishmen to come into India and build cities of their own.

Remember, Aurangzeb's grandfather Jahangir (World Seizer) had signed a trade treaty with England. This treaty allowed English merchants to build trading posts (ports where

English ships could land and load up with Indian goods) all through India.

Now, the English wanted to build a new trading post on the eastern shore of India, in an area called Bengal. They asked Aurangzeb for permission to build not only a place for ships to dock, but also a city and a factory at this new port. Aurangzeb agreed. After all, he was busy down in the south of India, and this new English city would only make India richer.

So the English began to build their city, which soon became known as Calcutta. They built a factory to make silk that they could then take to London and sell. More and more English men and women came to live in Calcutta. The city began to look more like an English colony than like an Indian city. Soldiers came to Calcutta to protect the English ships. The factories in Calcutta made gunpowder for the soldiers' weapons.

Aurangzeb didn't know it, but Calcutta would become the center of an English takeover of India—a takeover that would bring an end to Indian independence.

This takeover did not begin until after Aurangzeb's death. But at the end of his life, Aurangzeb began to realize that his attempts to make India into an enormous, rich, Muslim empire had actually made India weaker.

Just before his death, Aurangzeb was still down in the Deccan, putting down rebellion after rebellion. He had lost a fifth of his army in the war against the Deccan. His men were suffering from plague. He was under constant attack from Maratha guerillas. He was nearly ninety years old, weary and sick. Back in the north of India, the administrators who were supposed to be running the country in Aurangzeb's absence were spending money freely, neglecting the people, and allowing crime to flourish. Old, tired, and dying, Aurangzeb wrote to one of his sons, "I do not know who I am. I do not know what I have been doing. I have sinned, and yet I do not know what punishment awaits me." Aurangzeb's attempt to make India great had failed; he died knowing that India's end was coming.

England in the 17ᵗʰ Century

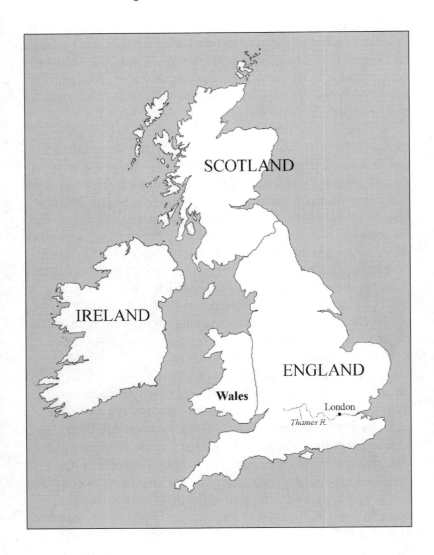

Chapter Twelve
Battle, Fire, and Plague in England

Charles Loses His Head

While the English were building trading posts in India, England itself was in turmoil.

James I, the king of England and Scotland, had died, and his son Charles had inherited the throne. But right from the beginning of his reign, Charles started to make the people of England angry.

His first mistake was to marry the French princess Henrietta Maria. Henrietta was a beautiful, high-spirited girl, but she was also a devout Catholic who had promised the pope that she would try to spread Catholicism throughout England. Most Englishmen, especially English Puritans, hated and feared Catholicism. When Charles got ready for his formal coronation ceremony, he was afraid to hold the traditional parade through the streets of London. He thought Puritans might gather along the way and shout out insults!

Instead, Charles planned to get to the church by sailing down the Thames River on a barge. But the coronation day was filled with chaos. When it was time for the king and queen to leave the palace, Henrietta refused to come out of her room. She declared that she couldn't attend a Protestant ceremony. When Charles's noblemen tried to force her through the door, Henrietta punched her fists through the glass windows of her room!

So Charles went to be crowned all by himself. He paraded out to the Thames, but the royal barge missed its landing and went aground. Charles had to ride in a much smaller boat instead. When he arrived at the church, he tripped at the threshold and nearly fell on his face. When he tried to put on the coronation ring, a large jewel fell out of it and disappeared. Near the end of the ceremony, the Archbishop told the gathered crowd to shout, "God Save King Charles"—but since most of them didn't hear him, Charles was greeted with silence. And as the ceremony ended, a small earthquake shook England!

The troublesome coronation was only the beginning of a troubled reign. Like his father James, Charles believed that God had placed him on his throne and that his subjects should obey him without question. But Parliament believed that its members, who represented the people of England, should make the laws. When Parliament met after the coronation, it refused to give Charles all of the money he wanted.

Charles was furious. He dismissed Parliament and ruled without it for eleven long years! In those years, he fought wars and made laws all by himself. He even told English and Scottish Christians how to worship God! He passed so many restrictions on Puritans that hundreds left England and went to the American colonies. He forced the Scottish church to use the English prayer book and ceremonies. The Scots hated this English command. In one Scottish church, the minister had to bring two loaded pistols with him and point them at the congregation while he read the English prayer book!

But while Charles was making the Scots and the English Puritans hate him, he was also running out of money. At the end of eleven years, he was forced to call Parliament back into session to beg for more cash. This Parliament refused to dissolve when Charles became angry. Because it went on meeting for eight years, it became known as the Long Parliament.

The Long Parliament wanted to pass laws that would limit Charles's power. But as time went on, the Long Parliament started to bicker with itself instead. The Puritans and non-Puritans in Parliament spent more and more time arguing about whether or not the Church of England was pure enough. Soon, Parliament was spending most of its time talking about God—not Charles.

Charles could see that the Puritan members of Parliament were irritating the other members. So he assembled five hundred soldiers and marched into Parliament, hoping to arrest the five Puritans who were his fiercest enemies. But the Puritans, warned ahead of time, were gone! Charles and his soldiers faced five empty seats. Embarrassed, Charles snapped, "The birds have flown!" and strode back to his palace.

This was a mistake.

When the news spread that Charles was willing to use his English army against other Englishmen in order to get his own way, more and more people turned against him. Charles realized that a rebellion was about to explode all around him. He fled from London and went up to the north of England, where his most loyal noblemen lived. The Puritans in Parliament took control of London.

Civil war had begun!

For six years, Charles's supporters, called *Cavaliers*, fought against supporters of Parliament, called *Roundheads* (because of their Puritan haircuts). Charles had most of the regular army on his side, but the Roundheads organized their own army, using the most modern weapons and training methods. This New Model Army was commanded by the most fervent Puritan of all, Oliver Cromwell.

Two years after the war began, Cromwell helped lead the Roundheads into battle against Charles's soldiers at a place called Marston Moor. Twenty thousand Scotsmen marched to fight for the Roundheads—because the Roundheads had promised the Scots that, if they won, they could use their *own* prayer book. Charles's army was defeated. Afterward, Oliver Cromwell wrote to his brother, "Truly England and the Church of God hath had a great favour from the Lord....Give glory, all the glory, to God."

This victory was the end of Charles's power. He avoided capture for months, but finally gave up and surrendered. The Roundheads put the king in jail. They had won the civil war!

But Oliver Cromwell was worried. From his prison, Charles was constantly sending messages to his supporters, begging them to rise up and put him back on his throne. The Long Parliament itself wasn't sure what to do with Charles. Many of the non-Puritan members thought that Parliament should make an agreement with Charles and rule alongside of him.

Cromwell wanted Charles and his tyranny gone for good. He and the other Puritans marched the New Model Army into Parliament and drove out everyone who had sympathy for Charles! Only about sixty members were left. This "purified" Parliament became known as the Rump Parliament, because only part of it was left!

The Rump Parliament decided that England would only be at peace if Charles were dead. It charged Charles with treason against his own country. A trial was planned. Soldiers were assigned to guard the court from angry supporters of the king. Remembering the Gunpowder Plot, they searched the cellars. The presiding judge got himself a hat lined with steel, just in case someone might try to shoot him!

When Charles was brought into the court, he refused to answer any questions. But plenty of witnesses testified against him. "The said Charles Stuart," announced the court, "...trusted with a *limited* power to govern...for the good and benefit of the people....hath traitorously and maliciously levied war against the present Parliament, and the people therein represented....[M]uch innocent blood of the free people of this nation hath been spilt."

The court declared Charles guilty and led him away. Three days later, on January 30th, 1649, the king of England was led out of his jail, toward a scaffold built in the center of London. The morning was dark and cold. As he walked toward the black-draped scaffold, drums beat mournfully.

Charles climbed up and took off his cloak, handing it to an official who stood nearby. "Wait until I give you the sign," he said to the executioner.

"Yes, Your Majesty," the executioner answered.

Charles put his head on the block. "I go from a corruptible to an incorruptible crown," he said. In a moment, he stretched his hand to the executioner—who swung his axe. Some of the people who crowded around were weeping; others cheered.

118

The executioner held up Charles's head. "This is the head of a traitor!" he shouted out. For the first time in a thousand years, no king ruled in England.

Cromwell's Protectorate

Now that the king was dead, England was no longer a *monarchy* (a country ruled by a king or queen). The Rump Parliament declared that England had now become a *commonwealth* (a country where the people rule, by electing leaders who will represent them). Parliament was supposed to listen to the people of England and pass laws that the English wanted.

But the Commonwealth got off to a bad start.

Many Englishmen and women hoped that Parliament's first action would be to *reform* (change for the better) the courts in England. It cost a tremendous amount of money to go to court, and the laws were so complicated that most English citizens had to hire expensive lawyers to help them. Only rich people could make full use of the courts.

But most of the members of Parliament were lawyers who liked the laws of England just the way they were—complicated and hard to understand. And although the Rump Parliament was supposed to dissolve itself so that new leaders could be elected by the people, it never did. Four years after Charles I was executed, the Rump Parliament was still arguing slowly about whether or not English laws should be changed.

Oliver Cromwell was fed up with Parliament. When one of his generals suggested that Parliament should be made up of hand-picked men, rather than elected representatives, Cromwell agreed. He and his Puritan friends decided that England's government should be an "assembly of saints"—men who agreed with the Puritan cause.

So Cromwell marched into the Rump Parliament with his soldiers from the New Model Army behind him and declared it dissolved. "You have sat here too long for the good you do!" he shouted. "In the name of God, go!" The soldiers drove the members of the Rump Parliament out at sword-point!

Just like Charles, Cromwell had used an English army to threaten other Englishmen. But Cromwell believed that *his* use of force pleased God. "Perceiving the spirit of God so strong upon me," he remarked later, "I would not consult with flesh and blood at all."

Now that Parliament had been dissolved by force, Cromwell and his army generals appointed a new Parliament, made up of 139 men "fearing God and of approved fidelity and honesty." This Parliament became known as the Barebones Parliament, after one of its members, a Puritan minister named Praise-God Barebones. It was also called the Nominated Assembly, because its members were hand-picked, or "nominated," by Cromwell.

Cromwell still called England a commonwealth, but now it was being ruled by his own hand-picked men, not by the people of England. Six months later, this Nominated Assembly of men loyal to Cromwell passed a new bill. This bill announced, "Parliament now gives all of its powers to Oliver Cromwell, to act on behalf of the people of England!"

Oliver Cromwell had become the new king of England.

He was never called "king." Instead, he was given the title Lord Protector of England. And he was supposed to call Parliament every two years and listen to what the members of Parliament advised him to do.

But Cromwell certainly *seemed* like a king. He moved his family into the royal palace. The ceremony to make him Lord Protector looked an awful lot like a coronation ceremony. His advisors often called him "Your Highness." And when Parliament refused to do exactly what he said, he scolded its members, telling them that he spoke for God and that they were opposing God Himself when they opposed the Lord Protector. "I undertook this government in the simplicity of my heart and as before God...to do the part of an honest man," he explained. "I speak for God and not for men." When Parliament continued to oppose Cromwell, he announced, "I think...that it is not for

120

the profit of [England], nor for [the] common and public good, for you to continue here any longer. And therefore I do declare unto you, that I do dissolve this Parliament."

Cromwell had the power to dismiss Parliament and the power to rule England as he pleased. But his power didn't make him popular. He directed his soldiers to break up all of the royal regalia used to crown kings (the crown, scepter, coronation ring, and bracelets)—and even though many Englishmen had hated Charles, they also disliked seeing these English treasures destroyed. He allowed his army to wreck churches which seemed too "Catholic." So wherever the New Model Army went, stained glass was broken, beautiful wooden carvings and statues were hacked apart, and lead ornaments were melted and made into bullets. And Cromwell made his Puritan convictions the law of the land. He believed that playing cards was ungodly—so cards became illegal. He thought that going to plays was ungodly—so all of the theatres in England were closed. He believed that God approved only of hymns—so the English were allowed to sing only hymns.

Cromwell became so unpopular that, three years after he became Lord Protector, an anonymous booklet was published, encouraging someone to assassinate him! But no one needed to assassinate Cromwell, because he was already growing ill. He had been wounded in battle many times and had never truly recovered. And he was suffering from malaria. When his favorite daughter died, in the fourth year of the Protectorate, Cromwell became even sicker with grief.

In September of 1658, Oliver Cromwell died. He was embalmed so that he could have a royal funeral, with his body lying in state while all of England filed past to see him one last time. But the embalming didn't work. Cromwell's body was too disgusting to put on view! So it was hastily buried in Westminster Abbey, and a wax figure was put on display. Afterward, an empty coffin was the center of a huge funeral. One observer remarked, "[It was] the joyfullest funeral that I ever saw; for there was none cried but dogs."

Oliver Cromwell's son Richard claimed the title Lord Protector. But the English were tired of the protectorate. It was just like a monarchy—except with more rules! Noblemen who served in the army started to argue with each other about who should rule England next.

One of the army generals realized that England was on the brink of the greatest civil war yet. He marched into London and called the members of the old Long Parliament back into session. This Parliament met together and decided to send a message to Charles I's son, who had fled England and was living in France, far away from Cromwell and his soldiers. "Come back and become king!" Parliament begged. But even while it planned to welcome Charles II back, Parliament also began to pass laws that would restrict the king's power. From now on, English kings would have to answer to Parliament for their actions.

On May 23rd, 1660, Charles's son, Charles II, returned to England. The English, tired of war and Puritan laws, welcomed him with cheers of joy. The years of the Protectorate were over. The king was back!

Plague and Fire

Now that Charles II was on the throne, the theatres re-opened. England's noblemen crowded to concerts, plays, and balls. The experiment of the Commonwealth had failed, but most Englishmen and women felt relief. The constant battles and upsets of Cromwell's years were finally over! The years of Charles II's reign are now called the Restoration, because England's traditional monarchy was restored to the throne—and England's traditional way of life was restored as well.

But although the first years of the Restoration were joyful, catastrophe was just around the corner.

London, England's largest city, had grown, and grown, and grown. At the time of the Restoration, London had nearly half a million people living in it! It was filled with rows and rows of wooden buildings, shoved close together. The houses even jutted out over the narrow streets, so that you could reach out your hand from a window and almost touch the house across the way. London was both crowded and dirty. Drains and gutters were ancient, often blocked with cracked stones and trash. Filthy water and sewage spread across the streets. Two or three poor families crowded into single rooms.

Just four years after Charles II's triumphant return, ominous rumors began to spread: A few men had died of plague on the far edges of London.

The plague, also called the Black Death, was no stranger to Londoners. Londoners had died from plague before—and in great numbers. London's packed, filthy streets were the perfect place for disease to spread! So Londoners waited, holding their breath, for news of more illness. They hoped desperately that the plague would simply die away. "It appeared to be only in the outskirts of the town," wrote the Lord Chancellor of London, "and in the most obscure alleys, among the poorest people."

But soon horrible news filtered through London's taverns. Whole families were dying. And the sickness was spreading across the city.

By Christmas, thousands of Londoners were dying every week. The plague raged on and on for months. By June of the following year, the sickness had spread into the city's center. Londoners tried to flee into the country, but villagers drove them away, terrified that they might bring plague with them. In London, few dared to venture from their houses. "Shops are shut in," wrote one Londoner, "…very few [people] walk about, insomuch that the grass begins to spring in some places, and a deep silence is almost every place, especially within the walls." So many people died that London began to run out of room to bury the dead. "The Churchyards are now so stuffed with dead bodies," another London observer wrote, "that in many places they are two or three feet higher than they were before." Men were hired to pull huge wagons called plague carts through the streets, shouting, "Bring out your dead!" so that the bodies could be collected and dumped into huge pits.

The English writer Daniel Defoe was only a child during the plague, but he used the stories of others to write an account of the plague. He wrote, "London might well be said to be all in tears....The Plague defied all medicines; the very phy-sicians were seized with it, with their [medicines]...in their mouths....There was scarce any passing by the streets but that several dead bodies would be lying here and there upon the ground....Death reigned in every corner."

The people of the seventeenth century didn't know that the Plague was spread by the fleas who lived on rats. Indeed, they thought that animals made the plague worse—but the wrong animals. The mayor of London ordered all dogs and cats killed. That meant that there were more rats, more fleas—and more plague! Samuel Pepys, an English aristocrat who kept a diary of these years, wrote, "Little noise [was] heard day or night but the tolling of [funeral] bells."

Finally, the plague began to die away. It had raged for a year. Over two hundred thousand people had died—two out of every five people in London! But as Christmas drew near, shops began to re-open. People once again walked in London's streets. Slowly, London was returning to normal.

But less than nine months later, another tragedy struck.

Late one September evening, in the year 1666, the king's baker was stoking his fire for the night in his bakery, in Pudding Lane. A coal fell out, unnoticed, and began to burn its way into a stack of brushwood nearby. The floor caught fire, and then the walls. The bakery dissolved into flames. The fire spread to the baker's house nearby.

Soon the Lord Mayor of London himself was woken by his servants and told that a fire was burning in London. True, only two houses were alight—but because London's wooden houses were so dry and close together, small fires could spread quickly. The Lord Mayor had been sound asleep, and he was cranky. He got grumpily into his coach and rattled down to Pudding Lane. He got out, walked down to the fire, and gazed at it. "Pish," he said. "A woman could put that out." And he got back into his coach and ordered it back home.

But barely had the Lord Mayor disappeared down Pudding Lane than the fire spread to the house next door—and then the house next to that. The summer had been dry, and the wind was blowing the flames along Pudding Lane.

Some of the people in nearby houses collected their precious belongings and carried them to the stone church nearby, where they might be safe from flames. Others formed lines down to the Thames River and passed water back up to the blaze in leather buckets, chamber pots, soup bowls, and every other container they could find. But the fire was spreading too quickly! Just down from the bakery, a shipbuilder's house stood, its cellar crammed with barrels of tar used to seal the seams of ships. When the cellar burned, the barrels exploded. The roof of the house blew off. Fire spouted upwards. Bits of burning shingle and wood flew out for dozens of yards and caught other houses on fire. It was, in the words of Samuel Pepys, an "infinite great fire....Everything, after so long a drought, proving combustible, even the very stones of

The Great Fire of London

churches....The churches, houses, and all on fire and flaming at once, and a horrid noise the flames made, and the cracking of houses at their ruin."

The fire spread across the city. It burned wharfs, stacks of timber, houses, and even Baynard's Castle, a stone castle filled with wooden furnishings. Taverns, shops, churches were burned. Hundreds of people fled to the enormous stone church at London's center, St. Paul's Cathedral. But the flames swept up the walls, burning timbers and melting the lead in the roof until it ran down toward the river like molten lava. The stones in the walls themselves began to explode from the heat!

The fire burned for three days. Finally, the soldiers fighting it began to blow up houses in front of it with gunpowder, pulling away the wreckage so that the fire would have no fuel. The wind began to die down. The fire hesitated, and it finally began to flicker out.

But four-fifths of London had been burned. Thirteen thousand houses, almost a hundred churches, and almost all official buildings—courts, jails, post offices, printing presses— were gone. Londoner John Evelyn, weeping, wrote in his diary, "London was, but is no more."

France During the Reign of the Sun King

Chapter Thirteen
The Sun King

The Sun King of France

The white walls of France's royal palace glowed in the warm afternoon sunshine. The king of France, Louis XIII, was deep in a meeting with his ministers. The queen was writing letters in her boudoir. Servants scurried through the corridors. Upstairs, in the nursery, one maid scrubbed at the grass-stained clothes of the Dauphin, the heir to the throne. Another polished the little boy's silver-plated breakfast dishes. Down in the kitchen, the Dauphin's nurse was telling the cook to fix Flemish soup (egg yolks beaten with wine and salt and then boiled) for the Dauphin's dinner; he'd been suffering from a slight cold, and she wanted him fed a proper invalid's supper.

Outside, the little boy himself wandered through the gardens alone. He was barely four years old, but somehow he had managed to escape from the palace without anyone noticing. He'd found a stick on the ground, and he poked at the grass along the path as he walked. Just ahead, a fountain bubbled down into a wide basin. The little boy bent over it, stirring the water with his stick. He leaned a little further over. His foot slipped. He fell—into water that was over his head! If a passing peasant hadn't heard the sound of splashes and hauled him out, the Dauphin would have drowned.

Not long after the little prince's swim, his father died. At the age of four years and eight months, Louis XIV was now the king of France. He was the lord of every French citizen and the master of every blade of French grass and clump of dirt.

You see, the French king claimed to be the owner of the country he ruled. The French called their king a "visible divinity"—God's representative on earth. So while Charles II struggled to keep his throne, Louis XIV ruled without opposition. His father and his father's minister, Cardinal

Richelieu, had made France into one of the most powerful nations in Europe. And Louis XIV was the most powerful man in this powerful nation.

While he was still young, Louis's advisor Cardinal Mazarin ruled for him. Mazarin had been trained by Richelieu to rule with a ruthless and strict hand, demanding that every French citizen obey the word of the king without question. He continually reminded Louis that the king should be treated almost like a god.

When Mazarin died, Louis announced that he would now rule absolutely, without a council of advisors. He would be his own "First Minister." His ministers were astounded! No French king had ruled without advisors for almost a hundred years. And no one believed that this elegant young man, skilled at dancing and court life, would be an efficient ruler.

But Louis himself knew what he wanted. In his memoirs, he later wrote, "In my heart I prefer fame above all else, even life itself." For the next fifty years, Louis ruled as absolute king of France. He worked all day long, every day, wielding absolute control over every part of his reign. He chose the sun as his emblem, to represent his power, and was called "the Sun King" by his courtiers. Only a nobleman of high rank was allowed to dry him after he had a bath. Other aristocrats fought over the privilege of handing Louis XIV his shirt and pants as he dressed! Louis thought that this was a very proper relationship for a king to have with his subjects. In a letter to his son, he wrote, "Letting your people lay down the law to you is the worst calamity that a man of our rank can suffer....When the people try to take power for themselves, the more you grant them, the more they want. The more favors you give to them, the more contempt they feel for you. And the ones who want power the most are always the stupidest."

The Sun King needed a palace worthy of his greatness, so Louis XIV decided to build a huge new house at Versailles, where a tiny hunting lodge stood. After almost fifty years of labor, this tiny hunting lodge had been transformed into an enormous palace, a quarter of a mile long. Canals were dug to bring water from the river and to drain the marshland. Versailles was full of elaborate rooms like the famous Hall of Mirrors, where seventeen huge mirrors stood across from seventeen large windows, and the Salon of Apollo, where a solid silver throne stood. Hundreds of statues of Greek gods such as Apollo, Jupiter, and Neptune stood in the gardens; each god had Louis's face! Every night, thousands of candles lit the palace into brilliance for balls, concerts, and floating parades held on the Grand Canal that ran through the grounds.

Louis XIV

To increase his power, Louis brought his noblemen to Versailles to live. He forced them to pay attention to court manners. The noblemen and women spent all of their time trying to please the king, rather than planning revolt. Noblemen would do whatever Louis asked, if it meant that they would receive a sign of his favor—permission to wear clothing reserved for the king's favorites, a position standing a little closer to the front of the throne room, or a more ornate chair at a royal dinner.

The Duc de Simon, who lived at Versailles for many years, wrote that Louis also encouraged his noblemen to spend money, in order to make them more loyal. "[The king] loved splendour, magnificence, and profusion in all things," the Duc remarked, "and encouraged similar tastes in his Court; to spend money freely on...feasting and at cards, was a sure way to gain his favour, perhaps to obtain the honour of a word from him....By making expensive habits the fashion, and, for people in a certain position, a necessity, he compelled his courtiers to live beyond their income, and gradually reduced them to depend on his bounty for the means of subsistence."

The Sun King spent most of his reign fighting wars to expand France's borders. During Louis's reign, France became the largest and most important nation in Europe.

But in the last years of Louis's life, his army began to falter. Other European nations joined together to oppose the ambitious French king. France lost some of its new territory. And then Louis's son, the Dauphin, died suddenly of smallpox.

Louis didn't mourn too much; he disliked his son, who was slothful and self-absorbed. "He feared nothing more in this world than to become king," the Dauphin's aunt remarked, tartly. "He was frightfully lazy, could sit the whole long day on a bed."

With the Dauphin's death, Louis's grandson became the new heir to the French crown. But not long after, the grandson's wife—a cheerful, affectionate girl, whom Louis XIV loved like a daughter—began to complain of toothache.

She didn't have a toothache. She had the measles.

After a week of illness, she died. A few days later, her husband died as well. Then one of Louis's grandsons fell from a horse and was killed.

Faced with so many catastrophes, Louis himself began to grow ill. One day, he went hunting and came back looking exhausted, complaining about pain in his left leg. His doctors told him nothing was wrong. But the doctors had missed an infection, growing below Louis's knee. In just a few days, Louis was suffering from gangrene. When he died, his only remaining grandson, a sickly five-year-old, inherited the throne of France.

The Sun King had made himself a god on earth—but he had also made a great mistake. He had made himself powerful by forcing the common people of France to pay heavy taxes to support his wars and his lavish palaces. French peasants and craftsmen had labored for decades to build Versailles; one

French aristocrat remarked that the hard work and swampy climate was so bad for the workmen that dead bodies of peasants had to be removed every morning. Thousands and thousands of Frenchmen had died in Louis's unending wars. And throughout the French countryside, anger was growing—anger which would eventually destroy the French crown forever.

Prussia During the Reign of Frederick I

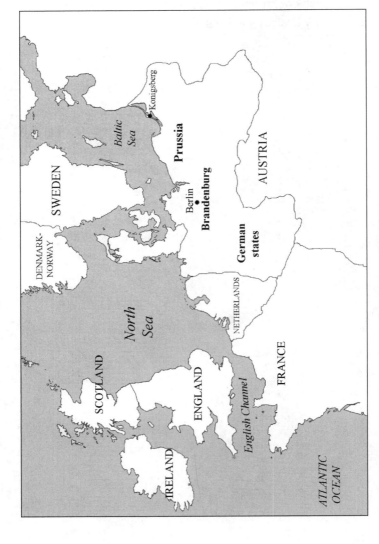

Chapter Fourteen
The Rise of Prussia

Frederick, The First Prussian King

Imagine that you're at a huge family reunion, where all of your aunts, uncles, cousins, second cousins, and third cousins are gathered together. Everyone is talking at the same time. Everyone wants to know what part of the family you belong to. "And who are you?" one of your third cousins asks you. "I'm a Smith," you might answer. You want everyone to know that you're not a Johnson, or a Lee, or a White. You and your parents and your brothers and sisters are all Smiths. That's an important part of who you are!

But now try to imagine that your family doesn't identify itself by its last name. Instead, you name yourselves after the room in the house where you spend most of your time. When your third cousin says, "Who are you?" you might answer, "I'm an Upstairs North Bedroom!" or "I'm a Downstairs Computer Room!" You're all still members of one family—but it's *more* important that you're a Downstairs Computer Room or an Upstairs North Bedroom.

That's how Germans thought of themselves, after the Thirty Years' War. If you lived in England, you were English. If you lived in Spain, you were Spanish. But if you lived in one of the little German states, you probably didn't think of yourself as "German." You were a citizen of your little state. And there were three hundred little German states, each ruled over by a prince.

But then one of those princes decided to build his little state into a kingdom—a German kingdom.

Prince Frederick ruled the German state of Brandenburg, in the eastern part of Germany. Frederick had also inherited another little kingdom—the kingdom of Prussia, even farther east than Brandenburg. Brandenburg lay within the borders of the Holy Roman Empire, so when Frederick was in Brandenburg, he had to obey the Holy Roman Emperor. But Prussia wasn't part of the Holy Roman Empire. When Frederick was in Prussia, he didn't have to obey anyone.

So Frederick asked the Holy Roman Emperor for permission to call himself "King of Prussia." The Holy Roman Emperor was grateful to Frederick, who had helped him fight off the armies of Louis XIV—and Prussia wasn't part of his empire anyway. So he agreed. But he only gave Frederick permission to call himself "King *in* Prussia." He wanted Frederick to remember that he could not behave like a king in Brandenburg—only in Prussia!

In January of 1701, Frederick rode to Königsberg, in Prussia, and held a coronation ceremony for himself. He dressed himself in scarlet robes and sat on a royal throne. He put the crown on his own head, put his scepter into his own hand, and announced, "I am now King Frederick I!" Then he marched to his wife's rooms and crowned her queen. Afterward, he held a huge royal feast. Now he was the Prussian King!

Frederick didn't actually have permission to be a king in Brandenburg. But when he paraded back into Brandenburg, he entered its largest city, Berlin, like a king. Cannons fired. All over the city, bells rang. Candles and torches and lanterns were lit in every window so that the city glowed like a star.

Like Louis XIV, Frederick wanted to be an absolute monarch, obeyed without question by all of his people. But he knew that the Holy Roman Emperor wouldn't approve—and he didn't have a strong enough army or enough money to wage wars, collect taxes, and behead his enemies.

So instead, Frederick just *behaved* like an absolute monarch. He called his entire kingdom "Prussia," so that all of his subjects (even the ones in Brandenburg) could call him their king. He spent enormous amounts of money on feasts and elaborate ceremonies. His court was one of the most splendid in Europe! His son later said, "My father had the appearance of kingship long before he was truly a king." But Frederick's play-acting helped the citizens of his kingdom—both inside *and* outside of the Holy Roman Empire—begin to think of themselves as members of one Prussian kingdom.

Imagine that your parents get tired of everyone calling themselves "Upstairs North Bedroom" or "Downstairs Computer Room" and decide, "We should all think of ourselves as Smiths!" But instead of commanding you to call yourself a Smith, they hold a big party to show how proud they are to be Smiths. Every morning, they parade through every room, singing, "We are Smiths! How lucky you all are to be Smiths!" After months of this, you might start thinking of yourself as a Smith, rather than a Downstairs Computer Room!

That's a little like what happened in Frederick's new kingdom of Prussia. Frederick encouraged *all* of his people to think of themselves as citizens of the German kingdom of Prussia.

Until this time, people in most countries were loyal to a piece of land (like the island of Britain) or to a monarch (like Louis XIV or Philip II of Spain). But Frederick knew that his kingdom was made up of two different pieces of land and that his power as monarch was limited. So he wanted Prussians to be loyal to something different: a *state*. Prussians learned to pay allegiance to an *idea* of a German kingdom, ruled by a German king. They used the word *Reich*—the German word for "kingdom"—to refer to this German kingdom!

Frederick spent most of his reign building this idea of a German kingdom called Prussia. He founded a great Prussian university, as well as a Prussian Academy of the Arts and a Royal Prussian Academy of Sciences. He gave this Academy of Science the job of studying the German language and teaching all Prussians how to use it properly!

Frederick's son, Frederick William I, took Frederick's ideas even further. He formally announced that both Prussia and Brandenburg were part of the Prussian kingdom. He made the army stronger. And then Frederick's grandson, Frederick II, took his grandfather's "kingdom in name" and turned it into a real power. He fought to add land to Prussia. He built himself a royal palace, not in Königsberg, but in Brandenburg itself. He gave Prussians a reason to be proud of their Prussian state! For this, Frederick's grandson became known as Frederick the Great. And one day, the Prussian kingdom that his grandfather had established would become the modern country of Germany.

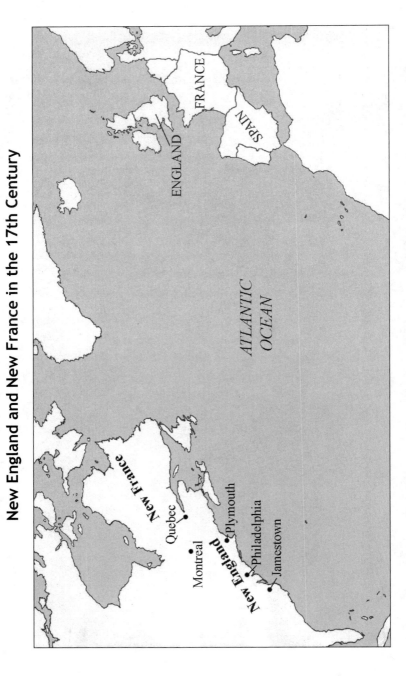

New England and New France in the 17th Century

Chapter Fifteen
A New World in Conflict

War Against the Colonies: King Philip's War

While the kings of Europe fought and schemed to make their kingdoms larger, the English colonies in North America were growing larger all on their own. More and more men and women were making the long journey across the Atlantic Ocean. New settlements spread across Massachusetts, over into the land we now call Rhode Island and Connecticut. New settlers built more houses, cleared more fields, and chopped down more trees.

They needed more space. And so they kept moving further west—and further into Native American lands—until the Wampanoag tribe decided to fight back.

At first, the Wampanoag and the English had been friends. When the English settlers first came to Massachusetts, the Wampanoag showed them how to fish, how to trap game, and how to survive the harsh northern winters.

But as the Massachusetts colony grew larger, the colonists no longer needed the Wampanoag. They grew their own crops, and traded their own goods to European merchant ships in exchange for the salt, weapons, and seeds that they needed. And they forced the Wampanoag to give them more land for their growing town.

The king of the Wampanoag tribe, Metacom, saw that his kingdom was vanishing. When his people went to fish in their favorite streams, the banks were crowded with colonists. When they walked in their hunting grounds, English hunters lurked behind trees, waiting for deer. "I am resolved," Metacom announced to a friend, "that I will not see the day when I have no kingdom."

One cold January morning, a young Wampanoag man left his tiny village and hurried down the icy dirt road, toward Plymouth Bay. He had grown up in Metacom's kingdom, but in his teens he had gone to the new little college built by the English to train Christian ministers. At this little college, which the English called Harvard, the Wampanoag boy had been given the English name John Sassamon.

John Sassamon knew Metacom well. Because John could read and write in English, Metacom had often asked him to carry messages to the English leaders. But now John Sassamon carried a warning.

John walked for hours, shivering in the grey winter air. His feet grew numb with cold. Finally, the tall wooden walls of the Plymouth fortress came into view. John Sassamon hurried through the gates. "Where is the governor?" he asked. "I must speak to him right away!"

The governor of Plymouth, Josiah Winslow, was busy with paperwork. But John Sassamon waited, anxiously glancing back at Plymouth's strong walls. When he was finally brought into the governor's office, he spoke so quickly that Winslow could barely understand him. "King Metacom is raising an army!" he blurted out. "He's asking every other tribe to join with him to fight against you. He plans to drive the English back to their home! I've come to warn you. But please, please don't send me back. He doesn't know I'm here, and if the warriors find out that I've warned you, they'll kill me!"

Winslow sighed. Like many English, he thought that the Wampanoag were stupid and not to be trusted. "You can hardly believe an Indian," he remarked to a friend, "even when they tell the truth." He turned to John Sassamon. "Go back home," he said. "Plymouth Plantation is safe."

Sassamon pleaded to stay, but Winslow refused. When Sassamon left the fortress, his eyes were filled with tears.

A week later, John Sassamon disappeared. His body was found, frozen into the ice of a pond. His neck was broken.

Josiah Winslow and the Plymouth Plantation leaders took alarm. Perhaps Sassamon's fears had been real! When two men came forward, claiming that they had seen three Wampanoag warriors kill Sassamon and throw him into the pond, the English decided to show Metacom who was *really* in charge of Massachusetts. English soldiers arrested the warriors and brought them to Plymouth. The Wampanoag warriors were tried, convicted of murder—and executed.

Metacom was furious! How dare the English invade his village and drag away his warriors? Three days after the execution, Metacom and his men attacked a little Plymouth settlement, burning houses and driving the settlers away.

War had begun.

The war between the English and the Wampanoag dragged on for months. The colonists had more guns—but the Native Americans were better at surprise attacks and ambushes. And Metacom convinced other Native American tribes nearby to join with him in his war against the English. Native American warriors burned English settlements, killed English colonists, and took others captive, only releasing them in exchange for money and weapons. One of these captured women, Mary Rowlandson, wrote about the attack on her house. "It was the dolefulest day that ever mine eyes saw," she lamented. "....[F]rom all...places [the Indians] shot against the house, so that the bullets seemed to fly like hail....Some in our house were fighting for their lives, others wallowing in their blood, the house on fire over our heads....Then I took my children...to go forth and leave the house: but as soon as we came to the door and appeared, the Indians shot so thick that the bullets rattled against the house, as if one had taken an handful of stones and threw them." Mary and her children were captured and held prisoner for weeks, until her husband paid money for her release.

After eight months of war, thirteen hundred Englishmen from Plymouth banded together to make the strongest attack yet against Metacom's forces. Metacom and his warriors had joined together with another tribe, the Narragansett, and were camped out in the middle of a treacherous swamp. The Englishmen sloshed through the swamp and attacked Metacom's camp. The battle, which became known as the Great Swamp Fight, almost wiped out the Native American warriors! Metacom himself fled west, into the colony of New York, and tried to convince the Mohawk tribe to give him fresh warriors and weapons. When the Mohawks refused, Metacom tried to keep on fighting with his remaining men.

But his shrinking war band could not resist forever.

Eight months after the Great Swamp Fight, English soldiers surrounded Metacom's camp. Metacom escaped, but his wife and nine-year-old son were

Metacom aims his arrow.

captured and sold as slaves to South America.

Metacom evaded the English for ten more days—but was surrounded in the middle of a swamp, unable to get away. A Native American warrior who had joined the English forces shot Metacom. The English then cut off his head, paraded back to Plymouth in triumph, and put Metacom's head up on a pole in the middle of the settlement—where it remained for years!

Because the English called Metacom "King Philip," this war became known as King Philip's War. Twelve English towns had been burned to the ground. One out of every sixteen men had died. Crops had been destroyed and farms leveled. In the following winters, many colonists died of starvation.

But more than three thousand Native Americans had died as well. Whole villages had been burned. Entire tribes had been killed; the few remaining members of those tribes scattered, many fleeing to the north. Now the English could continue to spread across North America, across land left empty by King Philip's War.

War Against the Colonies: Louis XIV Saves New France

Up north of Massachusetts, the French colonies were also fighting with Native American enemies.

The people of New France had done their best to be friends with the Native Americans nearby. Years before, Samuel Champlain had been careful to make friends with the nearest tribe, the Hurons. He gave them presents, slept and ate in their villages, and helped them fight against their enemies.

But the Hurons suffered from this friendship! The French gave the Hurons presents, but they also passed along a terrible new disease called *smallpox*. The Hurons had never been near smallpox before, so their bodies couldn't recognize the germs and fight them off. They began to grow ill. Rashes spread across their faces. They had trouble breathing and swallowing. Over half of the Huron tribe died from smallpox!

Another Native American tribe that lived nearby, the Iroquois, saw that the Hurons had become weak from illness. The Iroquois had always been more warlike than the Hurons. So Iroquois armies invaded Huron land, burned Huron camps and longhouses, and killed hundreds of Huron men and women. The Huron tribe disintegrated, and the triumphant Iroquois claimed their land.

Then the Iroquois set out to destroy New France— because the French had been friends and allies of the Hurons. Small parties of Iroquois warriors raided farms in Quebec, burning houses and killing settlers. Other war bands laid siege to Montreal, the largest settlement in New France. The settlers fought back. But the fierce and determined Iroquois were experts at forest fighting. They appeared and disappeared with bewildering speed, leaving death and destruction behind them.

The attacks went on and on. More and more French settlers left the dangerous lands of New France and went home! The colony shrank until it had almost disappeared.

But then the king of France, Louis XIV, stepped in to rescue New France.

Louis XIV, the Sun King, had spent years fighting wars to expand his French empire. He didn't intend to lose his colonies in the New World! So he sent soldiers from the French army over to fight the Iroquois. He promised these soldiers that he would give them land in the New World if they would save New France.

The French soldiers sailed to New France and marched off their ship, ready to fight. They had muskets and cannons. They had already fought bloody wars on the battlefields of Europe—and they were sure that they could defeat the "savages" of North America.

They were wrong! The battlefields of Europe hadn't prepared them to fight in thick woods and tangled brush. Even with their bullets and cannonballs, the French soldiers weren't able to defeat the Iroquois nation.

But they did manage to protect the settlements of New France from attack. Finally, the Iroquois agreed to observe an uneasy peace. They retreated back to their own land, and the French soldiers settled down on their new land, ready to begin new lives.

Now they were faced with a different problem. Louis XIV had sent hundreds of soldiers—all men—to New France. These soldiers wanted to start families and raise lots of little French Canadians. But there were six men for every woman in New France!

Once more, Louis XIV came to the rescue. He announced that he would pay young Frenchwomen large amounts of money if they would go and live in the colonies. Many young women accepted the king's offer and sailed across the Atlantic to New France—where they were greeted with great joy by French soldiers looking for wives! These young women became known as *filles du roi,* or "daughters of the King."

Now that New France was a safer place to live, the colony began to grow once again. Farmers called *habitants* cultivated the fields of the New World. Fur traders called *voyageurs* sailed up and down the rivers, trading for furs. Ships from France came to the ports of New France, bringing French goods, newspapers, and more settlers. The towns of Quebec and Montreal grew larger and richer. The streets were laid with cobbles; stone houses stood proudly in the middle of each town. Silversmiths, wigmakers, and tailors worked hard on their crafts. The gentlemen and ladies of New France, like the courtiers of Louis XIV over in France, decked themselves with silk, lace, powdered wigs, and jewelry.

But the Iroquois had not given up. Once again, they began to attack the rich towns and farms of New France.

One October morning, the farm of François Jarret lay peacefully under the mellow fall sun. François Jarret was a *seigneur,* an army officer who had been rewarded with a large farm. Jarret's farm was called Verchères. Many farmers lived on the lands of Verchères, cultivating Jarret's fields for him.

On this particular morning, François Jarret and his wife were both away from the fort, tending to business in the nearby town. Their fourteen-year-old daughter Marie-Madeleine was walking through the fields. She could just see the fort in the distance. Birds sang in the trees nearby, and the cool fall air moved against her face.

Suddenly, Marie-Madeleine heard gunshots in the distance. Then she heard a terrifying sound: the voices of farmers, screaming, "Save yourselves! The Iroquois are attacking!" She turned—and saw a band of fifty Iroquois warriors charging toward her. She ran toward the fort as fast as she could!

Later, Madeleine wrote down the events of that day. This is a simpler version of her story:

> The Iroquois who were chasing me found that I was too far ahead for them to capture. So they started to shoot at me. Bullets whizzed by me! As soon as I came close enough for the guards inside the fort to hear me, I started

shouting, "Get your weapons! Please, come and save me!" But no one appeared at the walls!

Just as I reached the gate, the fastest warrior caught me by the handkerchief around my neck. I yanked it off, leaving it in his hand, slipped through the gate—and pushed it closed! I looked around me. There were a few gaps in the walls of the fort. I started shouting at the others inside the fort, "Put posts across the gaps! Repair the walls!" I grabbed one of the posts myself and put it into place. When the others saw me carrying a post, they began to fix the walls themselves. So I went to find the guards. I found one hiding. Another was inside the room where the ammunition and powder was kept. He was holding a lighted fuse!

"What are you doing?" I shouted. He answered, "It's hopeless. We should blow ourselves up so that the Iroquois can't capture us." "Miserable man!" I screamed. "Give me that!"

He gave me the fuse. I could see that no one else would lead us—so I took off my bonnet, put on a hat, and grabbed a gun. I found my two little brothers, who were twelve and ten. "Come on," I said. "Let's fight to the death for our country!"

We loaded the cannons and shot them from the walls. The Iroquois were frightened by this and fell back a little. Inside the fort, women were crying. I ordered them to be shut up in an inside room, so that our enemies would not know that we were frightened. The sun was setting. The sky was filling with clouds; snow and ice had begun to fall. I knew that the enemy would attack again as soon as the night grew dark. All night, we stood on the walls, guarding the fort against the invaders. I took one corner. My two brothers took two more. The last corner was guarded by a man of eighty years old! For eight days, we held the fort against our enemy.

Finally, French soldiers from a nearby settlement arrived and drove off the attackers. For her bravery, Marie-Madeleine de Vercheres became a French Canadian heroine. Her statue still stands in Quebec today.

William Penn's Holy Experiment

While the colonies in New France and New England fought for survival, a man named William Penn was working hard to build a different kind of colony. Penn wanted this new colony, Pennsylvania, to be a place of peace, brotherhood, and love—not a place of war.

But the history of Pennsylvania was filled with trouble!

The story of Pennsylvania began in 1660, when William Penn was just sixteen and studying at the University of Oxford. The English had just decided to invite Charles II back to England. William's father, an officer in the English navy, commanded the ship that brought Charles II back to England. In gratitude, Charles II made William's father an admiral and a knight. And when Charles II was crowned in London, Admiral Penn loaned him sixteen thousand pounds for his treasury— more money than a farmer or merchant might earn in his entire lifetime!

Admiral Penn wanted William to have a position at the new royal court—perhaps as an ambassador or army officer. But in Oxford, William had started going to the meetings of a religious group called the Society of Friends of the Truth. The Friends were nicknamed "Quakers" because people whispered that they "quaked," or shook, in the presence of God. Quakers refused to belong to the Church of England. Instead they gathered together in plain meetinghouses where they sat and prayed quietly, waiting for God's words to come directly into their hearts. Quakers believed that every man and woman should be equal. So they refused to use the word "you" because, in those days, people used the word "you" when talking to superiors and the word "thee" when talking to equals. Quakers used "thee" when speaking to everyone. They wouldn't even take their hats off in the presence of the king! This looked a lot like rebellion—so Quakers were often arrested and put in jail.

Admiral Penn didn't want William to become a Quaker. So he ordered William to come home from Oxford, and sent him to France instead. In France, William met Louis XIV and learned French dress and French manners at the glittering, beautiful, French court. When he returned, he seemed content to lead the life of a wealthy aristocrat. He went to parties and balls. He decided to become a soldier and had his portrait painted in a full suit of armor!

But while William was playing the part of a fashionable young man, he was still thinking about Quaker ideas. Soon, William Penn was going to Quaker meetings once more. At the age of twenty-two, sitting in a Quaker meeting, William Penn was suddenly filled with joy. "The Lord visited me," he later said, "with a certain sound and testimony of his Eternal Word." Now William could no longer be a soldier; Quakers believed that fighting was wrong. And he certainly wouldn't be a royal ambassador; Quakers were not in favor at court. When Admiral Penn found out that his son had become a Quaker, he was so furious that he threw William out of the house and told him not to come back!

William Penn went to live with friends in London. He wrote tracts defending Quaker beliefs, preached in public, and was thrown into jail. When he was released, he learned that his father was dying. William Penn hurried home to sit by his father's side. Ten days later, Admiral Penn died.

William spent the next three years writing and thinking about Quaker ideas. Meanwhile, all over England, Quakers were put in jail because of their beliefs. William Penn knew that, over in North America, Puritans had formed colonies where they could worship as they pleased. Why couldn't Quakers have a colony as well?

So William wrote to Charles II, reminding the king that he still owed the Penn family sixteen thousand pounds. He asked for the king to pay him back, not with money, but with land in North America.

Charles II agreed—and he insisted that the land be called Pennsylvania in honor of William's father. In 1681, he gave William Penn a piece of land on the western bank of the Delaware River for his very own. The land was almost as big as the country of England!

William Penn planned to use this land for a colony where Quaker ideas would be followed. He wanted the settlers to be like brothers, all equal to each other. The capital city would be called the City of Brotherly Love—in Greek, *Philadelphia.* The colonists would govern themselves! To help them, he wrote out directions, called the Frame of Government, that explained how the colony would run. Colonists would vote to elect three groups of leaders: a council, an assembly, and a governor. The council would make laws, the assembly would vote on whether or not the laws should be passed, and the governor would make sure that laws were followed. That way, no one group of people would have all the power. Later, this Frame of Government would be a model for the American Constitution.

William Penn didn't forget about the Native Americans either. He sent them a message promising to pay them for any land that the colonists used. In the directions for his new colony, he wrote, "No man shall by any ways or means, in word or deed, affront or wrong any Indian....The Indians shall have liberty to do all things…that any of the [colonists] shall enjoy."

In 1682, William Penn himself came over to Pennsylvania, bringing a hundred colonists with him. In the next year, twenty-three different ships arrived, one at a time, bringing new settlers—two thousand in all!

But the governor of Maryland, the colony just south of Pennsylvania, watched Pennsylvania's growth with alarm. He thought that the Pennsylvania colonists were settling on land that ought to belong to Maryland. Just two years after William Penn's arrival, the Maryland governor announced that he was going to sail to England and ask the king to give him part of Pennsylvania's land.

William Penn didn't want to leave his colony so soon. But he had no choice. He had to follow the Maryland governor back over to England and defend Pennsylvania's right to its land! So, sadly, he boarded a ship and set out on the long journey across the Atlantic.

He would not return for fifteen long years!

When he arrived in England, he found that Charles II was too ill to see him. Not long after, Charles II died—without leaving a son behind him. His brother, James II, claimed the throne.

William Penn

But James II was Catholic. The people of England were horrified. Did this mean that England would become a Catholic country? And then something even more alarming happened: James II and his wife had a son. They planned to raise this little boy to be a good Catholic—and James's heir. Now, England might be facing a whole dynasty of Catholic kings!

The English Protestants revolted. They sent a message to James's older daughter, Mary, who lived in Holland. Mary was a Protestant, and she had married a Dutch nobleman, William III of Orange. Both were Protestants. "Come to England and seize the throne!" the English Protestants pleaded. "Be king and queen and deliver us from Catholic rule!"

William and Mary agreed to come. They also agreed to sign a paper, promising that they would not try to pass any laws without the approval of Parliament. In November of 1688, they sailed to England along with 14,000 Protestant soldiers. As soon as they landed, James's royal army deserted him and welcomed the new Protestant rulers! James, like his brother before him, had to flee to France.

The Protestants of England were delighted. They now had a Protestant king and queen who had promised not to be tyrants. The English called this takeover the Glorious Revolution. Their new monarchs, Mary II and William III, would never try to seize power from Parliament.

But the Revolution wasn't so glorious for William Penn. He was arrested three times because he was suspected of loyalty to the king. Each time he was released, he tried to get a ship to take him back to Philadelphia—and failed. Finally, he was forced to go into hiding. He stayed in hiding for years and years!

Finally, when fears of James II's return began to die down, William was able to come out of hiding and buy passage on a ship to North America. When he walked down its gangplank in the harbor of Philadelphia, he could hardly believe his eyes. In fifteen years, Philadelphia had grown to be the second largest town in all of North America! The city was filled with shops, tall brick houses, wide streets, and thousands of people. The Holy Experiment had succeeded.

Today, a statue of William Penn stands on top of Philadelphia's City Hall. The statue is thirty-seven feet tall! For many years, no building in Philadelphia was allowed to be taller than the brim of the statue's hat, so that William Penn would always be the highest spot in the city that he planned.

Europe During the Agricultural Revolution

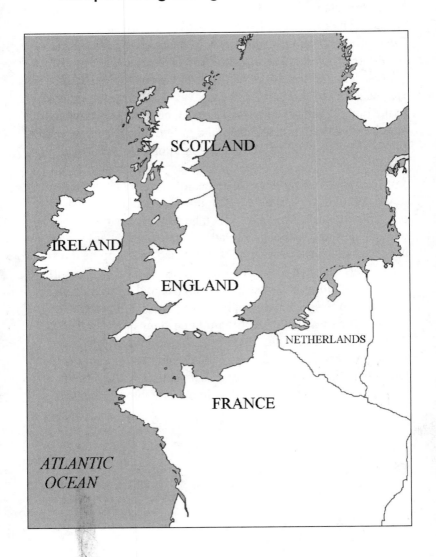

Chapter Sixteen

The Universal Laws of Newton and Locke

William Penn set out to build a colony where everyone was equal. And the people of England demanded that their new king and queen, William and Mary, only pass the laws that the *people* wanted. What happened to the days of knights and castles, when a king could do whatever he wanted, and when lords rode through their estates, commanding the peasants to obey?

In England and in Europe—that part of the world that we often call the West—those days were fading away.

The days of kings and lords first began to lose their brightness when philosophers and scientists realized that the ancient Greeks, who had long been held up as the wisest men in the world, were sometimes wrong. A hundred years before William Penn and William and Mary, the Italian scientist Galileo had studied the ideas of the ancient scientists Aristotle and Ptolemy. Both men wrote that the sun went around the earth. But Galileo realized that this idea didn't explain his own observations of the sky. He needed a new theory, and he made one: The earth actually goes around the sun! Galileo was one of the first scientists to use the *scientific method*. Instead of accepting old ideas, he carefully observed the world around him, and then tried to make a theory that would explain his observations.

Almost a hundred years later, in 1642, a weak, sickly baby was born in England. His parents didn't expect him to live—but they named him Isaac anyway, like the baby born to Abraham and Sarah in the Bible. Isaac *did* live. As a matter of fact, Isaac Newton lived to be eighty-four years old! And he used those eighty-four years to take Galileo's ideas even further.

155

As he grew, Isaac Newton became more and more curious about how the world worked. He read every book he could find. He did scientific experiments. He tried very hard to turn lead and copper into gold—but he never succeeded!

When Isaac was eighteen, the people of England invited Charles II to reclaim the throne. Three years later, Isaac Newton went to study science at the University of Cambridge. There, he was told to read the ideas of Plato and Aristotle—but Newton thought that the ideas of modern scientists like Galileo and Copernicus were closer to the truth. In his scientific notebook, Newton wrote, "*Amicus Plato amicus Aristoteles magis amica veritas.*" That is Latin for, "Plato is my friend, Aristotle is my friend, but my best friend is truth."

When Cambridge closed down because of the Plague, Isaac Newton went back home. He went on studying the world, trying to figure out why it worked the way it did. While he studied, thought, and wrote, Charles II ruled, grew ill, and then died, and James II came to the throne.

One day, Isaac Newton was sitting beside a window, thinking and staring out into the family apple orchards, when he saw an apple fall to the ground. He thought, "Why does it always fall down? Why doesn't the apple ever fall sideways, or up? Some sort of force must be pulling on the apple to make it always fall in exactly the same way!"

Newton went on observing, doing experiments, and thinking until he was able to describe the force that pulls on the apple. He called it *gravity,* from the Latin word *grave,* which means "heavy." This "heavy" force means that large bodies, such as the earth, have a force that pulls objects toward them. Isaac Newton learned that he could predict, using mathematics, how strong that force would be, anywhere in the universe. The next time an apple fell, Newton could tell you exactly how fast it would fall and when it would hit the earth!

Newton's new rules, which we now call the laws of gravity, showed that every motion or action in the universe had a law that governed it. The universe wasn't a huge, mysterious, magical riddle. Instead, people could figure out—and even predict ahead of time—what would happen. The universe was like a machine that always worked in the same way. In 1687, while James II was still on the throne (and growing more and more unpopular for his Catholic ways), Isaac Newton published his ideas in a book called *Principia Mathematica,* or "Principles of Mathematics."

Newton's ideas about laws that governed the whole universe didn't just affect other scientists. Other thinkers, such as *philosophers* (who think about ideas), *economists* (who think about money and how it works), and *political philosophers* (who think about the ways countries are governed) began to think that if universal laws governed objects, universal laws also governed people. If they could use the scientific method to observe people and make theories about the ways people acted, perhaps those universal laws could be discovered. Then, life would no longer be mysterious. They would no longer need to wonder why one country prospered while another became poor, or why one country won a war while another lost. Universal laws would explain all of these things!

Another Englishman, John Locke, was determined to discover these universal laws. When the English rebelled against Charles I, John Locke was seventeen years old. His father joined the anti-royalist forces, and fought against Charles's royal army during the Civil War. After Charles's execution, John Locke went to study at Oxford. He was supposed to study history and Greek philosophy—but like Isaac Newton, John Locke found these ideas old-fashioned. He wanted to experiment in science and read the new ideas of modern philosophers!

When Charles II came back to England, Locke had grown to be a man of twenty-eight. The king's supporters knew that Locke preferred a commonwealth to a king. Locke was afraid that he might be arrested, or even executed! So he left England and visited France, Holland, and other European countries, learning from other scientists and philosophers. He stayed out of England through the reign of James II. When Mary and William came triumphantly to England, John Locke returned to England as part of Mary's royal party.

Now that England was a *constitutional monarchy*—meaning that the king and queen themselves had to obey the laws passed by Parliament—John Locke didn't have to worry about being arrested simply because he preferred one form of government to another. Now, he was free to write down the ideas he had been thinking about for the past years. In 1690, the year after he returned to England, John Locke published a book called *Two Treatises of Government*.

In his book, John Locke explained that he had discovered universal laws that could predict how people should act. Every man and woman, Locke wrote, was equal. Every human being had, by "natural law," the right to seek "life, health, liberty, and possessions." No king could claim that God had given him the divine power to execute his subjects, throw them in jail, or take their property!

But Locke added that groups of people gathered together into cities or countries need *someone* to make and enforce laws. So people should join together in groups and draw up a contract. This contract gives some of them power to rule over others—but the rulers can only have as much power as the people are willing to give them. Rulers can't take away the "life, health, liberty, and possessions" of their subjects. If they "destroy, enslave, or…impoverish" their subjects, the people can join together, announce that the contract isn't valid any more, throw the rulers out of office, and appoint new rulers. "Men under government," Locke wrote, "…[should] have a standing rule to live by, common to every one of that society. . .and not to be subject to the inconstant, uncertain, arbitrary will of another man." In other words, even a king has to obey the laws—or else he loses his throne!

John Locke also thought that every ruler would be tempted to abuse his power. So he also wrote that a good government would have three parts, like William Penn's colony. One group would make the laws, another group would enforce them, and a third group would be in charge of fighting wars with other countries. That way, no king could ever make laws just for his own good—or start wars simply to make himself richer or more important.

Isaac Newton, John Locke, and many other men and women in England and Europe began to accept these ideas about government, and also to believe that universal laws, discovered through observation, governed every part of human life. Today, we often talk about these ideas as "Western ideas." Sometimes we talk about the years when these ideas became popular as the "Enlightenment."

But in the days of John Locke, the eastern countries of the world often did not agree with the West. As a matter of fact, when Japan closed its harbors, one reason was to prevent Enlightenment ideas from coming in—and from encouraging Japanese citizens to question the power of the shogun!

Scientific Farming

It's five o'clock on a cold, dark March morning. Frost covers the stone steps of a farmer's cottage in the south of England; smoke has just begun to rise from the chimney. A huddle of sheep crowd against a stone wall nearby, looking hopefully toward the cottage. Occasionally one *baas*.

William Barkely has already been up for an hour. He's emptied the chamber pots, brought in wood, and stoked the fire. His wife Joan is already kneading the day's bread; it will rise near the fire until ready to bake for lunch. The three children are still sleeping, but Joan is listening for the first cry from baby Matilda. William takes a rope down from the wall and lights his lantern. He's headed out to the cattle barn to slaughter one of the cows for the evening meal. He's already eaten his breakfast, standing; a piece of yesterday's oat bread, soaked in a dish of ale.

Far away, in a comfortable London manor, Isaac Newton—now seventy-nine—is still sleeping. In an hour or so, a maid will bring him his morning tea and stoke his bedroom fire. He'll sit up in bed, the blankets wrapped around his shoulders, and drink his tea, waiting for his valet to arrive and lay out his clothes. Once dressed, he'll sit down to a breakfast of grilled fish, dried apples, and fine white bread. His carriage is waiting for him, the coachman huddled on the driver's seat, shivering in the cold morning air. When Newton finishes his breakfast, the coachman will take him to the Mitre on Wood Street, a warm and comfortable tavern where he'll preside over a meeting of the Royal Society of scientists. After the meeting, he'll dine on sizzling roast beef, cold sage soup, wine, and apple tart, and then he will nap in a leather chair in front of the tavern's roaring fire.

The life of a wealthy philosopher and scientist seems very different from the life of a hard-working farmer! But although Newton, Locke, and the other thinkers who tried to discover universal laws were wealthy men who could afford to spend their days writing and thinking (rather than working with their hands), the Universal Laws they laid out changed the lives of farmers like William and Joan.

As William goes through his day, he'll be farming in a different way than his grandfather and great-grandfather. He'll be using new, *scientific* methods of farming—thanks to the universal laws of nature.

The idea that laws could be discovered to explain the natural world soon began to change the practical details of everyday life. After all, if the universe was governed by universal laws, and people were governed by universal laws, surely crops and animals were also governed by universal laws? If farmers knew those laws, they could use them to raise larger crops, and healthier animals.

William Barkely is getting ready to slaughter a cow so that his family can eat meat. Twenty years earlier, no poor farmer would expect to eat meat in the winter or early spring! But William has plenty of meat for his family—because he knows some of the universal laws that govern plants and animals.

For centuries, farmers had known that fields planted with wheat year after year would give less and less grain. The wheat plants were using up all of the minerals in the soil—and as the minerals disappeared, wheat plants grew small and

160

spindly. So farmers would plant wheat one year, barley the next, and then let the fields lie empty the third year, so that the minerals in the soil would return.

But when English and Dutch farmers began to investigate the universal laws of plants, they discovered that different kinds of plants use different kinds of minerals. Lord Charles Townshend, an English gentleman farmer with a large estate, came up with a new rotation of crops. Since turnips and clover actually *return* minerals to the soil, he suggested planting first wheat, then turnips, then barley or oats, and finally clover. Farmers who used this four-year rotation could plant their fields every single year. They had more grain—and more food for cattle, since cows liked turnips and clover. Soon, most English farmers were using Townshend's crop rotation—and Townshend had earned himself the nickname "Turnip Townshend."

Since farmers now had more grain and more cattle food, they could afford to keep larger herds of cattle alive all year round. Now they could eat meat any time of the year!

William Barkely and his family will eat beef for dinner tonight. After William Barkely prepares his meat to be cooked, he heads over to the sheep pen to feed the flock. William's sheep are big, round ewes with plenty of thick wool. William has spent the last few years carefully breeding his best sheep together, hoping for large, healthy lambs. Now his flock is the finest in the countryside!

William's grandfather couldn't breed his best sheep together. In *his* day, farmers didn't have private, fenced-off fields where they could raise crops and put flocks out to pasture. Open fields were owned by towns, and everyone in the town farmed the fields together. Everyone's sheep and cows grazed on common pasture land together.

But with the new interest in scientific farming and crop rotation, each farmer wanted his own field to till in the most modern way possible. So the English government passed laws called Acts of Enclosure. These Acts divided the common fields up into smaller private fields, each one fenced off. Enclosure meant that each farmer could rotate his crops and fertilize his fields—and could control which animals mated together. A

161

sheep farmer could breed only his best sheep. A dairy farmer could breed only the fattest beef cattle and raise more cows ideal for meat. As a matter of fact, one farmer named Robert Bakewell cross-bred the fattest cows from several different herds and created a whole new kind of cow, called the New Leicestershire. This animal put on fat quickly, so that Englishmen could feast on roast beef with plenty of fat gravy all year round!

The Acts of Enclosure didn't please every farmer. When a town enclosed its lands, government officials arrived to divide up the fields. The farmers receiving the fields had to pay the government officials—and they also had to pay for new hedges or stone walls to surround their land. When William's town was enclosed, he had enough money to pay the fees, but other poorer farmers nearby didn't have enough money. They had to sell their farms to richer neighbors. William bought one. Now his farm is twice as large.

After feeding his sheep, William goes to harness his plow horse. It's time for the job that will occupy the rest of his day—sowing his early spring crop of wheat. He hitches his horse to a square wooden machine with two boxes on top and two sharp, hollow wooden blades below. This new invention has made his fields even more productive! His father sowed wheat by walking through the fields, throwing seeds all around him. Some of the seeds sprouted—but many were wasted. Birds ate some. Others baked in the sun before they sprouted. And the plants that *did* come up didn't come up in orderly rows, so that William's father couldn't walk between the rows of his crop to care for and weed it.

But then a scientist-farmer named Jethro Tull invented the seed drill. When William's horse pulls the seed drill through his field, the two hollow wooden blades will cut narrow, even furrows into the ground. Seeds will drop out of the boxes, called *seed hoppers*, and fall into the furrows. Protected from the sun and from scavenging birds, fertilized by the rich earth where turnips were planted the year before, William's wheat

162

crop will yield bushels and bushels of grain. He'll sell some of this grain; the rest will feed William's family, his sheep, and his cows.

All over England, farmers like William are using these new, scientific methods of farming. Ancient ways of growing crops and tending animals are disappearing. An Agricultural Revolution is taking place!

Russia During the Reign of Peter the Great

Chapter Seventeen
Russia Looks West

Peter the Great

If English farmers and European philosophers lived in the West, and the people of Japan and China lived in the East, who lived in the middle?

The Russians!

The enormous country of Russia lay between the Western countries of Europe and the Eastern countries of Asia. In medieval times, Russia was much more Eastern than Western. Russian men wore long, eastern robes and beards. Russian women didn't mingle with men; they stayed in separate rooms and wore veils. And Russia's kings, called *czars,* ruled with absolute power, like the emperors of China and the shoguns of Japan.

But then a young man of seventeen took control—and turned his gaze to the West.

Peter I, who became known as "Peter the Great," became Czar of Russia in 1682, one year after William Penn founded the colony of Pennsylvania. The young czar was only ten, so his older sister Sophia took control of the royal palace in Moscow and ruled as his regent. Peter was sent to the country, where he spent hours climbing trees, roaming through the fields—and playing war games. He divided his friends into regiments and gave them uniforms, flags, and drums. When Peter was eleven, he was allowed to use real cannons in his war games!

Meanwhile, Sophia ordered Russian troops into battle, had herself painted wearing the crown of the czars, and behaved more and more as though she were the *real* czar of Russia. When Peter was seventeen, Sophia tried to convince her royal guard to attack Peter and his mother in their country home. But the royal guard refused! They had grown tired of Sophia and her tyranny. Instead, the royal guard swore allegiance to Peter, the rightful czar of Russia. Sophia, frightened of her brother, fled to a convent—where she would spend the rest of her life.

Now Peter was truly czar of Russia!

Peter had always been fascinated by the West. But not very many Europeans traveled to Russia, and those who settled in Russia lived apart from the Russians, in special colonies for "foreigners." Peter had spent hours in these colonies, talking to the Westerners who lived there. He had even found an old, rotten English sailboat in a shed—and was fascinated by it. Peter wanted ships like the English had. He wanted to build a navy that could sail to Europe. He wanted a fleet of merchant ships that could take Russian honey, wax and furs to Europe, and bring back all the luxuries of the West for Russians to enjoy.

But Peter knew that Russia would never be able to visit the West without a good port for ships to sail in and out of. Russia's northern coast was so cold and icy that ships couldn't even reach it for most of the year. And Peter's only port city, the city of Archangel, was so far north that it was frozen solid for half the year. During the cold dark Arctic winters, the sun only rose for five short hours a day. And the air was so cold that if you spat on the ground, your spit would freeze before it landed!

Russia needed a warmer port, and Peter had his eye on one: the port of Azov. The Sea of Azov led right into the Black Sea, which led to the Mediterranean. Azov belonged to the Ottoman Turks, but Peter was sure that the Russian army could defeat the Turks in battle and claim Azov for Russia.

So Peter marched his army down to Azov and laid a siege around the fortress that protected the port. He wrote out a demand for surrender, attached it to an arrow, and ordered an archer to shoot it into the city. But the Turks simply laughed at Peter's demand. Peter soon saw why. Turkish ships could sail right into Azov to bring food and weapons to the Turks inside the fortress. Meanwhile, the Russians camped outside the walls began to run out of food and ammunition. And the weather was growing colder. A savage winter was coming!

Peter realized that he would never be able to capture Azov unless he could stop Turkish ships from reaching it. So he withdrew his army and ordered his men to build twenty-five warships and hundreds of barges—all before spring! The Russian soldiers labored all winter, building this huge fleet and learning to sail it. When spring came, the brand-new Russian navy drove away the Turkish galleys that arrived to save Azov. Meanwhile, Russian soldiers began to build a pile of rubble high against Azov's walls. When the mound was high enough, soldiers poured over it into the fortress. The Turks waved their turbans in surrender. Azov had fallen!

Now Peter had his port. He still couldn't trade freely with the West, because the Ottoman Turks also guarded the *strait,* or narrow place, that led out of the Sea of Azov toward the Mediterranean. Peter planned to drive the Turks away from this strait too. Then, his path to the West would be open!

But Peter needed help if he was going to keep on fighting against the Turks. So he decided to visit Europe. He would be able to see how Western countries ran their navies and their trading companies. And he would try to convince the nations of Europe to join with him in war against the Ottoman Turks. He would be the first Russian czar to travel to the West.

Peter collected an enormous group of noblemen, officials, servants, soldiers, and sailors into an expedition and set off for the West. He planned to visit Poland, just to the west of Russia, and then to travel on through Germany, Holland, and England. His journey took a year and half! Peter spent months learning all about the accomplishments of Western countries. In Prussia, he studied gunnery for weeks. In Holland, Peter worked at the docks of the East India Company, in Amsterdam, for four whole months. When he visited England, he spent another four months working in English docks. He visited the Tower of London and the Mint. He listened to the meetings of the Royal Society. He even went to a Quaker meeting and met William Penn! (But afterward he remarked to one of his courtiers, "What use is a bunch of men who won't fight for their country?")

The Westerners who met the Czar of Russia admired his curiosity and his quick brain, but they also thought he seemed savage and foreign. He drank a lot: brandy, vodka, wine, beer, and more. His clothes were patched, darned, and not too clean. He punched and kicked his friends and advisors if they displeased him. He even made one of his aides eat an entire tortoise, just for fun. "One could wish," wrote one aristocratic German lady who met Peter at a ball, "that his manners were a little less rustic….One can see also that he has had no one to teach him how to eat properly."

Peter returned to Russia full of new ideas. He shaved off his beard, so that he would look more Western. Then he ordered his noblemen, called *boyars,* to shave their beards too. He thought that all those Russian beards made them look too old-fashioned and too eastern.

Russian noblemen hated this idea. They didn't want to look like Europeans! Many believed that their beards symbolized a special relationship with God. Some were even afraid that they wouldn't be able to get into heaven without beards—so they kept the shaved beards in special bags, hoping to put the beards in their coffins. But Peter was adamant. He carried a pair of scissors with him everywhere. If he saw a nobleman with a beard, he would begin to cut it off!

Peter the Great flies into a temper

Peter also ordered his noblemen to wear Western clothes. If he saw a courtier with a long Eastern tunic, he used his scissors to hack off its bottom and its flowing sleeves! He also wanted women to take off their veils and mingle with men at social gatherings. He even wanted them to have tutors and be educated like men.

But although Peter hoped to make Russians look and act more Western, he didn't want them to *be* Westerners. Western philosophers in countries such as France and Spain were insisting that all men and women were equal—and that rulers, even czars, shouldn't have the power to do exactly as they pleased. Peter didn't want Russia to become *that* Western!

Peter's Port to the West

Peter's journey to Europe was a success—he learned all about the countries of the West. But it was also a failure—because he couldn't convince England and Holland to join him in a war against the Turks. Peter owned the Port of Azov, but he still couldn't get into the Mediterranean. And now Peter had eighty-six warships—with nowhere to go!

Peter knew that if he kept on fighting the Turks without help, he would probably lose. He studied his maps, looking for another clear path to Europe. But the only other way to send his ships to Europe would be to launch them into the Baltic Sea.

Unfortunately, Sweden owned the shores of the Baltic!

So Peter declared war on Sweden. Sweden's neighbor, Denmark-Norway, joined with him. Once, Denmark, Norway, and Sweden had all been ruled by one king—but Sweden had broken away, and now was growing larger, stronger—and greedier. The people of Denmark-Norway hoped that, together with Russia, they could beat off the swelling Swedish empire.

Peter believed that he could beat Sweden in a few short weeks. After all, the Swedish army was led by their nineteen-year-old king, Charles XII. Charles was known for wild parties and reckless stunts (such as making his whole court go out and hunt bears, armed only with wooden pitchforks). Peter didn't think that this noisy boy would be able to plan and carry out a disciplined military campaign.

Once again, Peter was wrong. His war with Sweden, the Great Northern War, began in 1700—and lasted for the next twenty-one years.

The war started badly for Peter. He started off to attack Narva, a Swedish city on the eastern banks of the Baltic, but his army was hauling so many cannons and siege weapons that the journey took months. Meanwhile, Charles invaded Denmark and scared the Danish into surrendering. And when Peter's army finally reached Narva, the cannons wouldn't work properly. Russian gunpowder was so bad that cannonballs often staggered out of the cannons and plopped harmlessly to earth. Other times, the gunpowder over-fired and blew up entire cannons!

While the Russians struggled with their cannons, Peter decided to return to Moscow to check on how the government was working in his absence. Just hours after he rode off, the Russian army learned that a huge Swedish army, under Charles's command, was only six miles away from Narva! They scrambled frantically to prepare for battle. But just as the Swedes came into view, a huge snow squall opened right above the Russians. In the blinding, violent cloud of snow, the Russians couldn't get into line—or even face the right direction. The cavalry rode the wrong direction, fell into the nearby Narva River, and drowned. The general and his officers galloped toward the Swedes, doing their best to surrender as quickly as possible!

Charles XII was delighted with his victory. He ordered a medal made, celebrating the triumph. The medal showed Peter the Great running away, holding a handkerchief to his eyes—which were squirting out streams of tears!

The Russian army retreated, but Charles decided not to chase them. Winter was coming, and he knew that his army might freeze to death in the icy Russian wilderness. So the Swedish troops started to wait out the long winter. Meanwhile, Peter returned to prepare his own army for spring. He ordered new cannons forged and ships repaired. He drafted more soldiers for his army and taught them to fight with both guns and bayonets. By the time fighting began again, the Russians were strong enough to hold off the Swedes. Battle followed battle. Peter the Great took a personal role in the war, traveling from front to front, leading attacks, sailing on warships, and even helping to repair the ships in the shipyards.

In 1702, Peter finally managed to capture a small Swedish fortress on the Neva River, which led into the Baltic Sea. He still couldn't sail into the Baltic, which was guarded by the Swedish navy. But he was sure that he would win the Baltic from the Swedes. Then, ships could sail from the little Neva fortress to Europe. The banks of the Neva River could be Russia's "Window to the West."

So Peter planned out a brand new city on the shores of the Neva. He named his city St. Petersburg after his patron saint, Peter.

The land where St. Petersburg would be built was swampy and muddy, filled with water birds, reeds, and mosquitoes. There were no trees for lumber, and no stones for foundations. There were no buildings—except for Peter's new royal palace, a little hut with three rooms, no stove, and rickety wooden walls painted to look like brick.

But Peter wasn't discouraged. In his imagination, he could already see the skyline of a great city, as great as any European city! As the war with Sweden dragged on, Peter ordered every soldier who could be spared to work on building St. Petersburg. He forced peasants and Swedish prisoners of war to work on it too—and paid them so little that they had to steal and beg in order to have enough to eat. Every piece of wood and every stone had to be dragged to St. Petersburg from far away. And there were no wheelbarrows, so the workers carried loads of stones in the laps of their long shirts.

While Peter built, Charles XII plotted his strategy. Six years after Peter began work on St. Petersburg, Charles invaded Russia.

The Russian army fell back. The Swedes chased them deep into Russia. But it was already fall—and cold weather threatened. Charles's soldiers began to whisper about the horrors of a Russian winter. It would become so cold, they told each other, that birds would die flying through the air, and hit the ground like stones!

Charles, excited by the prospect of victory, told his men to go on. The Russian army kept on retreating, until the only shelter nearby was a tiny walled town with one small door.

And then the temperature plummeted.

One of the coldest spells in memory had struck the Russian plains! The Swedes clustered toward the narrow door of the town—but it took three days for the whole army to file through. Meanwhile, more than three thousand soldiers froze to death. Frostbite took the noses, ears, fingers, and toes of thousands more. The whole time, the Russians were camped safely nearby; their heavy furs and warm boots and their winter-proof tents kept them safe. When the weakened Swedes finally met the Russians in battle, the Russians were triumphant. Ten thousand Swedish soldiers were killed or captured. The Russians ruled the field!

Charles XII refused to surrender. The war sputtered on. But four years later, Charles was killed by a bullet during a meaningless battle. Without Charles, the Swedes gave up. They surrendered the eastern shore of the Baltic to Peter. Now Peter's Window to the West was wide open.

For the next few years of his reign, Peter worked hard to make Russia as rich as any Western nation. He built canals, factories, salt works, iron mills, and mines. He brought European craftsmen to Russia to teach Russians how to make cloth, lacquer ware, and other goods. He worked hard on St. Petersburg, which he declared to be his new capital city. In 1714, twelve years after the city began, a Western diplomat sniffed that the city was no more than "a heap of villages linked together." But only ten years later, in 1724, the same diplomat marveled that St. Petersburg had become a "wonder of the world," filled with "magnificent palaces."

But Peter had only a short time to enjoy his city. In that same year, 1724, he was sailing to visit a Russian factory when a nearby boat ran aground on a sandbar and began to sink. Peter leapt into the icy water to pull the sailors to safety. The icy water brought on fever and illness. Peter never recovered. He died while trying to write down the name of his successor.

When Peter died, the empire of Russia stretched from Archangel in the north, over past the Ural Mountains in the east, down to the Caspian Sea in the south, over to the borders of Poland and Sweden on the west. Moscow and St. Petersburg had become cities filled with Western merchants and diplomats. Russian diplomats visited every European court. Peter had made Russia larger. But even more important: he had made Russia part of Europe. No wonder he became known as Peter the Great!

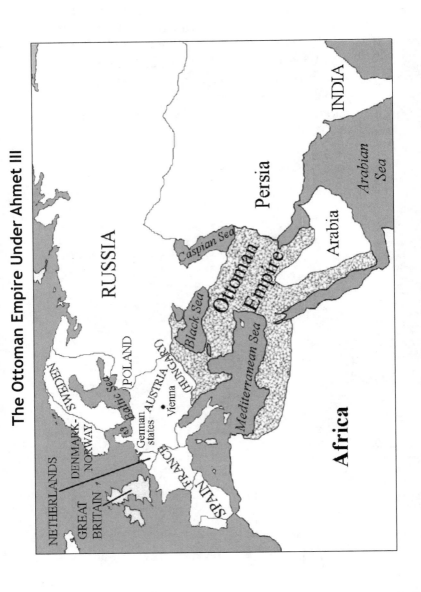

The Ottoman Empire Under Ahmet III

Chapter Eighteen
East and West Collide

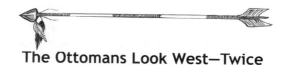

The Ottomans Look West—Twice

Peter wasn't the only Eastern king to look toward the West. To the south of Russia, Peter's enemies the Ottoman Turks were also ruled by a king who hoped to make his empire more Western.

But even before that king came to the throne, the Turks tried to become more Western—by conquering the West.

When Peter became czar of Russia, the Ottoman Empire stretched from the modern-day country of Iraq all the way over to the borders of Austria, the German state where the Holy Roman Emperor lived. The Ottoman Turks were a proud Eastern people, followers of Islam. Their king, or *sultan,* ruled over the empire without question—and also guarded the holy cities of Mecca, Medina, and Jerusalem. The sultan kept private royal guards called the *Janissaries* who would carry out any deed their sultan ordered!

In 1683, the year after Peter became czar, the Turks decided to make the West part of their Eastern empire—and began to march toward Europe! A quarter of a million Turkish soldiers were headed toward Vienna, the capital of the German state of Austria. The Holy Roman Emperor lived in Vienna! If the Turks could capture Vienna, they would own the heart of the West.

The Viennese people panicked! All of the noblemen fled with their treasure. Houses in front of the walls were knocked down so that there would be room to fight. The Holy Roman Emperor sneaked out of the city along with his family. The Viennese stood on the walls, waiting for the worst. And then they saw the long, frightening line of Turks rise slowly over the horizon. The footsteps of this enormous army shook the earth. "They broke against the earth like waves of the sea," one Viennese man wrote.

The Ottoman army set up a siege camp all around Vienna. The army's leader, the *vizier* (prime minister) Kara Mustafa, put up a whole network of tents with fancy silk covers, rich rugs, and gardens planted around them. Kara Mustafa did not intend to leave his camp any time soon!

The Turks started digging trenches toward the walls of Vienna, sheltering themselves by pulling timbers and earth over their heads. The Viennese were told to listen carefully for any sound of tunneling from underneath the city's pavements. As soon as they heard the sound of digging, German soldiers would try to break through the stones into the tunnels, fighting the Turks hand to hand in the dark cramped underground before they could break through into the city!

One morning, long before dawn, two bakers were preparing the day's bread. One baker kneaded the dough, while the other stoked the oven. Vienna still slept; the city was quiet.

Suddenly, the kneader paused. He could hear an odd sound. *Click. Scoop. Click. Scoop.* Turkish soldiers were tunneling beneath the bakery!

"Help!" he yelled. "Invaders! Help! Stop them!" German soldiers came running. They pried up the bakery's stones and leapt down into the tunnels below, shouting and firing. The Turkish tunnelers were driven back. Vienna was safe for one more day! According to legend, the bakers invented a new kind of bread in honor of the occasion: rolls shaped like the crescent emblem on the Turkish flag, which they called *croissants*.

But no one thought Vienna would last much longer. The siege dragged on. The people had run out meat; they were eating donkeys and stray cats. Many had begun to grow ill. And no one seemed to be coming to the rescue! The Turks went on digging trenches. At any moment, a huge assault could pour over Vienna's crumbling walls and bring the city down.

Meanwhile, an army of French and Polish and German soldiers was slowly assembling. Finally, on September 11th, 1683, the army was in position. The next morning, the

European attack began. German and Polish soldiers pressed their way into the Turkish camp. The camp collapsed! Kara Mustafa fled. Despite all that Turkish strength, the army had stayed too long. It was slow, disorganized, and easy to drive away. When Kara Mustafa returned home, the sultan ordered his head brought to court in a velvet bag.

The attack on Vienna was the last great attack of the Ottoman Turks. The empire began to shrink. The German armies drove them back east, out of the modern country of Hungary. The western side of the empire disappeared. The distance between East and West was widening, once more.

But twenty-five years later, a new sultan and his grand vizier tried once more to narrow that distance.

Like Peter the Great, Ahmet III admired Western culture and Western ideas. He was a particular fan of Dutch tulips! Tulips had been a wildflower in central Asia, where the Turks originally came from. As a matter of fact, a wild tulip was the sign of the Ottoman ruling house. Dutch explorers found the tulips and took them back to the Netherlands, where Dutch gardeners grew them, cultured them, and turned them into one of the world's greatest flowers.

Now, Ahmet brought tulips back to the Turks. He had thousands and thousands of tulip bulbs brought from the Netherlands and planted at his royal palace. Hundreds of gardeners tended the bulbs. In April, when the tulips bloomed, Ahmet threw enormous parties among his tulip beds. Colored lamps hung in the gardens; beautiful music was played from the garden's edges. He invited Western diplomats to these parties! The French ambassador described the scene he saw: "Beside every fourth flower is stood a candle….Along the alleys are hung cages filled with all kinds of birds. The trellises are all decorated with an enormous quantity of flowers of every sort, placed in bottles and lit by an infinite number of glass lamps of different colours…." Streams ran between the tulip beds; giant turtles swam in them, bearing candles on their backs.

For his love of tulips, Ahmet III became known as the "Tulip King" and his reign became known as the Tulip Period. For ten years, the Tulip King and his grand vizier, Ibrahim

177

Pasha, tried to shape the Ottoman court after the courts of the West. The Sultan's new palace, *Sa'adabat* or "the Palace of Happiness," was modeled after a French palace. Ibrahim Pasha sent ambassadors to French cities and factories to find out more about European art and science. The ambassadors brought back a printing press! For the first time, the Turks began to publish books: dictionaries, books about science, and a book about the military strategies of Western armies!

Ahmet's court never became as Western as Peter the Great's. Women in Ahmet's empire still wore the robes and veils dictated by their Muslim faith. The Ottoman Turks kept their distinctive turbans and beards. They continued to worship in the ways of Islam. But the court became too Western for the Janissaries! In 1730—five years after the death of Peter the Great—the Janissaries had had enough of Ibrahim Pasha, Ahmet III, and the luxury of the royal court. They rioted, burned down Ahmet's palace, and threw the sultan in jail. They put Ahmet's nephew Mahmud I on the throne instead!

Under Mahmud I, the Ottoman Turks were in no danger of becoming Western—but neither did they prosper. In the years to come, territories that belonged to the Turks—the states that we now call Balkan, such as Greece, Serbia, Bulgaria, and Montenegro—broke away, one by one. Today, the country of Turkey is the last remnant of the huge Eastern empire of the Ottoman Turks.

Ahmet III is known as the Tulip King

The Declining Indian Empire

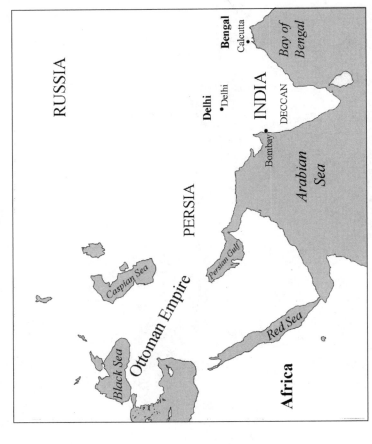

Chapter Nineteen
The English in India

The Indian Empire Falls Apart

The Ottoman Empire wasn't the only Eastern empire losing its lands. Southeast of the Ottomans, the empire of India was also shrinking away.

We've already read about the three great Moghul emperors of India: Jahangir (World Seizer), Shah Jahan (King of the World), and Aurangzeb (Conqueror of the World). These three emperors made India into a huge and wealthy nation. But the last of these emperors, Aurangzeb, made three fateful decisions. He decided to make Islam the law of India and to destroy the temples of Hindu worshippers. He decided to spend his whole reign fighting to conquer the Deccan, the southern lands of India—while ignoring the northern part of his kingdom and his capital city, Delhi. And he gave the English permission to build a trading post in the Indian province of Bengal, on India's eastern coast.

Aurangzeb didn't know that the English trading post in Bengal would help bring an end to the empire of India. But when he died—at the age of eighty-nine—he could already see that India was torn apart by Muslim hatred of Hindus and by the bloodshed caused by years of war. He was sick, weary, and filled with grief. "I have not done well," he wrote, just before his death, "by the country or its people."

Aurangzeb was right. India was soaked in misery. And as soon as Aurangzeb died, the misery got worse.

The moment the emperor drew his last breath, three of his sons all claimed the throne. Aurangzeb's oldest son had been waiting to inherit the crown for sixty-four years! He wasn't about to give way to his brothers. Instead, he killed them in battle, crowned himself Emperor Bahadur Shah I, and moved into the royal palace at Delhi.

For a little while, Bahadur tried to mend India's woes. Aurangzeb had destroyed Hindu worship places; Bahadur allowed Hindus to worship as they pleased. Aurangzeb had spent years fighting against the tribes who lived in the south of India; Bahadur tried to make peace with them. But Bahadur died only five years after becoming emperor.

His son claimed the throne of India—and spent the next eleven months paying more attention to his favorite dancing girl than to his duties as emperor! The new emperor made all of his dancing girl's friends—including poor musicians and an old vegetable seller—into state officials. He spent hours cutting down trees for fun, sinking boats on the canals nearby just to watch the passengers struggle to shore, and sitting on top of his fort, throwing rocks at people who passed by.

Finally, two Indian noblemen, brothers named Husain Ali and Hasan Ali, had had enough.

The Ali brothers hired assassins to break into the emperor's bedroom and strangle him. They picked another young man who had Moghul blood in him and decided to make *him* emperor instead! They rushed the new "emperor" into Delhi and arranged to have him crowned after an elaborate coronation parade. The Ali brothers planned to be the *real* rulers of India. Their new "emperor," Farrukhisiyar, was supposed to do only what the Ali brothers ordered him to do.

But Farrukhisiyar turned out to be cowardly and suspicious. He was afraid of everyone—even his own servants and the children who played on the palace grounds. He accused the Ali brothers of planning his death, and threatened to have them executed! So Husain and Hasan sent their assassins to the palace once more to get rid of this useless king. When he saw the assassins coming, Farrukhisiyar hid beneath his mother's skirt. The assassins found him anyway. They dragged him out and put him to death, but nobody cared. "He was feeble, false, cowardly, contemptible," one writer who lived at the time explained. "It is impossible to regret him."

The Ali brothers put another Moghul "king" on the throne, but he died of a seizure after ruling for only four months. They put a third king on the throne. This one died in even less time! Finally, Hasain and Hasan crowned a seventeen-year-old Moghul boy, Mohammad Shah, as emperor of India.

Mohammad was healthy and energetic. As a matter of fact, he was so energetic that he convinced a few other ambitious Indian noblemen to get rid of the Ali brothers. For the next thirty years, Mohammad Shah would rule all alone over India.

But Mohammed Shah didn't actually bother to *run* his empire. He spent most of his time going to animal fights and watching bears and wild boars gore and slash at each other. He even paid to have wild animals brought to Delhi to amuse him. In one fight, he ordered bears, goats, rams, and a wild boar dressed up in tiger skins so that they could then fight to the death against a wild elephant!

Meanwhile, all of the officials in India were busy dividing up the land that they had once governed for the emperor—and ruling it themselves. India, once an empire under a single Moghul emperor, had become a handful of little independent provinces ruled by petty kings, each pretending to pay allegiance to an emperor who never bothered to visit them or give them any orders.

Just thirty years after Aurangzeb's death, the Persians invaded this weak and divided India.

We read about the patchwork of the Persian empire not too many chapters ago. Remember, Persia lay between the Ottoman Empire and the empire of India. During the years that the Ali brothers were putting one emperor after another on the throne of India, Persia was governed by a shah named Nadir. Nadir Shah had been a highway robber from the part of Persia that we now call Afghanistan. But after he helped fight against the Ottoman Turks, Nadir grew popular enough to claim the throne of Persia for himself! He was anxious for the countries around him to recognize his power as shah. So he sent messengers to Delhi, hoping that the Indian emperor would hail him as Persia's rightful ruler.

But the Indian court was so disorganized that no one ever sent a messenger back. Nadir Shah was furious. "How dare the court of India ignore and insult me?" he thought to himself. "How dare they treat me like a bandit king? I'll teach them a lesson they won't soon forget!"

He marched his army down through the north of India toward Delhi, conquering Indian cities as he went. The frightened Indian army finally stumbled out of Delhi to meet him. But they were so terrified of Nadir Shah's giant war camels and guns that they couldn't even get into line to meet his attack. Twenty thousand Indian soldiers fell on the battlefield!

Nadir Shah captured Mohammad Shah and forced him to follow the Persian victory parade back into Delhi, bowing and saluting the whole way. Once in Delhi, Nadir Shah ordered the city burned and the people put to the sword! "The streets were strewn with corpses like dead leaves," one eyewitness wrote, later. "The city was reduced to ashes and looked like a burnt plain." Nadir Shah then took the key to India's treasury, plundered the Taj Mahal, and marched back to Persia, loaded down with silver, gold, jewels, and elephants. He even took the famous Peacock Throne of India back to Persia and broke it up for its jewels. "The accumulated wealth of three hundred forty-eight years changed masters in a moment," mourned one Indian who watched.

The Indian empire was gone. Mohammed Shah remained on the throne, but he reigned over a ghostly city filled with charred walls, deserted houses, and open graves.

The Shopkeepers' Invasion

When India fell apart around them, the English decided that it was time to take charge.

Just five years after the Jamestown colonists arrived in North America, English merchants had built the first English trading post in India. In a rickety wooden building in Surat, a rich, busy port city on the western coast of India, English merchants huddled over their accounts, counted bales of cotton, silk, and indigo leaves, and arranged to load these Indian goods onto the English ships anchored in the gulf nearby. The English made so much money trading for Indian goods that they opened more trading posts—in Bombay, a little to the south, and then in the province of Bengal, on the other side of India. To build these ports and to pay for ships and sailors, English merchants banded together into a group called The East India Company. Each member of the Company helped pay for the buildings and ships of the trading posts—and got part of the profit in return.

But then Aurangzeb died, and India began to collapse. Local officials called themselves kings and fought against each other. Hindu tribes from the south of India invaded the northern parts of the country. The Persians marched down to Delhi and destroyed it!

The English watched from their trading posts—and worried. How could the English merchants keep on carrying silk, muslin, and indigo from the center of India to the ports, when they were likely to be attacked along the way? And what if Hindu tribes, Muslim rebels, or Persian invaders attacked the tiny wooden English trading posts?

The English decided that it was time to become soldiers as well as merchants. They would fight to protect their trading parties and their trading posts. They started to build forts in Bombay and in Bengal.

That's when the trouble began.

Like other Indian officials, the governor of the province of Bengal now called himself the ruler, or *nawab,* of Bengal. Now, the nawab, whose name was Siraj, saw that the English were building themselves a fortress in Bengal, right in the little English settlement called Calcutta. They had named it Fort William—the name of an English king. They were placing guns along the walls. And they had never even asked his permission! Siraj grew more and more suspicious. Why did the English need a fortress in Calcutta? Were they planning on taking over his little kingdom of Bengal?

Siraj wasn't sure that his Bengal army could defeat the English, but he had an idea. There were plenty of French traders in India too. He would offer the French land in India if they would join with him to chase the English out of Calcutta.

The French were delighted to help get rid of the English. They joined with Siraj and marched to Calcutta. The fort at Calcutta was barely finished, and few English soldiers stood on its walls. Siraj's army captured it in less than four days!

When Siraj's men poured into the fort, Siraj ordered all of the English captives—145 men and one woman—thrown into Fort William's dungeon. The little dungeon, down in the cellar of the fort, was nicknamed the "Black Hole." It was only 24 feet long and 18 feet wide, perhaps twice the size of your bedroom. But Siraj's soldiers forced every last Englishman through the door and bolted it.

There was no food or water. The Indian night was hot and still. There was no room in the Black Hole to sit—or to breathe. One of the captives who spent the night in this dungeon, John Holwell, claimed that by morning, 120 of the prisoners had died from suffocation. When he was released and returned to England, he wrote an account of that night. "Figure to yourself the situation of a hundred and forty-six wretches...crammed together...in a close sultry night, in Bengal!" he exclaimed. "What words shall I adopt to tell you the whole that my soul suffered?" Holwell's account described men dying from thirst and heat while standing straight up, wedged together.

Later, some historians would suggest that Holwell was exaggerating, and that so many people could never have fit into such a small space. But it didn't really matter. English men and women heard the story of the Black Hole of Calcutta. They were furious! How could Englishmen ignore such savagery? The East India Company decided to do something unheard of: send an army into India to punish Siraj and the Indians of Bengal.

This was an astounding decision. After all, the East India Company wasn't a country or a king. It was a *company*. Imagine a big company like Microsoft or Wal-Mart hiring its own army and invading a city because its employees had been treated badly! That's what the East India Company did. Its members hired an army and a general to lead it.

This general, Sir Robert Clive, marched his army over to India, ready to meet Siraj's soldiers. But he didn't leave the victory to chance. Ahead of time, Sir Robert Clive sent a secret message to Siraj's chief general, Mir Jafar. The message said, "When you see the English army advancing, make some excuse to hold most of your army back from the battle. If you do this, I will make *you* the ruler of Bengal once Siraj is dead!"

Mir Jafar listened to the message, and made no promises. But when the Indian army met the East India

Company men in battle, Mir Jafar leaned on his spear, at the battle's edge. He issued no orders. His soldiers, waiting for his command, kept retreating. Soon they broke their formation and fled in panic! Siraj himself was killed.

Robert Clive brings English rule to Bengal.

Robert Clive announced that Mir Jafar would now be the nawab of Bengal. But Mir Jafar owed his throne—and his power—to the East India Company. And so he had to do what the English wanted him to do. When Mir Jafar resisted the company's orders, another, larger army arrived in Bengal and attacked him. When the second battle was over, the East India Company ruled the province of Bengal in the name of England.

The weak Indian emperor, afraid of these energetic invaders, gave the English authority to collect taxes in Bengal and spend them. Bengal followed English law and had its cases tried in an English court of law with an English judge presiding. Calcutta was declared its capital city. Now the English were more than merchants. They were rulers!

Over the next few years, as the Indian empire continued to fall apart, the English claimed more and more land. Eventually, they took the emperor himself under their "protection." The last Moghul emperor was a prisoner of the English. India had fallen to the shopkeepers.

The Expanse of China

Chapter Twenty
The Imperial East

Emperor Chi'en-lung's Library

The streets of Peking, far, far to the northeast of India, are still and dark. The inn-fires are banked for the night; travelers sleep motionless in their rooms. The Forbidden Palace, the walled and secret city-within-a-city where the emperor and his royal family live, is blanketed with quiet. On the walls, the watchmen doze, standing with their backs against the red walls.

But deep inside the Forbidden Palace, the emperor's windows glow with lamplight. Chi'en-lung, the fourth Manchu emperor of China, is bent over his desk, a brush in hand and a scroll in front of him. Carefully, he inks the brush and strokes down, sideways, and over. Another Chinese character has been added to his poem!

Chi'en-lung leans back and gazes at the painting that hangs on the wall across from him. A branch of blossoming plum sweeps across the paper, each flower and twig outlined with exquisite care. The Chinese artist who painted this plum branch, Zou Fulei, has been dead for three hundred years. But Ch'ien-lung can still read the poem Zou Fulei brushed onto the painting's left side:

In this tumbleweed shack, where can I seek spring's return?
I charge the chilly toad to keep the old plum company.
As laments of mist subside, my empty room grows cold,
Traces of ink preserve the shadows that come to my window.

Zou Fulei's poem tells how he painted the branch: as he sat in his bare room, the moon—a mysterious bright place where a magical toad was thought to live—cast the shadow of a plum branch against the paper windows. Zou Fulei copied the pattern onto his painting!

The emperor is composing four more lines to round out the old artist's poem. He stares back at his paper, at the line he has just finished.

In a single breath, the springtime goes but must return
He bends back over the paper and adds,
But who has conveyed these tidings to the chilly plum?
He smiles, pleased with his poem. *When I finish this poem,* he thinks to himself, *I'll copy my own lines onto the right-hand side of Zou Fulei's painting. His lines and mine will live forever!*

Chi'en-lung, emperor and poet, is the grandson of the great Manchu emperor K'ang-hsi. He has already governed his grandfather's empire for years. In the decaying Ottoman empire, the Tulip King has already fallen; Mohammad Shah still sits on his shabby throne, watching the power of the English in India grow.

But China is stronger and richer than ever. Chinese soldiers watch for rebellion, ready to crush resistance. Painters and poets flourish under the benevolent guidance of the court. Chinese porcelain, painted in rich glazes of copper red, green, and rose, is prized all over the world.

Chi'en-lung rises and walks to the window. He gazes out over the dark gardens and halls of the Forbidden City, past the walls that protect the palace, out toward the dark rooftops and streets of Peking. This city, on the northeast edge of the Chinese empire, is the largest city in the world. Over a million people live in Peking! Chi'en-lung's empire stretches from the border of Russia down to the Himalayan mountains that separate China from India.

Chi'en-lung wants the whole world to know the greatness of China. And although the countries all around can see China's huge size and marvel at the millions of people who live within its borders, the emperor knows that China's greatest accomplishment—its books of poems and philosophy, its novels and histories—are still scattered throughout this vast country, hidden away in libraries.

In 1772, after he had been on the throne for over thirty years, Chi'en-lung decided to gather all of China's greatest literature together in one enormous collection. He appointed two scholars to head up this task. They hired dozens more. For years, these scholars traveled throughout China, examining the libraries of every town and the private collections of every rich man. Finally, they assembled a list of all the great Chinese books written.

The scholars and Chi'en-lung studied these lists together. After weeks of discussion, they settled on a final selection of the most important books in four categories: classics, history, philosophy, and literature. Now, an even greater task loomed: These works had to be copied out into a single huge set!

Copying out Chinese books was more complicated that copying English books. The English alphabet has twenty-six letters, and with those letters, you can form every word in English. But Chinese has symbols for different sounds and words. A Chinese dictionary published in the days of Chi'en-lung listed over forty thousand of these symbols! A Chinese artist had to master eleven distinctive brush strokes in order to form these characters properly. Beautiful calligraphy was considered so difficult that no foreigner could ever master it.

Artists began to copy out the collected works. The set of books turned out to have 36,275 volumes. And Chi'en-lung wanted seven copies of the set! That meant calligraphers would have to write out a quarter of a million volumes total.

Ten years after the search for books began, the first copy of the series was finally completed. It was given the Chinese name *Ssu-ku ch'üan-shu,* which means "The Complete Library in the Four Branches of Literature." It took five more years to finish all seven copies of the Complete Library. Four copies were placed in the four imperial palaces; the last three were put in libraries where scholars could study them.

But even while scholars were saving all of these books, preserving them for centuries to come, Chi'en-lung ordered other books destroyed. He knew that many Chinese still resented the rule of the Manchu, who had come down from the north so many years ago and claimed the Chinese throne.

So the scholars who made lists of China's great books were also given the job of looking for any books which made unflattering remarks about the Manchu dynasty. They made lists of these books and brought them to the emperor. Chi'en-lung wanted these books destroyed! For the next fourteen years, he sent command after command to governors in every province of China, ordering them to check and recheck every library for these banned books and to burn every copy found. The emperor of China loved books—but he loved his power even more.

The Land of the Dragon

Chi'en-lung ruled China for sixty years. All this time, strong Western countries were grabbing more and more land for themselves. Spain ruled over much of South America and some of North America too. France owned land in North America. England had colonies in North America—and now it was spreading into India as well!

Meanwhile, China was doing plenty of grabbing of its own! The center of the Chinese empire lay around the Yellow and the Yangtze rivers, where the ancient Chinese civilization had first grown. This "China of the Eighteen Provinces" was home to millions of Han Chinese and Manchu people.

But this "center" was only part of China.

Imagine that you're standing on the roof of the Forbidden Palace, looking out over the endless roofs of Peking. You hear a swish behind you. You turn—and see that an imperial dragon has landed behind you. This imperial dragon, the symbol of the emperor's power, has five toes on each foot. His body is long and snakelike; his tail is the tail of a fish. He dips his head, crowned with the sharp antlers of a deer. His eyes glow red!

You climb aboard the scaly body. He bends his snaky neck around to see whether you're comfortable, and sees that you're too small to straddle him comfortably. So, obligingly, he

194

shrinks a little. Imperial dragons can change size whenever they like. They can also turn themselves into waterspouts and whirl across the sea; you hope this dragon won't turn himself to water while you're aboard!

The dragon flaps its wings and rises. You're sailing over those endless rooftops, toward the north, with the rising sun behind you. The red light falls first on the walls of Peking and then on hills and mountains, carpeted with rough scrubby trees and long wiry grass. Ridges and peaks pass beneath you. You're flying over the Uplands of China, where peasants farm rice on the warm southern sides of the mountains, and wheat in the drier north.

But then the hills and fields drop away into a flat brown plain. The dragon swoops down. You see sand beneath you, yellow and white, shifting in the howling winds. A sand rat scuttles away into its hole. A vulture, hunched on a single low tree, flaps resentfully away as the dragon approaches. You're flying over the Gobi Desert, a huge dry plain—and the edge of Mongolia, homeland of the descendents of Genghis Khan and his Mongol horde.

Beneath you, a group of nomads comes out of their felt *yurts* and looks up, mouths open with amazement. They recognize the dragon, because now Mongolia belongs to China! Chi'en-lung's grandfather K'ang-hsi invaded Mongolia and forced its government to pay allegiance to him. Now, Mongolia sends tribute every year to the Chinese emperor. The dragon flies further north, leaving the desert behind. Ahead of you lies Mongolia's capital city, Ulan Bator. The dragon banks along its walls and turns southwest. As you leave Ulan Bator behind, you peer down at its streets; Chinese soldiers patrol the alleys, watching for any sign of rebellion!

Now you soar further south, toward the lands where Turkish tribes fought to spread the Turkish empire. But the glory days of the Ottoman Turks are gone. China now rules over part of this Turkish land; it is called Chinese Turkestan. Below you, the dome of a mosque glitters white in the sun. These Turks are still Muslim—but they pay allegiance to the Buddhist emperor of China. In the forests beyond the mosque, you see a white puff of dust. The dragon swoops down again, so that you can see the war band of Chinese soldiers, headed deep into Turkestan. The Turks are restless; Chi'en-lung fights continually to keep them under his control!

You've traveled halfway along China's borders; now the sun stands overhead, and the dragon is beginning to turn back toward the east. Below you lies the highest mountain in the world, Mount Everest! It casts its shadow over the land to its north. This ancient country, Tibet, is a mysterious and little-known place; old people whisper of a hidden kingdom in its snowy mountains, called Shangri-La. Those who live in Shangri-La are never hungry; no one grows old in Shangri-La, and no one dies!

The Tibetans are a peaceful people, governed not by a king but by a Buddhist monk called the Dalai Lama who rules alongside a Mongol prince. China hasn't completely conquered this southern land, but the emperor is scheming to add it to his collection of countries. Just a few years ago, the Mongol prince who was supposed to help the Dalai Lama rule fought with other Mongols who wanted to control Tibet. The emperor sent Chinese soldiers into Tibet to protect the Dalai Lama. Those Chinese soldiers are still in Tibet, even though the revolt is over. Their leaders, two Chinese officials called "High Commissioners," are "helping" the Dalai Lama rule. Slowly, the High Commissioners are gaining more and more power!

You leave Tibet behind and fly further to the east and the south. Here, a huge piece of land juts down from the Chinese mainland into the ocean. You are so high that you can see the water on both sides: the Bay of Bengal on the western side of this land and the South China Sea on the east! The land below you sparkles silver and red. The dragon swoops down once more so that you can see the country of Burma, on the Bay of Bengal's edge. Rivers wind between mountain peaks, slowly widening out into flat glittering flood plains where men and women stoop over the rice fields. The sun, now beginning to sink behind you in the west, shines brightly on houses made of red glazed brick and of timber with bright tin roofs. In the streets of the villages, men in blue robes and women with gold and jade in their hair walk toward the Buddhist temple. But you see Chinese soldiers marching toward the north of Burma, ready to fight. The emperor is worried about Burma. It's growing a little too powerful! In the next three years, those soldiers will invade Burma four times; they'll never own the country, but the people of the north will be forced to pay tribute.

You fly straight across toward the South China Sea, and a long thin country that lies along its edge: the country of Vietnam. Chinese soldiers trudge north through wet rice fields, headed home. For years, China has been trying to take over Vietnam. For the moment, the invasion has failed. The royal family of Vietnam has driven the Chinese invaders out once more! The imperial dragon snorts in frustration. He veers suddenly out over the water, almost dumping you into the surf below. You cling to his neck, hoping that he won't dissolve into a waterspout! But he's just headed out toward an island that lies off China's coast: the island of Taiwan. Here, the Chinese effort to conquer its neighbor has succeeded! Taiwan has become part of China's southern province, Fukien. You see boats sailing from the mainland toward the Taiwanese coast. Chinese settlers are streaming into Taiwan; the island's population has swelled by half a million people. The dragon expands a little with pride. He veers inland to show you one more successful Chinese conquest: the country of Korea, now paying tribute to the emperor.

When the dragon sets you gently down back on the rooftop of the Forbidden Palace, you have traveled around the edges of the largest empire in the world. At this time, perhaps nine hundred million people live in the world; over three hundred million of those people belong to the Chinese empire. France and Spain and England are powerful countries—but one-third of all the people in the entire world live under the flag of the imperial Chinese dragon!

North America During the Time of the Three Wars

Chapter Twenty-One
Fighting Over North America

Three Pointless Wars

China's empire was the largest in the world—but the countries that had to pay tribute to China were constantly hoping to be free. Chinese soldiers were always fighting to keep Mongolia, Turkestan, Taiwan, and other Chinese "protectorates" loyal!

The empires of France, England, and Spain were no more peaceful. But instead of fighting to keep their colonies, these three empires—so close together in Europe—fought with each other. These three countries fought three wars. Each one of these wars started over in Europe and then spread to the colonies in North America. Each war had two names—one used by Europeans and another used by colonists.

And none of these three wars accomplished anything!

The first war started when Louis XIV, the Sun King of France, tried to expand France's power in Europe. The other countries of Europe—the Netherlands, the German state of Austria, and England—banded together in an alliance to stop him. They called their war The War of the Grand Alliance. While English soldiers fought against the French in Europe, the English government also paid the Iroquois of North America to attack French settlements in Canada! And in response, the French settlers (who knew perfectly well that the English were behind these Iroquois attacks) attacked English settlements. For eight years, English settlers in New York and New England fought against French settlers in New England and Canada. The settlers called *their* war—the North American part of the War of the Grand Alliance—King William's War, after King William of England.

After eight years of fighting, neither side had won! But over in Europe, France and England finally made peace with each other. The settlers were ordered to stop fighting. So they did. Eight years of fighting, from 1689 to 1697, had given the French and English colonies nothing except hatred for each other.

Four years later, Louis XIV managed to make his grandson king of Spain, which gave him more power than ever. England and the Netherlands declared war on France again— and this time on Spain as well. This War of Spanish Succession went on for years and years in Europe. Once more, the French and English colonists in North America fought with each other, just as their parent countries in Europe were doing. They called *their* war Queen Anne's War after the new Queen of England; William and Mary had died, and Mary's little sister Anne had inherited the throne.

During Queen Anne's war, the English managed to capture several French settlements. The French settlement of Acadia, east of Quebec, now belonged to the English. And English troops marched down into Florida and burned the Spanish colony of Pensacola. England seemed to be gaining the upper hand in North America.

But once again the war ended without any real victory. Over in Europe, the English and the French made peace after thirteen years of fighting. Once more, the French, English, and Spanish colonists stopped fighting.

For a little while, France and England were at peace. Both countries had new rulers. Two years after the end of the War of Spanish Succession, Louis XIV died. His five-year-old great-grandson inherited his throne. England's Queen Anne died too, without an heir. So Parliament voted to pass the crown to the great-grandson of James I, the "Bible King." This great-grandson was named George Louis, and he was a good Protestant prince.

Unfortunately, he wasn't English!

George's mother, James's granddaughter, had been born in Germany and had grown up to marry a German prince; George Louis grew up in Hanover, speaking only German and thinking of himself as German. But Parliament was so anxious to avoid having a Catholic king that they were willing to crown a German as their king! So George Louis arrived in England and was crowned George I of England. He didn't even speak English! And none of his ministers spoke German. So they had to do all of England's business—in French!

England and France were at peace while George I and Louis XV reigned. So were the English and French colonies in North America. But after George I died of a stroke and his son George II inherited the throne, war broke out for a third time. This time, the war was between England and Spain, not England and France. And it started over an ear.

Spanish and English sea captains had never been good friends. English ships often prowled the waters between South America and Spain, hoping to catch Spanish galleys carrying gold from the South American mines—and rob them. Spanish sea captains suspected all English of being pirates; Spanish ships guarded the waters near South American ports, searching—and sometimes robbing—English merchants who were following the law!

One grey fall day, sea captain Robert Jenkins stalked into a meeting of Parliament, a jar in his hand. Members of the House of Commons, meeting together to discuss the Spanish harassment of English ships, watched him walk to the wooden table at the center of the room. Jenkins pulled his long, grizzled hair back behind his ear. One ear was pierced with a gold hoop. The other ear was gone. Jenkins slapped the jar down on the table. His ear floated in it—pickled in a pint of whisky.

"You see this?" Jenkins shouted. "The Spanish boarded me off the coast. Came aboard, tied us up, accused us of being pirates. Me, a law-abiding English merchant! And when they couldn't find no stolen goods, their captain sliced off my ear! And then he yelled, 'Were the King of England here...I would do the same for him!' Then they robbed our ship, climbed back aboard their own, and set us adrift without oars or sails!"

Parliament was furious at this treatment of a law-abiding English merchant! The Spanish pointed out that Robert Jenkins was a thief and a liar and that none of this had ever happened—but no one listened. In 1739, England declared war on Spain.

This war, called The War of Jenkins' Ear, soon grew much bigger. Charles VI, the Holy Roman Emperor, had just died, and his heirs were fighting about who would inherit his power. The English supported the Austrian heir; France didn't want Austria to have any more power. So France joined Spain in its war against England. Then Austria joined England, and Prussia joined France. The War of Jenkins' Ear had turned into The War of Austrian Succession.

Once more, Europe was at war! And once more, the war trickled over into the colonies. The English colonists in Georgia marched down and attacked the Spanish colonies in Florida. Up north, the French and English colonists started fighting with each other. Once more, the colonists gave *their* war the name of the English king: King George's War. The fighting went on for four years!

Finally, England, France, and Spain all signed a peace treaty and told the colonists to stop fighting—again. The third pointless war had ended. Hundreds of colonists and Native Americans had died in King William's War, Queen Anne's War, and King George's War.

But nothing had changed.

The Seven-Year War

After three wars, France, England, and Spain were no closer to settling their fight over North America! France had colonies far north, in Canada, and far south, where the state of Louisiana now lies. England had colonies all along the eastern coast. Spain had colonies in Florida and in Santa Fe, New Mexico. But huge areas of North America still lay open. Which country could drive the others out and win the continent?

One more war would settle the question once and for all. This time, the war started in North America—and spread all over the world.

In 1753, five years after the end of King George's War, the governor of the English colony of Virginia heard alarming news from English scouts. The French were building roads into the Ohio Valley (today, western Pennsylvania). The governor, Robert Dinwiddie, knew that England wanted the rich, timbered Ohio River Valley too! If the French claimed the valley, the English might never get their hands on it.

So Governor Dinwiddie sent a message to King George II. "What should we do?" he asked. King George II sent an answer back: "Send a messenger and tell the French to leave. If they won't leave, go chase them out—and build an English fort to protect the land!"

Governor Dinwiddie sighed. He had very few fighting men, certainly not enough to take on all of France. And who would be willing to travel through hundreds of miles of wilderness, risking capture, carrying a letter telling the French to retreat?

A young Virginian volunteered. George Washington, only twenty-one years old, had been born in Virginia to an English tobacco farmer. He had spent the last few years working as a surveyor, measuring farms and drawing up maps for their owners. But George Washington wanted to be a soldier, not a surveyor. He begged Governor Dinwiddie for permission to carry the message. On Halloween, the governor agreed. Washington found a wilderness guide and a translator to accompany him and set off that same day—not even waiting for morning!

It took three weeks for the little party to ride through the mountains, up through the Ohio River Valley and to the headquarters of the French. When he was just days away, Washington found himself at the richest place in the whole valley: the Ohio Fork, where three rivers joined together. Washington thought to himself, "A fort built here could command the whole valley!"

He traveled on, finally reaching the French headquarters north of the valley. When he gave the French commander the governor's message, the commander simply laughed and told the young man to go back to Virginia.

Washington set off. By now, it was the middle of December, snowing and growing colder by the minute. His little party was running out of food. Their horses were starving and so weak that Washington finally left them behind. As he trudged through the snow with his wilderness guide, a Native American ally of the French leapt out and shot at him! Washington was afraid that the French had regretted letting him go—and had sent assassins after him. He hurried on to the shores of the Allegheny River. He had to get across right away. But the river was filled with rolling cakes of ice!

Washington and his guide built a raft and launched it out into the river. Ice slammed against it, overturning it! Washington fell, clutching for the raft's edge. He barely caught it and hauled himself back up, dripping. The guide still clung to the raft. The two men came aground on a little island at the middle of the river—and there they spent the night, with no fire or food. The temperature dropped more and more. Ice rattled down on them. Washington's clothes froze solid.

But in the morning, the river was a sheet of thick ice. The two men walked across it to the opposite shore. Finally, they reached a settlement where English traders lived, and they managed to get fresh horses for the ride home.

When Washington arrived back at Governor Dinwiddie's palace in Williamsburg, he told the governor about the French refusal. Dinwiddie sent a message to England, asking for more soldiers. Meanwhile, forty men were sent to build a fort at the place where three rivers met. Dinwiddie promoted Washington to a higher rank and sent him to protect the new little fort along with a small band of colonial soldiers. But the French were already too strong. They took away the little fort and defeated Washington's tiny army. Washington surrendered—and was allowed to retreat.

The English weren't about to give up! Two thousand English "regular" soldiers arrived from London, under the command of an English general, Edward Braddock. Edward Braddock was sure that his "regular and disciplined troops" would quickly beat off the French and their Native American allies. He invited George Washington to come along with him as his aide to see the English victory.

But Braddock had no idea how to fight in the rough woods and mountains of North America. He marched his men toward the Ohio River Valley in a long line, beating drums and waving banners, blasting rocks out of the way.

The French were ready. They ambushed Braddock's soldiers from behind trees, just ten miles away from the Ohio Fork. The soldiers' red uniform coats made them easy targets. And when the English soldiers tried to hide and shoot from behind trees, Braddock ordered them back into line! A thousand English soldiers fell, and the rest ran away in terror. Washington himself had two horses shot out from underneath him. When he undressed that night, he found four bullet-holes through his clothing.

The French and Indian War had begun.

Soon other countries in Europe chose sides and joined in. The war spread across Europe, even into India, and across the oceans of the world. The French and Indian War was given a new European name: the Seven Years' War.

At first, France seemed to be gaining the upper hand. But the Prime Minister of England, William Pitt, was determined that England would triumph. He made sure that the English troops in North America had plenty of money, ships and ammunition—and that the colonial soldiers and the "regulars" from England fought together, rather than bickering with each other. And the English "redcoats" began to figure out how to fight in the woods and fields of North America. They took off their red coats, turned them inside out, and covered the insides with clay. They rubbed soot and dirt on their shiny, ship-shape gun barrels so that they wouldn't glint in the sun. Then they started fighting in small groups, from behind trees. The Indian allies of the French were disgusted. "Those redcoats," they told the French, "no longer stand still and let us kill them!"

The French were having troubles at home, too. Louis XV had grown up into a weak and wasteful man. He spent most of his time chasing women and wallowing in luxury—and becoming more and more unpopular. In 1757, three years after the war began, an assassin sneaked into the royal palace of Versailles and tried to kill him with a pocketknife!

Soon the English were driving the French out of North America. George Washington led a successful attack on the Ohio River fort and won it back for England. It was renamed Fort Pitt, after the Prime Minister. Today, the city of Pittsburgh stands where the fort was first built.

Then the English conquered Quebec, the capital of New France. The next year, Montreal fell to England as well. New France belonged to England! The French agreed to a surrender. In 1763, the Treaty of Paris ended the Seven Years' War. Louis XV agreed to give up all of France's lands in North America, except for the territory called Louisiana. Many settlers in New France moved back to France—or down to New Orleans, in the Louisiana colony. Some stayed, still speaking French, but now under British rule.

Louis XV had lost the huge empire that Louis XIV had saved. His people hated him for it. When he died of smallpox, not long after, his courtiers poured quicklime on his body and buried him at night, with no ceremony. He had become the most unpopular person in France!

England, France, and the American Colonies

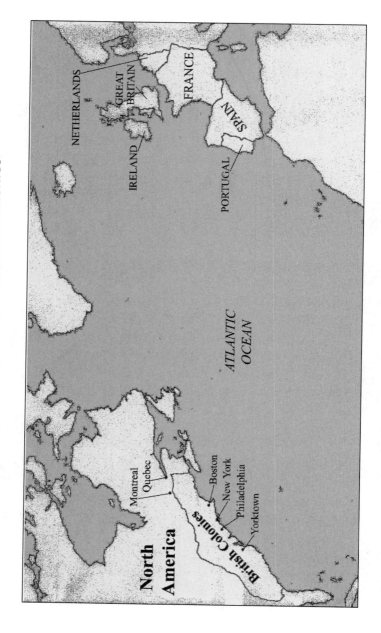

Chapter Twenty-Two
Revolution!

Discontent in the British Colonies

The English empire was growing. England owned the eastern coast of North America, all the way up to Montreal. France had abandoned India to the English as well. And during the reign of Queen Anne, Scotland and Wales had been joined together with England in the Act of Union. From now on, we can speak of the English as "the British"—Englishmen, Scotsmen, Welshmen and Americans, all sailing and marching together under the red, white and blue flag of Great Britain.

But the Americans would only be British for thirteen more years.

During the Seven Years' War, Britain had spent hundreds of thousands of pounds defending the American colonies. The British thought that it was high time for the colonies to put some of that money back into England's treasury. And the simplest way to do that was to pass laws requiring the Americans to pay extra taxes.

So Parliament and the king's ministers wrote a series of new tax laws, called Acts. The first tax law, the Sugar Act, was passed just one year after the Treaty of Paris. Now, Americans had to pay extra money for all sugar and molasses that came into American ports—unless the sugar came from Britain. The Americans hated the Sugar Act. And they hated the Stamp Act, which was passed the following year, even more. The Stamp Act told them to pay extra money to Britain every time they bought newspapers, pamphlets, dice, or playing cards. And every time a legal document like a will or diploma was written, the colonist who owned it had to pay a fee to get it "stamped" and made official.

All of this money went to Britain.

More Acts were passed. Americans were ordered to provide rooms and food for British troops sent to North America—and to pay for those rooms and food themselves. New taxes on glass, paper, paint, and tea were passed.

More money flowed into Great Britain's pockets.

The Americans began to argue about these tax laws in their *General Assemblies*—meetings of all the colony leaders. Many of the leaders thought that Parliament should have asked the assemblies to approve the new taxes before making them law. In Virginia's assembly, a hot-tempered leader named Patrick Henry stood up and shouted, "The inhabitants of this colony are not bound to yield obedience to any law or ordinance whatever designed to impose any taxation whatsoever upon them, other than laws or ordinances of the General Assembly!"

Patrick Henry argued that according to British law, no British citizen could be forced to pay a tax unless his *representative* (a man elected to argue for his rights) in Parliament agreed. But since there were no Americans in Parliament, the colonies didn't *have* representatives. Any tax passed by Parliament was illegal, because it forced the British citizens of America to pay a tax without representatives in Parliament agreeing. "No taxation without representation!" became the cry of Americans all up and down the coast of North America.

The new king of Great Britain, George III, agreed to *repeal*, or take away, some of the taxes. George III was the grandson of George II, who had died suddenly of a stroke not long before the end of the Seven Year's War. George III came to the British throne ready to enjoy peacetime. He hadn't counted on all of this trouble with the colonies!

George III's repeal of a few taxes didn't do any good—because Parliament insisted that the tax on tea remain. Parliament wanted the Americans to know that the colonies were part of Great Britain and that the government of Great Britain could pass whatever laws it pleased, without asking the colonies for permission. The Americans were furious. The British soldiers stationed in the large port cities grew more and more unpopular.

One cold March morning in 1770, a group of Americans in Boston were throwing snowballs at British soldiers when one of the soldiers panicked. He shouted out an order to fire. The soldiers lifted their weapons and shot into the crowd of unarmed Americans. Five people were killed, and dozens more wounded. For the first time, British soldiers had fired at their own colonists.

Immediately, colony leaders gave this event a huge, horrible name: the Boston Massacre. Only five people had died, which made this the smallest massacre ever. But soon, all over the colonies, Americans were talking about the Boston Massacre.

Resentment of Parliament grew and grew. American merchants decided to boycott all English tea. They refused to unload cargos of tea. Tea parties became coffee parties. "Farewell the Tea-board," one poem written during this time begins:

> To my cream pot and tongs I now bid adieu....
> No more shall my teapot so generous be
> In filling the cups with this pernicious tea,
> For I'll fill it with water and drink out the same,
> Before I'll lose LIBERTY, that dearest name.

But in Boston, the governor insisted that ships bearing tea be allowed to unload and sell their goods.

The Americans rebelled. On the evening of December 16th, 1773, sixty men wrapped themselves up in Indian blankets and feather headdresses, marched to the wharf where three British tea ships lay at anchor, and dumped 342 chests of tea into Boston Harbor.

Parliament was furious at this "Boston Tea Party." It passed a series of laws which the colonies called the "Intolerable Acts." Until Boston paid for the tea, the port would stay closed. British soldiers commanded by the British general Thomas Gage would run Boston. No town meetings could be held without permission.

At this, leaders from every colony gathered together in Philadelphia in a big meeting called the First Continental

Congress. This Congress gathered in Philadelphia in 1774. Patrick Henry was there. So was George Washington!

The Continental Congress wrote out a petition and sent it to George III and Parliament. This petition asked the British government to remove the British soldiers, reopen the port, and repeal the taxes. The Continental Congress also warned that the colonies would no longer obey laws passed without their

The Boston Tea Party

permission. For the first time, the American colonies were acting all together.

No one knew exactly what would happen when the petition reached England. But many Americans were sure that war would follow. They began to collect weapons and bullets and to store them away. Patrick Henry went back home from the First Continental Congress and told the Virginia Assembly, "We have done everything that could be done to avert the storm which is now coming on. We have petitioned; we have remonstrated; we have supplicated....If we wish to be free...we must fight! I repeat it, sir, we must fight!...Gentlemen may cry,

212

Peace, Peace—but there is no peace....Is life so dear, or peace so sweet, as to be purchased at the price of chains and slavery? Forbid it, Almighty God! I know not what course others may take; but as for me, give me liberty or give me death!"

The American Revolution

The petition to Parliament didn't bring peace. Instead, the British prepared to fight the Americans to keep their empire together.

British leaders knew that Americans were also preparing for war. They could see young American men practicing with their weapons in fields outside the Massachusetts settlements of Lexington and Boston and the town of Concord. These young men called themselves Minutemen, because they were ready to fight at a minute's notice. The British knew that the Minutemen were storing up muskets and bullets, ready to fight—and that the biggest collection of weapons was in Concord.

On April 18th, 1775, a troop of British soldiers marched out of Boston under cover of dark. They planned to march most of the night and to arrive at Concord suddenly, surprising the Americans and taking the weapons away.

But the Americans found out about this plan. Two Boston men, Paul Revere and William Dawes, were given the job of riding to Concord ahead of the British troops and warning the Americans there. They galloped all night, calling out the news as they rode: "The British are coming! The British are coming!"

All along their path, Americans grabbed for their weapons. Minutemen gathered together at Lexington, halfway to Concord, waiting for the British troops to march into view.

The soldiers arrived at Lexington early on the morning of April 19th. It was a cool, foggy morning. The officer in charge saw the Minutemen, gathered in the mist, blocking his way. He pointed his sword at them.

"Lay down your arms, you rebels, or you are all dead men!" he shouted.

The Minutemen stared back at him, their muskets ready.

"Fire!" the officer shouted.

Muskets began to sound. Eight Minutemen fell. The rest retreated. But when the British arrived at Concord they found more Minutemen gathered. Both sides fired their weapons. More Minutemen fell to the ground. So did British soldiers. The British tried to find the weapons but could see nothing. They started back toward Boston. All the way, the Minutemen followed them, shooting from the cover of trees nearby. Before the journey was over, over two hundred British soldiers were dead—and the War of American Independence had begun.

The news spread all through the colonies. Men got ready to fight. The Second Continental Congress met together and made George Washington the commander of the whole colonial army.

Meanwhile, on June 17th, 1775 , the first huge battle of the war took place. The British attacked the American soldiers camped on Bunker Hill, a high hill above Boston. After three charges, the Americans were defeated, and the British were in control of the hill. But the British had lost three times as many men as the Americans.

Then Washington arrived in Boston and took on the job of turning this ragged collection of Minutemen and volunteers into an army ready to face the British! He didn't have enough weapons or enough food. Many of the soldiers didn't even have shoes. Most of them could leave the army whenever they wanted—and many did. But Washington built a military camp and drilled his army into shape.

The Americans fought on. More and more Americans began to argue that the war should lead, not to representation in Parliament—but to actual independence. The American writer Thomas Paine published a pamphlet called *Common Sense*, pleading for the Americans to break completely from England

and to publish their reasons for doing so for the world to see. "While we profess ourselves the subjects of Britain," Paine argued, "we must...be considered as Rebels. Were a manifest to be published...setting forth the miseries we have endured, and the peaceful methods which we have ineffectually used for redress...such a memorial would produce more good effects."

Thousands and thousands of Americans read *Common Sense* and agreed. In May of 1776, the colony of Rhode Island became the first to declare itself independent of Great Britain. A new Continental Congress met in Philadelphia to write out the reasons why the colonies, now called *states*, needed to form their own new country. A Virginian named Thomas Jefferson was given the job of writing the first draft of this *manifest*.

On July 4th, 1776, the Continental Congress approved Thomas Jefferson's manifest, called the Declaration of Independence. "When in the course of human events," it began, "it becomes necessary for one people to dissolve the political bands which have connected them with another, and to assume among the powers of the earth, the separate and equal station to which the laws of nature and of nature's God entitle them, a decent respect to the opinions of mankind requires that they should declare the causes which impel them to the separation!" The Declaration went on to list all of the wrongs done to the colonies by Great Britain. "These united colonies are, and of right ought to be, free and independent states," it concluded. "They are absolved from all allegiance to the British Crown, and...all political connection between them and the state of Great Britain is and ought to be totally dissolved."

In response, the British landed thirty thousand men in New York and attacked Washington's army. The Americans were defeated and forced to retreat for miles and miles, with the British following in triumph. Washington only had three thousand men left. Volunteers had left; others had deserted!

Washington knew that he could never face the British army and win. So he decided on a surprise attack. On Christmas night, 1776, Washington's army was camped on one side of the Delaware River. German troops hired by King George III were celebrating on the other side, drinking beer and dancing.

In the middle of the night, Washington marched his men to the river and shipped them over, a boatload at a time. "It is fearfully cold and raw, and a snowstorm setting in," one of his aides wrote. "Some of [the soldiers] have tied old rags around their feet; others are barefoot....The storm is changing to sleet and cuts like a knife." The boats were in danger of overturning or losing their way. The men were in danger of freezing to death.

Washington persisted. The Americans reached the other side, surprised the German troops, and defeated them, taking over a thousand prisoners. "It is a glorious victory!" the aide exclaimed. "It will rejoice the hearts of our friends everywhere and give new life to our hitherto waning fortunes!"

The war wasn't over yet. Everyone watching was sure that the American resistance would soon collapse. After all, the British empire had just won the Seven Years' War! The colonies would not be able to resist much longer.

But then, in 1778, the tide turned: France decided to join the battle and fight with the Americans against her old enemy England. And then the Netherlands and Spain joined in the revolt as well. The English began to tire of the war. Once more the colonies were draining Great Britain's treasury!

In 1781, Washington's army managed to corner the largest British force at Yorktown, on the coast of Virginia. A French fleet sailed up to the shore, cutting off the British retreat. Finally, the British commander, Lord Cornwallis, decided that he had no choice but to lay down his arms. According to tradition, the military band played an old tune called "The World Turned Upside Down" as the British surrendered:

> If buttercups buzz'd after the bee,
> If boats were on land, churches on sea,
> If ponies rode men and if grass ate the cows,
> And cats should be chased into holes by the mouse,
> If the mamas sold their babies
> To the gypsies for half a crown;
> If summer were spring and the other way round,
> Then all the world would be upside down.

None of these things seemed more ridiculous than the idea that the American colonies could win a war against Great Britain!

216

In 1783, Great Britain signed an agreement giving the colonies their independence. The Americans were no longer colonists. Now they were citizens of a new country!

The United States of America in 1788

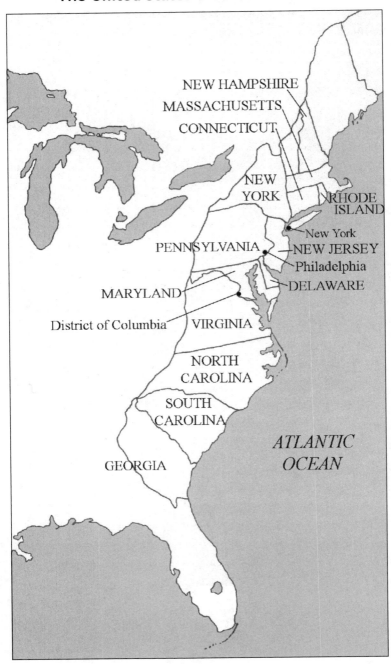

Chapter Twenty-Three
The New Country

The American Constitution

Have you ever driven to a different state? Did you see soldiers guarding the state border as you crossed it? When you stopped at the next gas station, did the clerk refuse to take your money because it was strange and foreign?

Probably not. Today, an American can travel from state to state as easily as walking from the kitchen to the living room. But right after the American revolution, things were different.

After the peace treaty with England was signed, the thirteen American colonies became independent states. Each of the thirteen American states began to pass its own laws and write out its own *constitution* (a set of rules explaining how a country will work).

Trouble started right away. Each state was busy planning how to make treaties with foreign countries—thirteen different treaties. Each state wanted its own navy—thirteen different navies with thirteen different admirals. Virginia and Maryland were quarrelling about who had the right to claim the Potomac River, which ran between them. Not all of the states were even using the same kind of money. And although the colonies had borrowed money from France to help pay for the War of Independence, none of the states wanted to pay that money back. Each state thought that *another* state should pay the debt!

American leaders like Alexander Hamilton from New York, James Madison from Virginia, Benjamin Franklin from Pennsylvania, and George Washington himself saw that the new states would soon be in trouble. If they continued to act like thirteen different countries, the new nation wouldn't be able to negotiate foreign treaties, build a strong navy, or send merchant ships abroad. "We are fast verging," George Washington warned, "to anarchy and confusion."

It was time for all of the states to join together and make a *federal* government—a government that had authority to act for all thirteen states.

Many Americans hated the idea of a federal government. After all, they had just fought a war to be free of the federal government of Great Britain. How could they be sure that a federal government wouldn't take away the power of each state to do as it thought best?

Finally, twelve of the states offered to send their leaders to Philadelphia for a Constitutional Convention that would discuss the need for a federal government. George Washington didn't want to go. He was sure that the leaders, or *delegates,* would just argue and argue. But the other Virginia delegates begged Washington to come. Everyone respected George Washington. If anyone could get the leaders of all the states to agree together, Washington could.

The delegates arrived in Philadelphia in 1787. They gathered together in Independence Hall, the red-brick building at the center of the city. George Washington was elected chairman of the meeting. Benjamin Franklin, now eighty-one, was too old to walk to the daily meetings. Instead, he hired four prisoners who were let out of jail to carry him to and from Independence Hall in a chair.

The delegates talked and argued for days and days. No one else was allowed to listen. The windows were even nailed shut so that no one outside could eavesdrop!

The delegates wanted to make sure that the new Constitution would give the United States of America the power to act together—but also to act separately. Finally, they agreed on a plan that would divide the government of the United States into two "houses," like the House of Commons and the House of Lords in the English parliament. These houses would be responsible for writing out laws and voting on them. One house would be called the Senate. Each state, no matter what its size, could elect two representatives called Senators to sit in the

Senate. That way, each state would have an equal voice. No state could have more power than any other.

But each state would also get to elect one representative for each thirty thousand people. These representatives would meet together in the House of Representatives. The House of Representatives showed that all of the people of the United States, no matter what state they lived in, were part of one country. Every person in every state would have the same amount of power to send a representative to the House. States with more people in them would have more representatives—but the same number of senators.

All the laws of the country would have to be approved by *both* houses—by the states, and also by the people. Together, these houses would be called Congress. Congress would be the *legislative* part of the new federal government, able to pass laws, declare war, and make treaties with foreign countries.

But the English Parliament also had two houses. And Parliament had still passed taxes, even though the English in America objected. What would keep Congress from doing the same thing?

The delegates decided that a leader should have the power to *veto,* or stop, any law that Congress might pass. This leader would be called the President. He wouldn't have the power to make any laws, but he would be able to stop Congress if Congress got carried away! Now the American federal government had two parts: Congress, the legislative branch, and the President, the *executive branch.*

But who would make sure that Congress and the President would both follow the laws that they passed?

The federal government needed a third branch: a court of judges who would decide whether or not laws were being properly observed. This "Supreme Court" became the *judicial branch* of the federal government. Its members had to be chosen by the President—but Congress had to approve them! Now, each of the three parts of the government had to cooperate with the other parts. No one branch of the government could grab all of the power for itself.

The delegates wrote all of these rules down in a new Constitution, signed it, and then published it in newspapers in every state. The Constitution began, "We the people of the United States, in order to form a more perfect union, establish justice, insure domestic tranquility, provide for the common defence, promote the general welfare, and secure the blessings of liberty to ourselves and our posterity, do ordain and establish this Constitution for the United States of America." Then the Constitution explained how the three branches of government would work.

The delegates had decided that nine states would have to agree to accept, or *ratify,* the Constitution. The first state to agree was Delaware, on December 7th, 1787. By January of 1788, Pennsylvania, New Jersey, Georgia, and Connecticut had also ratified it. It took four more months for Massachusetts, Maryland, and South Carolina to agree. When New Hampshire, the ninth state to vote, ratified the Constitution in June of 1788, the Constitution became the law of the United States of America.

Not everyone was pleased with the Constitution. Quick-tempered Patrick Henry from Virginia called it a "horridly frightful" document. He was afraid that the President would become a king and that Congress would be able to use too much power against the people. He wanted the Constitution to have a *Bill of Rights* attached to it—a list of powers that the government could never use against the people of the United States.

Many other Americans wanted a Bill of Rights too. "All power is subject to abuse," James Madison remarked, "[and so we must] fortify the rights of the people against the encroachments of the government."

Four years later, a Bill of Rights was added to the original Constitution. The Bill of Rights, ten *amendments* (additions) to the Constitution, said that Congress could never forbid American citizens to speak their opinions, to worship God as they pleased, to assemble together in public, or to keep weapons to defend themselves. No one could ever be seized by the government and kept in jail without a public trial. The Bill of Rights said that the federal government could never behave like a king toward its people—even if there seemed to be good reasons for doing so.

The Constitution was finished. Finally, the United States was truly a nation.

The First American President (1789-1797)

After the Constitutional Convention was over, George Washington went home. He was almost sixty years old. He'd fought in the French and Indian War. He'd led the War for Independence. Now, he wanted to stay on his farm in Virginia, feed his animals, work in his garden, and sit with his wife in front of the fireplace in the long, quiet evenings.

But the delegates who had signed the Constitution begged George Washington to become the first President. Many Americans were nervous about this new office. They were afraid that the President would soon become a king. And the delegates knew that George Washington would never try to become the king of America.

Washington didn't want to be king of America. He didn't even want to be President. "It is my great and sole desire to live and die, in peace and retirement on my own farm," Washington told Alexander Hamilton. "I call heaven to witness that this very act would be the greatest sacrifice of my personal feelings and wishes that ever I have been called upon to make."

But George Washington also believed that he had a duty to the people of the United States. If they wanted him to be President, he would have to accept.

The first elections for a President of the United States were held in February of 1789—and Washington won unanimously. As he had promised, he accepted the job of first President. But he wrote in his diary, "[I begin the presidency] with a mind oppressed with more anxious and painful sensations that I have words to express."

Washington had to ride to New York, the temporary capital of the new United States, to be sworn in, or *inaugurated,* as President. He was hoping for a quiet journey—but every time he got near a town, people ran out and cheered. Little girls threw flowers. Men took off their hats. Church bells rang! When he rode through Philadelphia, he had to parade under triumphal arches built just for his honor. Finally, he arrived in New Jersey, where a barge would take him across the water to New York. He found the dock covered with a red carpet, soldiers standing at attention all along it. The barge he would ride on was covered with flags and rowed by thirteen men, each representing one of the thirteen states. As the barge pulled away from the dock, a whole parade of ships fell into line behind it: a Spanish warship, with its crew cheering; a floating choir singing songs in honor of Washington; and dozens of small ships filled with cheering Americans.

The barge docked near Wall Street. When Washington stepped onto New York's streets, he saw the roofs and sidewalks crowded with people, cheering and shouting his name. "The streets were lined with the inhabitants as thick as the People could stand," one man wrote back to his wife, describing the scene. "Men, women and children—Nay, I may venture to say Tens of Thousands....Heads standing as thick as Ears of Corn before the Harvest." Women hung out of windows, calling, "The great Washington is here!" Little boys in the branches of trees screamed, "Hurrah! Hurrah!" Some people fainted. "I have seen him!" one woman yelled. "I would fall down on my knees before him!"

Washington was taken to the City Hall, renamed Federal Hall, in a coach surrounded by soldiers. Standing on a second-floor balcony, where all the crowd could see him, he laid his hand on a Bible and took the first oath of office. "I solemnly swear," Washington announced, "that I will faithfully execute the office of President of the United States and will, to the best of my ability, preserve, protect, and defend the Constitution of the United States."

"God bless our Washington!" the crowd shouted. "Long live our beloved President!" Bands played. Fireworks exploded

224

in the sky. George Washington had to walk back to the house where he was staying, because there were so many people celebrating in the streets that his carriage couldn't get through!

Washington found all of this attention embarrassing—and frightening. He said, "I greatly fear that my countrymen will expect too much of me." But along with his new Vice-President, John Adams, Washington started on the huge job of governing the United States. In his first week as President, he had 718 soldiers, 75 post offices, and a few clerks. There was no other government!

Washington had to build the federal government from nothing. He chose four helpers, or *secretaries*, to help him run the country. Alexander Hamilton became Secretary of the Treasury. Thomas Jefferson became Secretary of State. Washington also chose a secretary of war to take care of the army and navy, and an attorney general who would help him understand and follow the Supreme Court's decisions. These four men became known as the President's Cabinet.

Washington hired almost a thousand people to carry out all the federal government's jobs—from running post offices to keeping lighthouses lit! He also signed an Act declaring that the United States would have a new capital city. None of the states wanted a city in another state to become the capital of the United States, because then one state would be more important than all the rest. So Washington convinced Virginia and Maryland to give up a little bit of the land between them. This land, the District of Columbia, would be the location of a new capital city. Congress and the Supreme Court could meet there. The President would live there! The cornerstone for the President's new house was laid in 1792 in the District of Columbia. Eventually, this President's House would become known as the White House. It would have 132 rooms and 35 bathrooms!

George Washington certainly seemed to have kinglike powers! He had chosen almost everyone in the new government. At his inauguration, a song in his honor had been composed—and sung to the tune of "God Save the King." The plans for the new President's House made it look like a palace. The new capital city was named Washington in his honor!

But Patrick Henry's fears didn't come true. George Washington didn't try to become a king. Congress suggested that he be called "His Exalted High Mightiness" or perhaps "His Highness the President," but Washington simply went by "Mr. President." He only wanted to be president for four years, because the job was so hard. His hands developed rheumatism. His hair turned white. He wanted to go back to his farm. At the end of his four-year term, the people of America re-elected him—even though he didn't run.

Washington agreed to serve one more four-year period, or *term*. But then he refused to be President again. He knew that America didn't need a President holding power for life! He wanted the Constitution to be the ruler of the land, not the President. Washington walked away from the power of the presidency—something no European king would ever do. When he heard the news, George III of England marveled, "[He is] the greatest character of the age!"

The Great Southern Continent

Chapter Twenty-Four
Sailing South

Captain Cook Reaches Botany Bay

In a London lodging house, Captain James Cook was writing up a list of supplies for a long, long voyage. He had been hired by the English government to make a scientific expedition: to sail to Tahiti, on the other side of the globe, and look at the planet Venus. Telescopes, measuring instruments, mapmaking supplies: all sat around him in boxes, ready to be packed neatly away into the hold of his ship, the *Endeavour.*

Sailing to distant places was like meat and drink to James Cook. In his thirty-three years, he had already been over much of the world, drawing maps and investigating strange new islands and coastlines. During the Seven Years' War, he had mapped out the coast of Canada, so that the British could sail up to Quebec and capture it. He had sailed on coal ships and on warships, on flagships and on barges.

But this trip was something different. James Cook knew that observing Venus was a valuable assignment. When Venus passed between the sun and the earth, the passage, or *transit*, couldn't be seen in England—only from the southern part of the planet Earth. The Royal Society was counting on Cook to take careful measurements so that they could study this transit, which wouldn't happen again for a hundred years!

Yes, Venus was interesting. But more interesting to Cook was the sealed envelope in the bottom of his sea chest. A royal messenger from the court of George III had given it to him. The envelope contained secret orders, a mysterious mission which Cook would undertake—but he wasn't allowed to open it until he had finished watching Venus.

When the *Endeavour* was ready, Cook and his crew set off. The men couldn't wait to get to Tahiti, rumored to be full of warm beaches, fresh food, and the most beautiful women in the world. Eight months later, the *Endeavour* arrived at Tahiti's white sand shores. The islands were even more beautiful than the sailors had imagined! The natives of Tahiti garlanded them with flowers and brought them fruit and coconuts. While the sailors rested and repaired the ships, Cook ordered a little hill cleared of trees and a watching post built. He put all of his astronomical equipment on this post and waited for the transit. Two months later, the big day arrived. The tiny black speck of the distant planet moved slowly across the sun's face. Cook watched carefully, taking measurements and recording them for the scientists of London.

Now he could open his sealed instructions!

Late that night, alone in his quarters, he lit a candle and broke the seal. He read the royal command twice, and then three times. "You are to sail south," the orders read, "and find the Great Southern Continent for England!"

The Great Southern Continent! Geographers had long believed that a huge, hidden continent must lie on the bottom of the earth. Otherwise, they were sure that the world would overbalance and tip over from the weight of all the land on the north half of the globe. No one had ever found this mysterious land—but the year before, an English sea captain sailing through the Pacific had glimpsed distant mountains. George III exclaimed, "We must send ships to find it, and claim it for England!"

James Cook packed his reluctant men on board the *Endeavour* and turned south. It was three months before they sighted land—a long jut of mountains thrusting out into the sea. Was this a peninsula, attached to the Great Southern Continent? They sailed around it at a distance, examining the shore. But the mountains belonged to two islands, separated by a ragged gulf. Cook was sailing around the country of New Zealand.

Cook wrote in his journal, "As to a southern continent, I do not believe any such thing exists." He turned the *Endeavour* for home. He had been traveling for nineteen months, and his crew was tired and ready to return home. Cook decided that they would go west for the return trip. He knew that another

230

island had been sighted west of New Zealand, and he wanted to explore its coast on the way home.

Soon the island came into view. Cook anchored his ship in a peaceful bay so that his sailors could find fresh water and prepare for the long journey back to Europe. Meanwhile, he drew maps of the shore. The island was so full of strange new plants that Cook named it Botany Bay. (*Botany* means "the study of plants.")

When the *Endeavour* launched again, James Cook sailed along the coast of this island, mapping as he went. He decided to call it New South Wales, because it reminded him of the country of Wales in Britain.

Cook almost didn't make it back to England with his new maps. Late one night, the *Endeavour* ran aground on a coral reef—an iron-sharp ridge made up of the skeletons of tiny sea animals called *coral polyps*. This reef, the Great Barrier Reef, ran all along the coast of Australia. It ripped a hole in the ship's bottom. The sailors had to throw out all of the heavy cannons and iron, pump the ship out, sail it back to the coast, and mend it before they could continue on. They sailed up the rest of the coast, Cook mapping the whole way. Then he planted a British flag and announced that the whole coastline belonged to King George III of England!

James Cook didn't realize it, but he had found the Great Southern Continent. This island, New South Wales, was much bigger than he ever imagined. He had sailed up the coast of Australia, the seventh continent on earth.

When he returned to England in 1771, bearing his measurements of Venus and his map of New South Wales, Cook was welcomed and praised for his discoveries. But the next year, he made another voyage looking for the Great Southern Continent. On his second voyage, he went south into Antarctica and found only ice. He decided that looking for the Great Southern Continent was a waste of time.

So on his third voyage, he set off on a different mission: to look one last time for the Northwest Passage, that fabled path through North America that would lead to China. After all of these years, the British were still hoping to find it! Cook planned to look for the passage along the *western* coast of North America. In 1776, the same year that America declared its independence, Cook sailed to New Zealand and then around to the Pacific coast of North America.

Like other explorers, Cook couldn't find the Northwest Passage. He gave up and headed back south. His ships, the *Resolution* and the *Discovery,* were worn, battered with storms, their sails worn and split with travel, ropes frayed. Cook decided that they would stop in Hawaii to outfit the ships.

The Hawaiian natives welcomed the sailors with fruit, roast pig, and wreaths of flowers. The sailors thought that Hawaii was even better than Tahiti! They fixed the split sails and worn planks—and they ate, and ate, and ate.

Neither Cook nor his sailors realized that the Hawaiians were being so friendly because they believed that Cook was a god. Their legends said that their god of peace and happiness, Rono, would return to Hawaii in a floating forest. They thought that the masts of Cook's two ships were that forest!

But even a god can wear out his welcome. The sailors ate most of the natives' food. After two weeks, one of the sailors wrote later, the natives started "patting the bellies of the sailors…telling them partly by signs and partly by words that it was time for them to go."

Finally, the ships left the shores, repaired and shipshape, the sailors filled with delicious Hawaiian meat and fruit. But they had only been sailing for three days when a late-night storm cracked the mast of Cook's ship. Cook decided that they would return to Hawaii for more repairs.

Four days later, the ships limped into the harbor. "We were surprised to find our reception very different from what it had been on our first arrival," wrote the same sailor, "no shouts, no bustle, no confusion; but a solitary bay, with only here and there a canoe stealing close to shore." The natives weren't pleased to see that Rono and his fellow gods had returned. How much more food did the god of happiness want them to give him? They turned their backs and refused to feed the sailors. Some of them swam out to the ships that night and pulled nails out of the planks. Others pilfered iron tools from the ship's deck. Even one of the ship's boats disappeared, hauled away by unhappy natives.

Cook decided to take violent measures. He rowed to the shore with ten soldiers, planning to capture a Hawaiian chief and hold him hostage until the stolen boat was returned. The British party marched into the nearest village and demanded that the chief come with them back to their ship.

Reluctantly, the chief came from his hut and began to walk with the soldiers back toward the shore. A mob gathered to watch. Younger men began shouting out to the chief, "Don't go any further! This is wrong! Sit down in the sand!" The chief hesitated. And then it happened: one of the young warriors struck James Cook with a club. He stumbled and fell. Everyone could see the blood in his hair. This was no god! It was a mortal man!

Furious, the other warriors rushed forward with their spears and daggers. The soldiers scrambled back to the boat. But four of them—and James Cook—lay dead on the beach. Cook's voyage south had been his last.

The Convict Settlement

While Cook sailed south, England lost North America. Now England had no American colonies, no American tobacco—and nowhere to send its prisoners.

For years, Britain had been running out of jail space for all its prisoners, so judges had begun to send thieves, murderers, and swindlers to America for punishment. These criminals would travel to the colonies and work for a farmer or a plantation owner until their sentences were over.

But now the American states refused to take England's criminals. Where would all of these prisoners go?

The English government bought ancient ships, too old to sail, and moored them in rivers. Prisoners were sent on board these *hulks*. They were filthy, damp, dark, and filled with rats and insects. Thousands of prisoners died in the hulks.

But there were still too many for England's jails.

And then the English remembered New South Wales. Ten years after the War of Independence, eleven ships filled with supplies, jailers, and prisoners headed south for Australia. They were ordered to build a new colony in this land claimed by Cook—a colony of prisoners. The continent of Australia was about to become England's jail.

No one wanted to be sentenced to Australia. Australia had no cities, no ports, no ships. Mysterious people called Aborigines lived there—and might not be friendly. And Australia was so far away that a criminal sentenced to serve seven years would never come home. One judge, sentencing a criminal to be sent on this first voyage to Australia, announced, "I sentence you but to what I do not know, perhaps to storm and shipwreck, perhaps to infectious disorder, perhaps to famine, perhaps to be massacred by savages, perhaps to be devoured by wild beasts."

But the first governor of the Australian prison colony, Arthur Phillip, didn't intend to let the men and women on his eleven ships be massacred or devoured.

Phillip was a small man, dark-haired, quick and energetic—and persistent. When he landed at Botany Bay, he was in charge of a thousand people—three quarters of them convicted criminals. Many were women and children, sent to Australia because they had stolen a loaf of bread or a pair of shoes. Many were too sick to work. None of them really wanted to build a colony which would serve as their own prison!

Arthur Phillip was determined that they *would* build a colony and that the colony would prosper. But he could see that Botany Bay was the wrong place to settle. There was swamp all around and no fresh water. He ordered the whole group to move further up the coast to a cove where there was fresh water and flat land. He named it Sydney Cove, after an English government official. And then he set to work, building the colony of Sydney.

234

Most of the prisoners were city folk who didn't know how to tend animals or grow crops. They couldn't even cut down trees for houses; their tools, made to chop soft English wood, bounced off the iron-hard Australian tree trunks. And the prison guards refused to work side by side with the prisoners. They were only willing to guard them and issue orders.

So Arthur Phillip made some of the convicts themselves into colony leaders. The prisoners worked to build roads and huts. They pulled the plows themselves because there were no horses.

But despite all their hard work, the colony almost starved to death. Almost three years later, no English ship had arrived with fresh supplies. The prisoners hadn't been able to grow enough food for themselves. Arthur Phillip sent half of the colony to a distant island where they might find fish and birds to eat. He announced that everyone else would get only half of their usual rations. Starving prisoners started to steal food. Phillip, afraid that all the food would disappear, ordered the offenders flogged.

Finally, a ship came into view over the horizon. It was an English ship, bringing more prisoners—and more food. Sydney was saved from starvation.

But the ship had brought no instructions for Arthur Phillip. He had hoped that he might be allowed to return to England. Instead, he stayed, greeting shiploads of convicts, arranging to send ships to Calcutta for extra food, ordering fruit trees and vines brought from Africa, forcing the prisoners to keep working in the fields.

Despite the starvation and the hard work, some of the prisoners realized that life in Australia was actually better than life back in England. In England, they had been beggars with no way to get land of their own. But here, if they worked hard, Arthur Phillip would give them a farm of their own. The first convict to earn a farm, James Ruse, got forty acres! A thief named Simeon Lord spent fifteen years in the Sydney colony— and rose to be a wealthy trader with his own estate. A forger named Francis Greenway became Sydney's first architect, designing dozens of new buildings.

Slowly, the colony began to prosper. Four years after the prisoners arrived at Botany Bay, free settlers started to come to Australia. Hundreds of Englishmen and women decided they would be better off trying to scratch a living from Australia's red land than starving to death from poverty in England! Many of the convicts who had finished their sentences decided to stay in Australia and take up farming. Settlers moved inland and grazed sheep on the vast plains of Australia. These settlers were called *squatters* because they didn't buy their land; they just built houses on it and claimed it. Squatters could make good money sending wool to London to sell!

But life as a squatter wasn't easy. Squatters had to fight off burning sun, drought, unexpected floods, and loneliness. There were no doctors, no stores, no towns. Squatters only got their mail two times per year, when the supply wagons came. There was little else to do—and so they drank. More rum was brought to Australia than any other kind of food, drink, or merchandise!

And because so many more men than women were convicted of crimes, there were three men for every woman in Australia! Australia needed women. A committee in London was formed to send young women to Australia for only five pounds. Women who were too poor to find English husbands often went.

Phillip was finally allowed to return to England in 1792. He left a colony of 4,221 people behind him; 3,099 were convicts. Over the next eighty years, 160,000 convicts and many free people would come to Australia. Eventually, five English colonies would lie across Australia.

But although English Australia prospered, the native people of Australia were pushed out of their homeland.

Arthur Phillip had ordered the convicts of Sydney to live in peace with Aborigines. Any convict who killed an Aborigine would be hanged! But despite this, the convicts stole food and tools from the Aborigines. Squatters grazed their sheep on Aboriginal hunting grounds. As English Australia grew, the land of the Aborigines shrank. When Arthur Phillip landed in Botany Bay, three hundred thousand Aborigines lived in Australia. By the time that Great Britain claimed all of Australia for itself, fewer than eighty thousand remained.

France During the Time of the Revolution

Chapter Twenty-Five
Revolution Gone Sour

The Storming of the Bastille

In some ways, the Australian colony was a little bit like the new United States. In both of these new places, poor people had a chance to own land even though they weren't noblemen. And in both of these places, men and women could live away from the power of the king.

The nation of France watched the American revolt against the English king with fascination. The French even joined in to help the Americans win their freedom. But then they went home to an absolute monarch: Louis XVI, the great-great-grandson of the Sun King. Like his ancestors, Louis XVI claimed that he had a divine right to rule France and to do exactly what he pleased.

In the years after the American revolution, the French decided that their king was wrong.

France was an unhappy country. Louis XIV had spent most of France's money to build his huge palace of Versailles and to carry on long wars. Louis XV had lost the Seven Year's War and made France even poorer. Both of these kings had forced the poor people of France to pay more and more taxes—while the rich paid almost nothing.

The French thought of themselves as divided into three different parts, or *estates*. Roman Catholic priests were the First Estate. They didn't have to pay any taxes, because Catholicism was the official religion of France. The noblemen of France were the Second Estate. Many of them ruled over huge mansions and farms that had belonged in their families for hundreds of years. They spent months at Versailles with the king and served as his generals, ministers, and ambassadors. Most of them paid no taxes—or very little.

There were about thirty thousand people in the Second Estate. But there were twenty-six *million* people in the Third Estate. All of the merchants, shopkeepers, doctors, farmers, lawyers, judges, wagon drivers, peasants, bakers, tailors, and cobblers of France belonged to the Third Estate. These working people paid taxes on salt, soap, wine, tobacco, and leather. They paid taxes to the church. They paid rent to the noblemen who owned the land where they worked. They paid fees to grind flour, press grapes, or cross bridges. They were poor, and they were hungry; France was suffering from the worst wheat crops in hundreds of years, and there was no bread. An Englishman traveling in France was shocked at the hunger of the peasants. They looked, he said, like scarecrows.

Meanwhile, the noblemen went on spending millions on parties, clothes, coaches, and gambling.

Louis XVI suggested that the Second Estate start to pay taxes. But the noblemen refused! You see, Louis XVI looked like an absolute monarch—but he had to have the support of the noblemen and the army to carry out his wishes. And Louis had other problems. His young queen, Marie Antoinette, had nothing to do. So she spent her time dancing at balls, buying expensive dresses, and playing cards. She had a whole little village and farm built so that she could pretend to be a dairymaid, carrying a milk-pail made of priceless porcelain. Her brother, who had become the Holy Roman Emperor, called her a "featherhead!"

Marie Antoinette was not a cruel woman. She was a good and careful mother to her three children. She was so softhearted that she cried when she heard that peasants were starving. But she had no idea of how miserable most French peasants were—or how they felt when she spent millions of French francs on a party lit entirely by candles or on a "simple country dress" of priceless fabric. Marie Antoinette became more and more unpopular. The French whispered that she alone had caused France to be so poor, even though the country had been in debt long before Marie became Queen!

When the Declaration of Independence was published in America, it was translated into French and published in France as well. Millions of French people read its words about freedom and equality. And then they looked at their own wealthy queen and idle noblemen. Wasn't a shopkeeper or farmer the equal of a lazy aristocrat?

While the French grew more interested in the idea of revolution, France's treasury grew emptier. Once more, Louis XVI tried to make France's noblemen pay taxes. Once more, they refused. They would only pay a tax, they announced, if representatives from all three Estates met together and decided that new taxes were necessary.

Louis agreed. In May of 1789, delegates from all over France came to Versailles to talk about taxes. Some were clergymen. Some were noblemen. Some were merchants, shopkeepers, judges and lawyers from the Third Estate. One of those lawyers was named Maximilien de Robespierre.

The members of the Third Estate soon were fed up with the meeting. They were told that they could only wear black clothes, to show that they were less important than the members of the First and Second Estates. They could only use the side doors of Versailles. When all of the representatives went to church for a special Mass, there were only reserved seats for the First and Second Estate members; the Third Estate were expected to find places wherever they could.

And then the king decreed that each Estate would meet in a separate room and cast one vote about the proposed taxes. If the First and Second Estates voted together not to pay taxes, the Third Estate couldn't possibly win a vote against them—even though the Third Estate represented most of the people in France.

That was the last straw.

The Third Estate renamed the meeting The National Assembly and begged the priests of the First Estate to join them. Many priests, who had spent years working in poor towns where the people were starving, agreed. Even some of the noblemen agreed to join with the Third Estate. They realized that France would never be a healthy country if most of its people were hungry.

The remaining noblemen ran to Louis and begged him to halt the meeting before the National Assembly took over! So Louis locked the Third Estate out of their meeting room, so they couldn't vote!

So the new National Assembly met on a tennis court and took an oath called the Tennis Court Oath, swearing to make a new Constitution for France. Louis commanded them to go back to their own rooms, but they refused to leave! One of the nobleman repeated, "The King has ordered you to go!" But the National Assembly shouted back, "We are here by the will of the people, and we will not be dispersed, except at the point of bayonets!"

In Paris, only twelve miles away, word spread of the Third Estate's revolt. The common people of Paris began to arm themselves, ready to support the National Assembly. Louis XVI began to get worried! He was afraid that his French soldiers, who belonged to the Third Estate, wouldn't fire on the rebellious commoners in Paris. So he ordered the Swiss soldiers who were part of his royal guard to march to Paris and restore order.

The common people of Paris heard that the soldiers were coming. "Die rather than submit!" they shouted. But to fight off the soldiers, they needed gunpowder. Where could they find some?

"The Bastille!" someone yelled.

The Bastille, the royal prison of Paris, was an old fortress with eight towers and walls fifteen feet thick. The mob started to push cannons up and aim them at the walls. The keeper of the prison decided he'd better surrender. Only seven prisoners were inside, but the revolutionaries freed them, took the gunpowder, chopped off the keeper's head, and ran through the streets with it stuck on the edge of a pike.

It was July 14th, 1789. The Bastille had fallen—and so had the power of the French king. The Fall of the Bastille is still a holiday in France, just as July 4th is a holiday in the United States.

Now the commoners ruled in Paris. Throughout the countryside, peasants revolted, invaded the mansions of the rich, and murdered the hated noblemen of the Second Estate. Some noblemen and clergy decided to join the revolt. Others fled the country!

Louis XVI and his family were put in a carriage and taken to Paris, where they were kept in the palace of Tuileries and guarded. The National Assembly also went to Paris—and took over the government. Now it was time to write a new French Constitution. Like England, France would be a country where the king had to follow the laws. And like America, France would be a country where everyone was equal.

The Reign of Terror

Imprisoned in Tuileries, the royal family waited to find out what would happen to them.

Meanwhile, the National Assembly argued about France's new constitution. The clergy and the well-off members of the Third Estate—the doctors, lawyers, and merchants— wanted to put Louis XVI back on the throne, as long as the new Constitution gave him almost no power. But most of the Third Estate, led by Maximilien de Robespierre, insisted that France would be better off with no king at all. Robespierre made speech after speech, trying to convince the whole Assembly to get rid of the king.

The Assembly couldn't quite decide what to do with Louis XVI. But they *were* sure that they wanted to get rid of the Second Estate. So the Assembly declared that there would be no more titles in France. No Frenchman could be a duke or a baron. Instead, everyone would be given the title Citizen. And a month later, the Assembly announced that priests would have to be elected by voting, like politicians!

Now the First and Second Estates had been outlawed. But many in France still secretly hoped that the king would return to the throne and rule in the old way. Some of these *Royalists* plotted with Louis XVI to sneak the royal family out of the palace so that they could flee to the north of France. There, the king could gather Royalists around him and try to reconquer his country!

Louis, Marie and the children managed to get out of the palace and into a carriage. But as the carriage rattled through a little town called St. Menehould, a man by the side of the road peered in. He recognized the face of the man in the carriage. It was the same face that was on the money of France! The man leaped onto a horse, galloped ahead to the next town, and warned that the king was on his way. A mob assembled and stopped the coach. Louis and his family were taken back to Paris. They went on waiting, and waiting, and waiting.

Then, the commander of the Prussian Army sent a message to the National Assembly. "Hurt the king or his family," the message warned, "and Prussia will invade France and destroy all of Paris."

When the people of Paris heard about this threat, they shouted, "The king is a traitor! He has been sending messages to our enemies, begging them to invade his own country!" The fading hatred for the king was blown into a hot angry flame. Twenty thousand men and women stormed the palace of Tuileries, killed the king's Swiss guard, and dragged the royal family to a dark dungeon called the Temple. No one could escape from the Temple. Encouraged by fiery speeches from Robespierre, the National Assembly decided once and for all that France would be a Republic! The Assembly renamed itself the National Convention. Now France would be governed only by the National Convention, which would be elected by the people.

Hatred for the king spread to hatred of everyone who had aristocratic blood. French noblemen who had been part of the revolution started to flee from the country. Those in power wanted nothing to do with king *or* with nobility. There was only one remaining fate for the king. Like Charles I, he would have to be executed.

On January 21st, 1793, Louis XVI was taken out of his cell. "Don't seek revenge for my death!" he called to his son as he left. He was marched to the town square at the center of

Paris, where the guillotine, a sharp blade that dropped down on the necks of its victims, waited. The executioner cut his hair short so that the blade would slice cleanly. Louis tried to make a speech to the mob, but drummers nearby quickly started to beat their drums so that he could not be heard. He was pushed forward onto the guillotine. The blade fell. A soldier held up his head and shouted, "Long live the Republic!" People ran forward and soaked up the blood with handkerchiefs and bits of cloth so that they would have souvenirs of this great event!

The king was dead. But the French Republic was in trouble. Other European countries, watching with horror, hoped that this madness would not spread. Soon, England, the Netherlands, and Spain declared war on France. And in the west of France, many peasants who were loyal Catholics rose up and rebelled against the National Convention and its treatment of Catholic priests.

The National Convention was afraid that the Republic would fall. So it formed a new committee called the Committee of Public Safety, and put Maximilien de Robespierre at its head. Robespierre was given the power to arrest anyone suspected of disloyalty to the Republic—and put them to death.

Robespierre had all of the peasants who had rebelled in the west of France arrested and put to death. Then he began to send everyone who might have sympathy for noblemen, clergy, or kings to the guillotine.

The Reign of Terror had begun.

The National Convention passed a new law, called the Law of Suspected Persons. Under this law, anyone who was against the revolution—or who even seemed not too enthusiastic about it—could be executed! The first person convicted under this law was Marie Antoinette. On October 16th, nine months after her husband's death, Marie Antoinette was driven to the guillotine in a rough farm cart called a *tumbril*. She wore a white gown. She was only thirty-seven, but when the executioner held up her head, everyone could see that her hair had turned pure white.

Marie Antoinette was not the last of Robespierre's victims. He accused thousands of people of plotting against the

Republic: men, women, peasants, old people, even children! In town all over France, guillotines fell. Old women would sit beside the guillotines, knitting socks for the soldiers, chatting and laughing with each other and occasionally cheering as the guillotine fell. If blood sprayed on the knitting, so much better. The blood would fill the soldiers with revolutionary fire! "The guillotine was claiming both the innocent and the guilty alike," wrote Helen Williams, an English citizen in France who was arrested and then released. "The gutters seemed to stream with blood."

By the time that sixteen thousand French citizens had been guillotined, the National Convention started to worry about Robespierre. He had too much power. He had grown suspicious of everyone, even his own friends. Members began to whisper that it was time to remove this man, before he became a dictator even worse that Louis XVI.

Robespierre got wind of the Convention's doubts. He stormed before a meeting of the convention, yelling that a plot was being formed against him. "I know who is set against me!" he shouted. "They too will be rooted out and sent to the guillotine!"

The National Convention did not like to be threatened! The next day, one member after another stood up and made a public speech condemning Robespierre. Robespierre, unable to believe what he was hearing, sagged into a chair and grabbed his head with both hands. He was arrested and dragged away to the guillotine where so many others had died. The Reign of Terror was over. France had no more king, no more Robespierre—and no more leaders.

Russia During the Reign of Catherine the Great

Chapter Twenty-Six
Catherine the Great

Princess Catherine Comes to Russia

Over in Russia, the empress Catherine the Great watched in horror as king and aristocrats died by the guillotine.

Catherine the Great had come to the throne of Russia thirty years before. Like Peter the Great, who ruled before her, Catherine admired Western ideas. But she was still firmly convinced that kings ruled because God gave them power. France, she told one of her ministers, was "going to ruin." Catherine may have believed that God gave kings—and empresses—their power. But the empress herself had come to the throne by very human means!

Catherine wasn't even a Russian. Her father had been the prince of a little German state, and her mother was Swedish. But her mother's cousin had married the daughter of the great Russian emperor Peter the Great, and their son, Peter Ulrich, had been declared the heir. The Empress Elizabeth, Peter Ulrich's aunt, had seized the Russian throne years before. She thought that young Catherine would be the perfect wife for her nephew.

When Catherine was fifteen, the empress sent a message to Germany, inviting the young princess to come and visit Russia. Catherine's mother Johanna was thrilled. If her daughter married the future czar, she would be the mother of a queen! But Catherine's father shook his head in worry. "You will have to become a member of the Russian Orthodox Church!" he warned Catherine. "We have always been followers of Martin Luther's teachings. You must promise me never to leave the Lutheran church!"

Catherine promised. She wasn't sure she wanted to marry Peter Ulrich anyway. She had met him once before, when he was ten, and she remembered an odd, small, white-faced boy, bad-tempered and full of strange twitches. Even though he was only ten, he drank so much wine at dinner that he had to be carried away from the table. He had been unfriendly and rude to his servants, and seemed to want only to play toy soldiers with one of his attendants.

But the thought of a crown fascinated Catherine. And what was Peter like now that he was older? Catherine was willing to go and see.

So she packed her clothes and, with her mother, set off for Russia's capital city, St. Petersburg. St. Petersburg was almost a thousand miles away, and their road lay through the coldest, bleakest part of Europe. They traveled for six weeks. The roads disappeared under snow and ice and mud. They had to sleep at country inns where the guests piled together for warmth while dogs and chickens nosed around the straw-strewn floors. Catherine's hands and feet swelled from frostbite.

But when they finally arrived in St. Petersburg, they were welcomed with warm cloaks and celebration. The empress's fur-lined sled was waiting to whisk them to Moscow, where Peter was waiting. Finally, Catherine arrived at the enormous, candle-lit mansion where Peter stood in the front hall to welcome her. He was much taller and more handsome than when she had seen him last. And he was delighted to see her. "I wish I could have harnessed myself to your sled, so that you would have been here sooner!" he exclaimed.

But the more time Catherine spent with Peter, the less she liked him. He was rude to the servants and courtiers. When he went to church, he made unpleasant noises and told loud jokes during the service. Even though he would rule Russia one day, he refused to speak Russian; instead, he spoke German and told the Russians around him that he wished he could live in Prussia—a German state that Russians hated!

But everyone around her seemed to expect her to marry Peter. The Empress Elizabeth was a big, frightening woman, who flew into terrifying rages at her servants, and Catherine was afraid to tell her that she didn't really like Peter. She tried to tell her mother, but Johanna was looking forward to becoming the mother-in-law of a czar. She scoffed at Catherine's doubts!

Catherine's father would have agreed with her, but he was a thousand miles away.

Too afraid to refuse, Catherine agreed to convert to the Russian Orthodox Church and to be betrothed to Peter. The two went through a long, elaborate engagement ceremony. Catherine was given the title of a Russian Grand Duchess. Suddenly, everyone had to kneel in front of her, call her "Your Imperial Highness," and kiss her hand.

Four months after the engagement ceremony, Peter Ulrich came down with smallpox. Instantly, Catherine was whisked away to a distant palace so that she wouldn't catch the disease too. In those days, smallpox killed millions. Peter grew sicker and sicker. Smallpox sores covered his face and body. He wasn't expected to live.

But he survived. When Catherine saw him again, she gasped in horror. His face was swollen. His skin was a mass of scars. He was barely recognizable. "He had become hideous," Catherine wrote in her diary. "My blood ran cold at the sight of him!"

And just at this time, the Empress Elizabeth announced that it was time to set the date for the wedding!

Catherine dreaded the day of the ceremony, but she was afraid to break off her engagement. So the two were married, in an enormous celebration that the empress had planned for months. Ambassadors from all of Europe were there. The feasting went on for hours. Catherine was the wife of the future czar—and she was miserable.

Peter didn't improve after marriage. As a matter of fact, his behavior grew so strange that the Russian court whispered, "He's going mad!" His scars covered a face that was always grimacing and twitching. He talked loudly in church, insulted visiting ambassadors, and giggled uncontrollably at serious occasions. He liked to pour wine on the heads of his servants and play with his wooden soldiers. He ignored his wife!

Catherine had no friends, and her mother Johanna had returned home after the wedding. She spent nine lonely years reading books of history and philosophy, books about military tactics, books about the emperors of Rome and their strategies for ruling their empire. She made friends with the army officers. She rode through the streets of St. Petersburg and heard the Russian people murmur about her beauty. Next to weak, spindly, repulsive Peter, Catherine looked like a true queen!

Catherine's life at court grew lonelier and harder. Peter insulted her in public and threatened to send her into exile. When Catherine had her first baby, after being married to Peter for nine years, the Empress Elizabeth took the baby as soon as it was born and swept out of the room, commanding everyone to follow her. Catherine was left alone, exhausted and cold. No one even brought her a drink of water for three hours! The empress had decided to raise the future heir to the throne herself. She named the little boy Paul and put his cradle in her own room. Catherine didn't even see her baby for six weeks!

Catherine was furious. But, lying in her bed, she began to think.

The Empress Elizabeth was growing older and sicker. Peter was a fool and a madman. She was the mother to the heir of the throne—and she was a strong, intelligent, woman. The Russian people liked her. The army respected her. When the Empress Elizabeth died, why shouldn't Catherine rule in the place of her bad-tempered, childish husband?

When she was well again, Catherine began to make her plans. She reread her books about the Roman emperors and the ways they controlled their people. She spent hours talking to the empress's officials. They were impressed by her intelligence, and her understanding of affairs of state. Meanwhile, Peter drank more than ever. He staggered through the palace, screaming at the top of his lungs, beating his dogs and sometimes his servants in uncontrollable rages.

The old empress began to grow weaker. In December of 1761, sixteen years after Catherine's wedding, she took to her bed. Soon she was unable to move. She summoned Peter to her bedside. "Rule Russia well," she whispered. "Be kind to the servants. Watch over your son." Her eyes closed. But she still breathed. The whole court waited for days while the old woman lay motionless. Finally, on Christmas Day, the empress died. Peter Ulrich had become Czar Peter III of Russia.

Catherine did nothing. She was expecting another baby, and she was too tired and weak to lead a revolt. But she had waited sixteen years in this cold, strange country. She could wait a little bit longer.

Catherine the Great

The Empress Elizabeth's body was dressed in silver lace and a golden crown and taken to St. Petersburg's largest cathedral. For six weeks, services were held to mourn the empress's death. By the end of the six weeks, the body smelled terrible!

But Catherine pretended not to notice. She went to the cathedral every day. She wanted all of St. Petersburg to see how faithful and devout she was. Meanwhile, the new Czar didn't even bother to weep. He threw huge feasts and told the court not to wear mourning clothes. When he visited the empress's body in the cathedral, he told jokes and laughed loudly!

Now that Peter was in charge of the army, he announced that the soldiers would have to become more like Prussian soldiers. Peter had always loved the Prussian army. But the Russian soldiers had fought against the Prussian army for years, and hated Prussians! Peter didn't care. He declared that the Russians would have to get rid of their uniforms and dress more like Prussian soldiers. He planned to teach them to march and fight like Prussians. The soldiers were indignant. Many of them began to whisper that Catherine, who had often visited them in their army barracks, would make a better ruler than her husband.

By the time Catherine had her second baby, the army was almost ready to rebel against Peter. They hated their new uniforms and the new Prussian customs. And Peter had just ordered them to do something loathsome. He needed money for the royal treasury—so he sent the army out to seize land owned by the Russian Orthodox Church. He planned to sell this land and keep the money!

Church leaders protested. The Church had owned this land for hundreds of years! But Peter refused to listen. He ordered the soldiers to search Orthodox monasteries for treasure, even inside the monks' cells, and take everything that they found. Many of his soldiers were devout Orthodox Christians. They obeyed their czar—but they hated carrying out his commands.

Meanwhile, Catherine was recovering from the birth of her baby. In just a few weeks, she attended her first public banquet. Hundreds of guests—army officers, ambassadors from France and Prussia, state ministers—sat at long tables, glittering with silverware and golden dishes. Peter sat on a raised dais, drinking wine. He grew drunker, louder, and wilder as the night went on. At the end of the banquet, Peter lurched to his feet and screamed at Catherine, "Fool! Idiot! If I want to, I can throw you in prison for the rest of your life!"

Peter had finally gone too far. The army loved Catherine and hated their czar. The word spread through the army: It is time to put the empress on the throne.

On the morning of June 28th, 1762, Catherine got up early and dressed like an empress. Peter was away from St. Petersburg, staying at another town. The soldiers planned to surround the town so that the czar could not send for help, and then proclaim Catherine empress.

When Catherine was dressed, she went to the barracks of the soldiers and told them that she was afraid Peter would arrest her and send her into exile. Most of them knelt to kiss her hands. A few yelled, "Paul! Paul! The czar should be replaced by his son, not by his wife!" But the rest of the army followed Catherine through the streets of St. Petersburg, shouting, *"Vivat! Vivat!"* That meant, "Long live the new empress!"

Catherine went to the cathedral of St. Petersburg and asked the head priest of Petersburg, the Metropolitan, to bless her. The Metropolitan hated what Peter had done to the Russian Orthodox Church. He prayed over Catherine and pronounced her Empress! All over St. Petersburg, church bells rang. The people of St. Petersburg poured out of their houses to find out what was happening. Most were glad to hear that they were no longer ruled by the unpredictable, savage Peter!

In the meantime, the czar found himself surrounded! He tried to rally the army to his side, but as the day went on, Peter saw that the soldiers were no longer loyal to him. He spent the whole night drinking. By morning, he had realized that his throne was lost. He signed a paper, agreeing to give up his throne, and sent Catherine a letter. "Let me leave Russia," the letter begged, "and go live in Prussia, a country I have always loved!"

But Catherine knew that if Peter went to Prussia, he might be able to convince the Prussians to invade Russia and help him take his throne back. So she ordered her allies to take Peter to one of his palaces and guard him there.

Just a week after Catherine became empress of Russia, she received a scribbled note from one of the officers who was watching over Peter. "He is no longer in the world!" the letter began. "He started a quarrel with Prince Baritainsky at dinner, and before we could separate them, he was dead."

The ex-czar had been murdered.

His guards claimed that Peter had started a fight with Prince Baritainsky, one of the noblemen Catherine had sent to watch over him. The two had struggled. An accidental blow had killed Peter.

Catherine issued a proclamation to the people of St. Petersburg, announcing that the emperor had died suddenly of a stomach upset. "This is the will of God," the proclamation read. "The body will lie in state so that the people can pay their respects."

Thousands of people traveled to see Peter's body. But as they began to file by, loud gasps of horror rose into the air. Peter's face was purple. The body had a large cravat wrapped around its throat so that no one could see it. The emperor had obviously been strangled.

Strangled? The guards claimed he had died in a sudden fight. What had really happened? Had Catherine ordered her husband killed? Had she simply mentioned how good it would be if Peter were dead—so that her guards would act on her hint? No one knew—and Catherine never spoke of her husband's death afterward. But many Russians noticed that she didn't punish anyone!

Now Catherine was empress of all Russia. For the next thirty years, she would rule over her adopted country with as much energy as Peter the Great himself. She worked fifteen hours every day to make Russia stronger and bigger. Under her reign, Russia's borders expanded. The Russian army claimed the land of Alaska, north of Canada, took land away from the Turks and the Mongols, and seized part of Poland.

Like Peter the Great, Catherine liked many of the ideas of the West. She admired the French philosopher Voltaire, who wrote about equality and liberty, and wrote him many letters. She brought many Western customs to Russia. She rewrote Russia's confusing, ancient laws so that her people would have more rights. She told her ministers of state that no one could be tortured for information. She opened new schools and started the first college for Russian women. She even made a woman the director of the Russian Academy of Sciences. Catherine opened new hospitals and brought in doctors from the West to improve the health of the Russian people. Catherine's people began calling her "Catherine the Great!"

But although Catherine liked to think of herself as a modern, "Enlightened" empress, she didn't want the people of Russia to have the same rights as citizens of the United States or France. For Catherine, "equality" meant that all Russians had to obey the same laws. But the empress still got to *make* those laws, and she didn't have to ask anyone's permission! Catherine kept a close eye on her court during the French Revolution, looking for signs that the "French infection" had spread to Russia. She didn't hesitate to get rid of anyone she thought might be a threat to her power. One French philosopher, invited to visit Catherine's court, refused with the words, "I am not anxious to go to a country where people are apt to die so suddenly!"

By the end of Catherine's reign, Russia was a strong and wealthy empire. But Catherine had given her noblemen even

256

more power over the peasants and serfs who lived on their land—and these poor Russians had grown hungrier and more ragged than ever before. The "French infection" had not brought liberty and equality to Russia.

Europe and America in the Eighteenth Century

258

Chapter Twenty-Seven
A Changing World

Steam and Coal in Britain

Imagine that you're walking along a dusty dirt road, between two rows of poplar trees. The branches that stretch over the road are just beginning to bud with pale green spring leaves. A bird sings high above you, the sound carried to you on a chilly morning breeze. Just ahead of you lies an English village. The church bell is ringing: eight clear tones. It's still early in the morning, but the villagers are already hard at work.

At the edge of the village, the trees open up into fields. Two oxen pull a plow near the road's edge. Further off in the distance, you can just see a single horse pulling a seed drill. Farmers walk behind their machines, keeping the animals in a straight line. Stone walls close off the fields; against the rough gray of the nearest wall, two young men are shearing a flock of unhappy sheep. A pile of wool grows nearby. Three small children scurry back and forth, carrying the wool in baskets.

You hear a gentle *thump, thump, thump* from a cottage that sits beside the road. You peer through a window. A woman sits spinning wool into heavy thread. On the other side of the room, her husband bends over a loom, weaving cloth from the wool thread; the shuttle thumps against the loom's sides each time he passes it between the threads. A fire burns on the hearth. Beside the house, a young boy is chopping up stumps; each swing of the axe splits off another piece of firewood.

A *clang, clang, clang* sounds from further down the street. A blacksmith is making horseshoes. An apprentice blows at his fire with bellows, pushing the handles up and down and sweating despite the chill. The blacksmith swings his hammer over his head and beats at his softened iron, shaping it into a crescent. At the end of the village street, a windmill's sails revolve gently in the breeze. The miller inside is minding the grindstones, turned by the sails, as they grind the village's wheat into flour.

Muscle power makes the machines and tools in this village work! All over England, human and animal muscles produce the goods and food that Englishmen eat and use. Together, the people of a village can also harness the power of the wind; a village near a stream might be able to use a waterwheel instead.

A new source of power—neither muscle, wind, or water—will soon change village life.

In 1769, a Scotsman named James Watt perfected a machine called a steam engine. The steam engine works in a very simple way. Water is heated in a closed metal bowl called a *boiler.* When the water boils, it turns into steam. Steam takes up more space than water, so the steam pushes to get out of the bowl. The only way out of the bowl is through a narrow pipe called a *cylinder,* but the cylinder is blocked by a circular piece of metal called a *piston.* When the steam tries to go through the cylinder, it pushes the piston up. Then the steam cools off, condenses back into water, and falls back down into the boiler. The piston falls back down too. This happens over and over, so that the piston moves regularly up and down. The motion of the piston can be used to run machines!

The steam engine had been invented a hundred years before by a French scientist and built seventy years before by an English inventor. But James Watt figured how to make the steam engine put out more power for less fuel. Now steam could be used to run machines—mills for grinding grain, engines to pull plows and heavy loads, bellows, water pumps, even ships!

The steam engine changed the West just as much as ideas about liberty and equality did. Steam could run so many more machines so much more quickly than human muscles, windmills, or waterwheels! People grow tired, wind dies down, and drought dries up streams. But steam engines would run as long as they had coal.

As steam engines became more popular, more and more coal was needed to feed them. But although steam engines ran machines faster than ever, coal was still mined by hand. Miners had to dig tunnels down into the ground where coal lay and chop it out by hand. Deep down in the ground, there wasn't enough air for the miners to breathe. The miners tried to let air into the tunnels through trapdoors, but they still might stumble into airless pockets of the mine—and suffocate before they could get out! The miners called this lack of air "chokedamp." Even worse than chokedamp was "firedamp." Coal puts out a gas called *methane*. When methane built up in corners of coal mines, it would explode with a little bang. But that little bang would fill the air with coal dust, which acted like gunpowder and exploded again in huge shattering blasts that killed miners and collapsed tunnels.

Miners could be killed by suffocation, explosion, or tunnel collapse. But even those who survived often died later from a disease called "blacklung." After years of breathing coal dust into their lungs, miners couldn't breathe properly any more. They died when their lungs could no longer pull in enough oxygen to keep them alive! Miners used to sing, "I used to be a drill man, 'til it got the best of me....And now I've eaten so much dust that it's akillin' me!"

Women and children breathed coal dust too. Women pulled loads of coal out of the tunnels while the men worked. Children sat down in the pitch black of the mine, opening and closing the trapdoors that helped air move through the mine. "I have to trap without a light," one little girl, only eight, explained. "I'm scared, so sometimes I sing."

Coal miners hauled coal out of the mines for the steam engines. But then the coal had to be carried to the machines! Tons of coal were floated down England's rivers on barges. But what about machines that weren't near the water?

The answer: Railroads! A steam engine hooked to a train would burn coal to keep itself running—but by using a little bit of coal, it could pull tons more all the way across the country.

As steam engines grew more and more popular, railroads were built across more and more land. Farmers objected to the railroads. "All that noise will keep our cows

261

from giving milk!" they complained. "The chickens will stop laying eggs. The crops will wilt!" But railroad builders ignored these objections. Soon, coal trains were joined by passenger trains. Steam engines could take people from place to place much faster than horses and carriages! Millions of people began to use trains and to travel farther and farther away from home. Steam power was beginning to change life in England. And soon this change would spread across Europe and over to North America.

Cotton and Guns in America

Steam ran pumps and bellows, ships and trains. Over in America, it would soon run a new kind of machine: the cotton gin.

The warm, damp fields of the southern United States were perfect for cotton plants. Thread spun from cotton was used all over the world! Plantation owners could grow huge, healthy cotton plants covered with valuable cotton blooms. When the cotton fields were ready to harvest, slaves and hired men moved along the rows, plucking the fluffy cotton balls and dropping them into huge sacks.

But the cotton balls weren't soft and smooth like the ones you can now buy at a drugstore. They were filled with seeds. And the seeds were covered with little hooks, like sharp pieces of Velcro. Before the cotton could be used, all of the seeds had to be pulled out of the cotton balls, one at a time. One slave could work all day and only clean the seeds out of a single pound of cotton!

A college boy from Massachusetts named Eli Whitney came south, after the American Revolution, and set up his workshop near a plantation. Eli liked machines, and he liked solving problems. He watched the slaves struggle to pull the clinging, hooked seeds out of cotton blossoms. "There must be a better way to do that," Eli Whitney thought. And he started to experiment with different kinds of rollers and blades.

No one knows exactly how Eli Whitney solved the problem of cotton seeds. But according to a story told afterward, Eli was sitting on the back porch of a nearby plantation, idly watching chickens in a wire pen. A cat sat next to the pen, watching the chickens and hoping to make a meal of one of them. When a careless chicken wandered over to the edge of the pen, the cat pushed his paw through the wire and extended his claws. The claws scraped the chicken and pulled its feathers right off!

The chicken ran off squawking with a patch of bare skin. The cat stalked off with nothing but feathers. But Whitney had his idea.

He went back to his workshop and built a metal roller with teeth that rubbed up against a metal grill. The roller, turned by a handle, pulled up cotton and scraped it across the grill. The seeds dropped away. Now, a slave who turned the handle of this new machine, called a *cotton gin*, could clean fifteen or twenty pounds of cotton per day. A plantation owner who lived near a stream could hook the cotton gin to a water wheel and clean a thousand pounds of cotton per day. A steam engine could clean the cotton even faster!

With the help of the cotton gin, cotton growers could make more money than they ever dreamed. Plantation owners planted larger fields and bought more slaves. In the years to come, cotton would become the biggest industry of the South—and increase slavery a hundredfold.

Whitney wasn't finished inventing. He wanted to solve another problem too.

This problem had nothing to do with cotton. The United States government wanted the United States Army to have better guns. Guns were made by hand, one at a time. The parts of each gun fit *only* that gun—no other! If a trigger broke or a barrel twisted, the soldier who owned the gun would have to take it to a gunsmith and wait for a new part to be made.

Eli Whitney wondered: Why weren't guns designed so that every gun had the same size barrel, the same size trigger, and the same size bayonet? Then, he could make a hundred barrels, a hundred triggers, and a hundred bayonets. If part of a gun broke, the soldier could just grab a replacement part and put it in.

This probably seems like plain old common sense to you. Today, we're used to having parts that fit the same in any machine. A new light bulb will fit into any lamp or ceiling light in your house. If you have a pencil sharpener in your house, you can buy pencils in any city—and they'll fit into the sharpener. If you buy any roll of toilet paper from any grocery store, it will fit into your own toilet paper holder in your own bathroom! This is called *standardization*. Standardization means that parts are *interchangeable*. A light bulb from General Electric can be interchanged with a light bulb made by another company. Both will work!

But back in 1797, standardization was a brand new idea. Eli Whitney had to show a group of American government officials a whole stack of his new gun parts and invite them to put together a gun, using any of the parts. The officials—including Thomas Jefferson—chose their parts and started to fit them together. All of the parts snapped into place! The officials were delighted. They told Whitney to build a gun factory which could make guns for the whole United States army.

Eli Whitney claimed that his system of interchangeable parts was "unknown in Europe." Soon this way of making parts was called the "American system." Actually, a French inventor had already thought of this—but it was Whitney's factory that became famous. Soon, interchangeable parts were used for all sorts of goods: clocks, farm machinery, and cotton gins! The idea of interchangeable parts would soon help factories to spread across North America, just as cotton fields were spreading in the South. Like steam power, Whitney's two inventions would help to change everyday life forever.

China During the Rule of Chi'en-lung

Chapter Twenty-Eight
China and the Rest of the World

The Kingdom at the Center of the World

For sixty years, the emperor Chi'en-lung had reigned over China. He ruled in Peking while the Americans fought for independence, while Captain Cook sailed along the coast of Australia, and while the Bastille fell. When Eli Whitney invented the cotton gin, Chi'en-lung was still reigning in China.

While countries in the West invented steam machines and settled colonies, Chi'en-lung looked on without interest. China needed nothing from the West! The Chinese believed that the universe was centered on China. They called themselves the Central Civilization. Western ideas about equality and liberty didn't seem to have much to do with China, where the Manchu emperor ruled as the Son of Heaven and lived in his Forbidden City, far away from commoners. And the Chinese weren't particularly interested in Western inventions either. Western scientists wanted to find out about the laws of nature, so that they could force wheat, cows, steam, and cotton to serve people and their needs. But the Chinese had long followed the teachings of Confucius, who taught that the Chinese should accept nature and learn from it in a harmonious way, not try to master it.

So Chi'en-lung didn't send ambassadors to England and Russia, or build Chinese trading ships to go abroad. And he didn't allow Western ambassadors and merchants to roam through China, either. He announced that foreign ships could only come to one Chinese port: the port of Guangzhou, which the English called Canton. Foreigners who came to China had to follow laws called the Eight Regulations. The Eight Regulations told merchants exactly what they could and could not do. No foreign women were allowed to visit the warehouses on the dock at Canton. No foreign merchant was allowed to speak directly to a Chinese official; instead, he had to ask a Chinese merchant to speak for him. Traders had to leave China at the end of the trading season and go home. Foreigners were forbidden to buy Chinese books or learn the Chinese language!

Unfortunately for the British, they needed China much more than China needed them! The English loved their tea. Fifteen million pounds of tea every year came from China to Britain! And the English also wanted China's silks and spices. They wanted English ships to be allowed into all of China's ports.

So in 1793, George III sent an ambassador to China to ask Emperor Chi'en-lung to change the Eight Regulations. This ambassador was an earl named George Macartney. Macartney was an experienced ambassador. He had been all over the world on missions for George III. In Russia, Catherine the Great had liked him so much that she gave him a royal keepsake: a tobacco box studded with precious jewels.

As he sailed into Canton, Macartney shook his head at the muddy shores and shabby docks. How could any country refuse to send its ships all over the world for trade? How could an emperor still call himself the Son of Heaven, in an age when kings were asking their people for permission to rule? He told a friend, "The Empire of China is [like] an old, crazy…man-of-war [ship], which…has contrived to keep afloat for these one hundred and fifty years past, and to overawe their neighbours merely by her bulk and appearance….She may perhaps not sink outright; she may drift some time as a wreck and will then be dashed to pieces on the shore."

When Macartney arrived, he was expecting to be ushered to the emperor's palace and treated with respect, as the ambassador of the great British Empire. He didn't understand that the Chinese didn't see him as an ambassador at all! The emperor didn't receive ambassadors; that would mean accepting that other kings were as great as he was. Visitors to Chi'en-lung's court were bearers of tribute, not ambassadors!

Chi'en-lung ordered Macartney to come visit him at a *yurt*—a skin-covered tent near his favorite hunting lodge. Macartney had brought a whole ship full of English merchandise to show the emperor how much China could get through trade with Britain. He had brought telescopes, guns, chiming clocks, musical instruments, and a hot-air balloon, along with a balloonist who could give the emperor a ride. It took ninety wagons and forty wheelbarrows to unload all of it! But Chi'en-lung, treating all of these goods as gifts to his royal person, ordered that they be left at a nearby summer palace.

Without his goods, Macartney pressed on to the yurt. Finally, he was ushered into the presence of the emperor, the Son of Heaven. There was a short silence, while all of the Chinese courtiers gathered around waited, expectantly. Macartney was supposed to *kowtow*—to get down on his hands and knees and knock his forehead against the floor nine times to show the emperor's greatness.

Macartney had known that he would be expected to kowtow. So he had brought along a huge, life-sized oil painting of George III. "Great Emperor," he said, "if the men of your court will kowtow to my king, I will kowtow to you."

The Chinese weren't about to kowtow to the painting of a barbarian. So Macartney stayed on his feet too! He handed over the official letter from George III and explained that Britain wanted to send an ambassador to China to live in Peking. British ships wanted to sail into ports all up and down China's huge coast. The British wanted to build trading posts and settlements where English merchants could live year round.

But Chi'en-lung looked over the letter and shook his head. He motioned for his secretary. He would write a letter back to the English king, refusing every single one of the requests.

The letter read, "O King, you live beyond many seas. However, driven by your humble wish to take part in the glorious benefits of our civilization, you have respectfully sent your messenger, bearing your tokens of good will. This messenger has crossed the seas to pay me respects on my birthday. And you have sent offerings of the goods of your country to show your devotion to me. But we have no need of your goods. Strange and costly objects like these do not interest me; we possess all things. Our ways have nothing to do with

269

yours. Even if your messenger were competent enough to acquire some basic ways of ours, he could not then perform them in your barbarous country. We cannot do the things that you ask."

With that, Chi'en-lung sent Macartney back to England. The Kingdom at the Center of the World would not obey Britain's commands!

The Rise of the Opium Trade

The British had failed to convince the Emperor to open China's ports. English merchants were spending enormous amounts of money to buy tea, silk, and porcelain from China—but the Chinese weren't buying British goods in exchange.

What did England have that China wanted? There *was* one thing…opium.

Opium was a drug made from poppy juice, pressed into tablets or stirred into syrup. English doctors gave it to patients who were in pain. But opium did more than take away pain. It made patients feel peaceful and serene and sometimes gave them beautiful visions that lasted for days and days. "It Prevents and takes away Grief, Fear, Anxieties, Peevishness, Fretfulness," one English doctor explained.

Opium brought peace and took away pain, but it also made patients dull and confused. "It stupifies the Sense of Feeling," the same doctor warned, "[and] causes Stupidity…[and] Cloudiness." That wasn't the worst thing about taking opium, though. Patients who took it wanted more. The more they took, the less it worked, so they took larger and larger amounts. Then they couldn't stop. They had become addicts. An "opium eater" who wanted to quit would suffer from "Great, and even intolerable Distresses, Anxieties, and Depressions of Spirits, which in a few days commonly end in a most miserable Death, attended with strange Agonies, unless Men return to the use of Opium; which soon raises them again."

Many English men and women had become addicted to opium. At first, it seemed to promise them peace and beauty. The English poet Samuel Taylor Coleridge took opium because he had such wonderful visions! During one opium vision, he saw a fantastic scene that he described in poetry:

In Xanadu did Kubla Khan
A stately pleasure-dome decree:
Where Alph, the sacred river, ran
Through caverns measureless to man
Down to a sunless sea....
And there were gardens bright with sinuous rills,
Where blossomed many an incense-bearing tree;
And here were forests ancient as the hills,
Enfolding sunny spots of greenery....
Five miles meandering with a mazy motion
Through wood and dale the sacred river ran,
Then reached the caverns measureless to man,
And sank in tumult to a lifeless ocean....
It was a miracle of rare device,
A sunny pleasure-dome with caves of ice!

No one knows what this poem means—because opium visions seemed to make perfect sense while you were having them, but didn't make sense once you woke up!

The East India Company, which was owned by Britain, grew poppies in India. There, Indian workers made the poppy juice into opium and packed it onto ships which set out to China. Opium was sold through the port of Canton—and smuggled into other ports as well! The Chinese learned that smoking opium in pipes made the visions and the feelings of peace even stronger. They wanted more and more opium.

When the emperor saw what was happening, he made opium illegal. No British ships were to bring opium to China! For the Chinese to be "continually...sunk into the most stupid and besotted state," he declared, "is an injury to the manners and minds of men."

The British kept right on shipping opium into China—in secret. Finally, they were making money from Chinese trade. A chest of opium would sell for the same amount of money that a

London policeman would earn in three *years* of work! The British official in charge of India, who saw how much money India could earn by growing poppies, did his best to send even more opium. But even while he sent opium to China, he wrote to other Englishmen that opium was a "pernicious" drug which should be made illegal in India. He would sell the drug to the Chinese, but he didn't want his British subjects in India to smoke it!

More and more opium flooded into China. Merchants fought with each other to buy the opium and resell it for a profit. At first, only rich people had smoked opium, but now shopkeepers, soldiers, and even servants smoked the long pipes packed with poppy. In houses called *opium dens*, they lay on mats, smoked, and drifted away into week-long dreams filled with strange beasts and whirling colors. Opium poured money into English pockets, but laid waste to the south of China; Chi'en-lung had refused to let foreign ideas and merchants into his country, but he had not been able to keep the foreign poison out.

France During the Reign of Napoleon Bonaparte

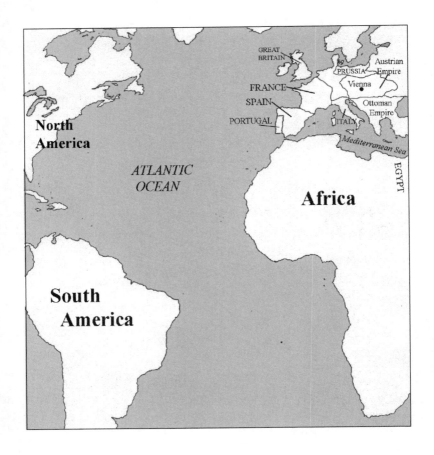

Chapter Twenty-Nine
The Rise of Bonaparte

Napoleon Comes to Power

While the British king and the Chinese emperor exchanged letters, the country without a king found itself ruled by a dictator.

After Robespierre was sent to the guillotine, the National Convention of France gave up on making France into a country governed by all of its people. The Revolution had removed the king and gotten rid of aristocrats—but it had also thrown the country into bloody years of war. Instead, the National Convention made France into an *oligarchy*—a country where only some of the citizens have power to rule. All soldiers and all Frenchmen who owned a certain amount of land were allowed to vote for leaders. These leaders were put in two houses, like the American Senate and House of Representatives. In France, though, the houses were called the Council of Ancients and the Council of Five Hundred. Together, the two houses chose five men to belong to a committee called the Directory. The Directory ruled France.

The Directory's first job was to protect France from the country of Austria, which had declared war on France during the Revolution and was still trying to invade it! The Directory needed one of France's generals to lead the French army in an attack on Austria.

The general they chose was named Napoleon Bonaparte.

Napoleon Bonaparte had already earned a name for himself. Several years before, Robespierre had sent Napoleon to round up hundreds of Frenchmen loyal to the king in the south of France. Then Robespierre had ordered them all killed. So Napoleon turned his cannons on them and then guillotined the rest. "If a man has to take sides in such a battle," he told his brother later, "he might as well take the victorious side. It is better to eat than be eaten." Napoleon Bonaparte would do anything to be on the victorious side!

When he got his orders from the Directory, Napoleon marched his army down into Italy. At that time, Italy was a whole collection of separate little states, and Austria controlled most of the northern part—the part close to France. If the French army could drive the Austrians back, France's border would be safe.

Napoleon's troops were sick of fighting. They were hungry and ragged, and their salaries hadn't been paid for months. They muttered and complained and wanted to go home. But Napoleon was ready to whip up their fighting spirits. "Soldiers!" he cried. "You are hungry and naked. But we are going to rich towns where you will find honor, glory—and wealth! Be courageous and you will have these things!"

Filled with visions of untold wealth, the soldiers followed Napoleon into battle. The Austrians were forced to retreat! Napoleon took control of northern Italy and announced to all the Italian people that France had come to set them free from their Austrian captors. "We come to break your chains!" he shouted. "We have quarrels only with the tyrants who have been holding you captive!" Then Napoleon ordered all of Italy's great paintings and statues sent back to France to be put in the Louvre in Paris. Many great Italian works of art are still in Paris today! Napoleon also announced that he respected the Catholic Church and would not rob any churches—but he *would* take their gold and silver vessels and their priceless paintings and "keep them safe." Perhaps it was then that an Italian saying became common: "Not all Frenchmen are robbers—but a good many sure are!"

Then Napoleon led the French army on toward Vienna, the capital of Austria. Vienna had stood against the Turks, but the Austrians didn't think they could beat back Napoleon. They gave him the countries of Belgium and Lombardy and swore a peace treaty with him.

Napoleon marched home in triumph. He was invited to parties and feasts, parades and ceremonies. He insisted that he had acted only for the good of France and its government. But to his close friends, he scoffed, "I am but at the opening of my career….Do you suppose that I have gained my victories in Italy in order to advance the lawyers of the Directory?"

The five members of the Directory knew perfectly well that Napoleon wanted power for himself. So they told him that his next task was to invade Great Britain.

Napoleon knew that invading Great Britain was the best possible way to get himself killed. Britain had the strongest navy in the world, and the French army was weak and tired. He suggested that it would be better to invade Egypt. After all, the Turks who ruled Egypt had never been friends of France. The Directory agreed. Egypt was far away from France, so Napoleon would be gone a long time.

Napoleon's men sailed down to Egypt. Meanwhile, the admiral of the English navy, Admiral Horatio Nelson, heard from his spies that the French were heading off to attack— something! He sailed through the Mediterranean, looking for Napoleon. He wanted to make sure that the French weren't attacking any English colonies or possessions.

Meanwhile, Napoleon landed in Egypt and invaded the cities of Alexandria and Cairo. "I have come to restore your rights and fight against the Turks who hold you captive!" he told the Egyptians. "I respect Muhammad and the Koran far more than they ever did!"

But Napoleon didn't have much time to enjoy his victory. The British navy finally caught up with him. The two navies fought; at this "Battle of the Nile," most of Napoleon's ships were captured. Napoleon left his soldiers behind, boarded a small ship which sneaked past the British navy in a thick Mediterranean fog, and sailed back to France. When Napoleon returned to Paris, the French—who weren't really sure what had happened in Egypt—again hailed him as a hero.

Napoleon was ready to take control.

With armed soldiers behind him waving their bayonets, Napoleon marched into the Council of Ancients and announced that the Directory was now too weak to protect France. Seeing all the bayonets, the Council of Ancients agreed—quickly—to remove the Directory and replace it with three consuls, just as in ancient Rome. Of course, one of the consuls was Napoleon himself. And it wasn't too long before Napoleon became the *only* Consul of France.

Some French citizens knew that they had exchanged a king for a dictator who would use his soldiers to do exactly as he pleased. But France had been torn by war, bloodshed, and suspicion for so long that most French were simply grateful that someone was going to bring some order into chaos. Napoleon himself believed that the French would give him power as long as he gave them safety, strength, and enough to eat. "A Republic?" he remarked to his friends. "What a notion!...[T]he French are infatuated [with the idea of liberty] but it will pass away in time....What they want is glory and the gratification of their vanity; as for liberty, of that they have no conception."

The Emperor Napoleon

Napoleon, the Consul of France, now ruled in Paris. The people of France still had the right to vote, but their votes didn't really matter; Napoleon and his Council of State had all of the power. Napoleon set out to rewrite the ancient, confusing laws of France so that France would be an orderly and law-abiding place. This new law code, the Napoleonic Code, ordered each person to be treated equally by the law—with some exceptions. If an employee had a disagreement with his boss, the boss would always win. And women had no rights at all. "Women should stick to knitting," Napoleon observed.

Napoleon then set about winning the loyalty of the Catholic Church. He told the pope that Catholics could worship as they pleased in France, and that France would even pay Catholic priests appointed by the Church—as long as they swore loyalty to Napoleon. The pope agreed. He also promised to add a new question and answer to the official Church teaching, or *catechism*:

Question: What should one think of those who fail to honor the emperor and do their duty to him?

Answer: They are resisting the order established by God Himself and are earning themselves eternal damnation.

Napoleon did not intend for anyone to resist *his* order!

Three years after becoming consul, Napoleon told his council to make him consul for life. He wrote a constitution that would govern France. But this constitution wasn't like the English or American constitutions. The new French constitution said that Napoleon could make any laws he wanted, declare wars himself, and decide on France's policies all alone. Napoleon ordered the people to vote on this constitution. Then he declared that the constitution had passed—three million votes to two thousand! (Napoleon made up those numbers himself.)

Napoleon was ready to expand his kingdom over more of Europe. But first he needed money. So in 1803, he offered all of France's land in North America to the United States. This "Louisiana Territory" was an enormous piece of land that stretched from the French colony of New Orleans up through the Midwest, through land where Arkansas, Missouri, Kansas, Nebraska, and other states now lie, all the way up into Canada. Except for New Orleans, no French settlers lived in this land. Napoleon knew that he wouldn't be able to start colonies and conquer Europe at the same time. So he sold the whole piece to the United States for fifteen million dollars. This "Louisiana Purchase" doubled the size of the United States in one day!

Then Napoleon decided that he should have the title of Emperor, with the right to pass the title on to any heir he chose. So he planned himself a huge coronation ceremony. He sat on a golden throne in the Cathedral of Notre Dame, holding a sword which he claimed had belonged to Charlemagne, the first Holy Roman Emperor. Then he took a golden crown of laurel leaves, put it on his own head, and proclaimed himself Emperor.

Now the Emperor Napoleon was ready to conquer an empire for himself. He planned to start with France's old enemy: Britain.

France arrested all British citizens in France. The British seized all French ships in British waters. French and

British ships prowled the seas, shooting at each other. Meanwhile, Napoleon started to build hundreds of boats on which he could load 150,000 soldiers who would row across the channel and invade England. They weren't very good boats; Napoleon was fairly sure that at least 20,000 men would drown on the way over. "But I would lose that many in a battle anyway," he explained, and went on building.

The English saw the boat building and prepared to fight back against "Boney's invasion." All over England, men were

pressed, or drafted, into the navy, and taught to be sailors on British warships that would fight against Napoleon. British soldiers readied themselves to fight off French invaders. Even England's farmers were ready to grab their pitchforks and fight against the French!

When the time for invasion came, Napoleon ordered his admiral to sail the French warships out into the English Channel and fight against the English fleet. Once the Channel was cleared of English warships, the flat, slow barges full of French soldiers could row safely across.

The commander of the English fleet was Admiral Horatio Nelson—the same admiral who had beaten Napoleon once before at the Battle of the Nile. He sailed his own ships out to meet the French, with his flagship the *Victory* in the lead. The signal flags on the *Victory* spelled out, "England expects that every man will do his duty!" The battle began off the coast of Spain. Nelson's ships outsailed and outfought the French. Not a single English ship sank. But twenty-two of Napoleon's ships had been captured; the rest fled. The boats with soldiers in them never even launched.

Napoleon Bonaparte

Admiral Nelson had saved England from the new emperor. But during the battle he was hit by a musket ball as he stood on the deck of his ship. Nelson died a few hours later. The French admiral died too: when he saw how badly he had been defeated, he killed himself.

This sea battle, the Battle of Trafalgar, put limits on the new emperor's power. He would never take England. But over the next ten years, Napoleon would do his best to spread his power across the rest of Europe.

Saint Domingue During the Time of Toussaint L'Ouverture

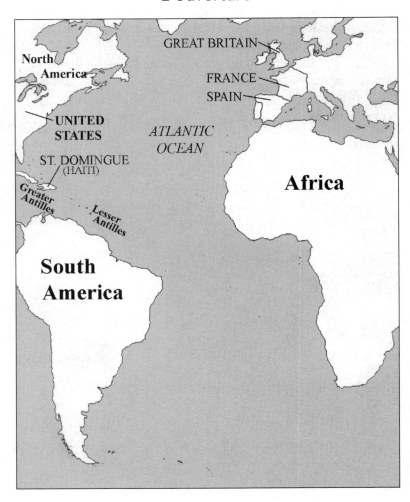

Chapter Thirty
Freedom in the Caribbean

The Haitian Revolt

Far away from Great Britain, a tiny island was about to defy the enormous strength of the Emperor Napoleon. And although it had no ships, no admirals, and few allies, the island of Saint Domingue would win its independence from France.

Saint Domingue lay in the north of the Caribbean Sea, above South America and below Florida. French settlers had lived on Saint Domingue for over a hundred years. They planted fields of sugar cane, squeezed the juice from the stalks, boiled it down into sugar, and shipped it to Europe and to North America. They grew coffee beans and harvested them. More and more coffee and sugar left Saint Domingue's ports. The planters grew richer and richer.

By the time Napoleon claimed power in France, this French colony was making almost half of the sugar used in the whole world—and almost half of the coffee. The planters and the colony leaders lived like French aristocrats. They dressed in silks and jewels and gave balls and parties. The western settlement, Cap-Francais, grew to be a city of twenty-five thousand, filled with theatres, huge mansions, and wide streets. The French called it the "Paris of the Antilles"! (*Antilles* was the name many people used for the cluster of islands between South and North America.) The planters of Saint Domingue grew so rich that the French courtiers at Versailles started to shake their heads and gossip about how much money was spent!

Meanwhile, slaves labored in the fields and sugar plants. Saint Domingue had thirty-six thousand white Europeans—and *half a million* African slaves.

Surrounded by all of these slaves (who were working hard and not getting any of the profit), the planters tried very hard to make sure that none of the Africans got any ideas about freedom or equality. French law said that a slave who earned his freedom would become a French citizen and have the rights of any Frenchman. But the laws of Saint Domingue said that everyone with African blood, slave or free, had to wear different clothes, sit in different parts of churches and other buildings, and be inside by nine o'clock every night. No one with African blood could become a goldsmith, or a jeweler, or an army officer, or a doctor. Slaves had no rights at all. They worked every day, often chained together, dying of weariness and illness, while more slaves arrived from Africa to replace them.

African slaves had only one comfort. They still gathered together to follow ancient African customs and to listen as African priests held ancient religious ceremonies. The planters who saw these religious ceremonies thought that the Africans were just dancing and singing. But while they danced and sang, the slaves were listening to their priests tell about the revolutions in France and in America—the revolutions that set men free. And while they danced, the slaves planned a rebellion.

On August 20th, 1791—three years after the Storming of the Bastille in France—the slaves broke out of their fields and their quarters. They set fire to every planter's mansion. They killed every planter they could find. They roamed across Saint Domingue, wrecking the fields where they had worked for so long.

One African, Toussaint L'Ouverture, watched the bands of slaves with worry. He saw no strategy, no attempt to make Saint Domingue free—just revenge. Toussaint had earned his freedom a few years before. Now, he helped the family of his old master to escape and then began to gather his own band of soldiers around him. Unlike most slaves, Toussaint had learned to read French. He knew a little bit about how armies should be run. He taught his men how to fight properly together.

Meanwhile, Spain had declared war on Napoleon. When Spanish soldiers came to Saint Domingue to help drive the rest of the French off the island, Toussaint joined them. Soon, he commanded four thousand men. Another ex-slave, Jean-Jacques Dessaline, became his lieutenant.

But Toussaint wasn't really an ally of Spain. He just wanted Saint Domingue to be free. When he realized that the Spanish who now occupied the island saw nothing wrong with keeping slaves, Toussaint announced that he would no longer fight for Spain. He would once again swear loyalty to France— to the France of the Revolution, the France which said all men should be equal.

The French, seeing a chance to get their island back, made Toussaint Lieutenant Governor of Saint Domingue. Toussaint turned his army against the Spanish and drove them out. Now he governed the island where he had once served as a slave!

Saint Domingue was wrecked. Towns were burned down. Roads were dug up. The fields had returned to weeds and young trees. Houses lay in ruins!

Toussaint announced that he would allow planters to return and that Africans must go back to work in the fields. But now, planters and Africans would work side by side. They would share the profits. No African could be whipped or punished.

Slowly, Saint Domingue began to produce sugar and coffee again.

But even though Toussaint claimed to be a loyal Frenchman, Napoleon refused to accept his loyalty. The Emperor hated Africans. He could not bear to leave an African governor in charge of the island which had once poured so much money into the pockets of France.

So Napoleon sent twenty thousand men to reconquer Saint Domingue! He put his own brother-in-law, Charles Victor Emmanuel Leclerc, in charge of the invasion.

On February 5, 1802, Leclerc's army landed on the island. Toussaint's soldiers fought back, killing thousands of Frenchmen. But Toussaint could see that his men would never be able to keep on fighting against the enormous forces of France. Leclerc promised Toussaint that he could retire to a plantation and turn the island over to Dessaline.

So Toussaint agreed to surrender. But instead of letting him settle peacefully down, Leclerc had him arrested at once.

The liberator of Saint Domingue was sent to a cold distant prison in the French Alps. He died there, less than a year later.

The people of Saint Domingue—four hundred thousand ex-slaves—waited nervously to see what Leclerc would do next. They didn't know that Napoleon had already sent his orders: They were all to be put back into slavery!

On a warm June morning, Leclerc was just finishing his breakfast when his aide appeared at the door of his quarters. "General!" the aide gasped. "Come quickly! Come and see."

Leclerc was puzzled. He followed the aide to the tent nearby where the French wounded lay, cared for by the army's doctor. Near the door, one of his officers lay on a cot. His face was drawn and yellow; his arms and legs shook.

"Yellow fever!" the aide gasped.

The French dreaded "yellow fever"—their name for *malaria*. Malaria was spread by mosquitoes in the warm tropical islands. Malaria gave its victims high fevers, chills, sweats, and hallucinations.

Malaria could kill a whole army.

In four weeks, four thousand French soldiers were dead. Leclerc himself grew ill. And as his army shrank, word got out among the ex-slaves of Saint Domingue: They were all to be returned to slavery.

At once, Toussaint's officers began plotting to begin the fight again. They would die rather than be enslaved once more! Leclerc sent desperate messages to France, begging Napoleon to send more men. He died before any help could arrive.

Instead, the English sailed into Saint Domingue's port, ready to help drive the French away. The surviving French commanders were forced to surrender. Jean-Jacques Dessaline declared the colony independent from France on January 1st, 1804. He renamed it "Haiti" and became its first ruler: Jacques I of Haiti. And then he pulled down the French flag and ripped out its white center. The flag of Haiti would no longer contain any white—the color of French kings. Instead, a red and black flag would fly over the new country.

Britain and the United States During the Rise of Factories

GREAT BRITAIN

ATLANTIC OCEAN

Boston
New York

UNITED STATES

Chapter Thirty-One
A Different Kind of Rebellion

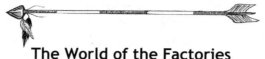

The World of the Factories

Do you remember walking down the road between the poplar trees, into the little English village where a weaver sat behind his loom and his wife spun thread? A nineteenth-century writer named Andrew Ure described the weaver's life as a healthy, happy way to earn money. The "dwelling and small gardens [were] clean and neat….the family well clad," he wrote. "The workshop of the weaver was a rural cottage from which, when he was tired of sedentary labour, he could sally forth into his little garden."

Across Europe, millions of people worked at home along with their whole families. If the mother and father wove cloth, the children worked too: a ten-year-old sorted cotton; a teenaged daughter spun thread; an older son tended the sheep and sheared their wool. Even a toddler might help by winding thread carefully onto a roll! When the family finished making their cloth, they would travel to market and sell it, using the money to buy food and tools. In the summer, they might spend more time tending their garden plot of carrots, cabbages, and beans; in the winter, when frost covered the ground, the family would go back to making cloth all day long.

Now let's go forward in time thirty years. Andrew Ure describes the very same village where the small gardens and cottages stood: "There are hundreds of factories….At the side of each factory there is a great chimney which belches forth black smoke and indicates the presence of the powerful steam engines….The houses have become black on account of the smoke. The river….is so tainted…that the water resembles the contents of a [black] dye-vat."

What has happened to England?

Factories are springing up all over the countryside. Now, machines can spin, weave, and knit better than the men and women who once made thread and cloth. Thanks to steam power, these machines never need to stop. Cloth is spun, woven and cut faster and faster and faster. Rich men, who might once have rented out their land to farmers, now have a better way to make money. They can buy a factory and hire workers to run the machines. The factory will make so much cloth that the owner can sell the cloth, pay the workers the same amount they would have earned making cloth at home, and still have plenty of money left over!

All over England, wealthy landowners began to buy and build factories. Soon, they discovered that they could sell the cloth made in factories much more cheaply than the cloth made by village workers in their homes. More and more people bought the cheap cloth, not the handmade cloth.

Now, weavers who worked at home couldn't get anyone to buy *their* cloth unless they sold it for less. Since they made less money from each piece, they had to work longer. Weavers worked for sixteen hours a day, their fingers sore and their eyes red—and still couldn't make enough money to buy food.

They had only one choice: leave their homes and go to work in the factories.

Today, most people "go to work." But back at the beginning of the nineteenth century, "going to work" was a brand new idea. Families had always worked together in their homes. Now, they were leaving their homes to go somewhere else in order to make a living.

The work at factories was different than the work at home. Weavers were used to making cloth from beginning to end: getting the wool, combing it, spinning it, weaving it, cutting it, and selling it. But in the factory, each worker only did one task—like tying threads on a spinning machine—over and over again, all day long.

An old-fashioned weaver didn't need anyone to *make* him work. If he made many pieces of cloth, he earned a lot of money when he sold his goods. If he was lazy or took a nap instead, he didn't make any money at all—and he went hungry! That was enough to make him work hard.

But in factories, workers couldn't be paid for each piece of cloth finished. Each worker was only doing one small part of the work. So they had to be paid by the hour instead. Now, someone had to watch over them to make sure that they spent all of their time working hard! These watchers were called *overseers*. Overseers treated factory workers with cruelty to make sure they were earning their money. Workers had to pay fines for looking out of windows, speaking to each other, or taking more than fifteen minutes to eat a meal. Sometimes they weren't allowed to go to the bathroom all day long!

All too soon, factory owners realized that women and children could run machines just as well as men—and that they were cheaper to hire! Men could no longer make a living working at home. Now, they often couldn't get factory jobs either. But children worked long hours so that their families would have enough money to live. They had to stand all day in front of machines—so long that many children had bow legs, deformed from standing. They had to pay fines if they talked or made faces at each other. In cotton factories, the cotton gave off fine white dust that the children breathed in all day. Their lungs quit working properly. Many of them died!

The English poet William Blake protested that the factories, or *mills*, were turning England from a "Jerusalem," a Christian kingdom, into a country that God would judge. He wrote,

> And did the Countenance Divine
> Shine down upon those clouded hills;
> And was Jerusalem builded here
> Among those dark Satanic mills?

The poet William Wordsworth complained that the lives of people were being sacrificed to make money:

> Men, maidens, youths,
> Mothers and little children, boys and girls,
> Enter, and each the wonted task resumes
> Within this temple, where is offered up

To Gain, the master idol of the realm,
Perpetual sacrifice.

The British government did try to pass some laws to make the factories better places. But the rich men who made money from the factories objected! They protested so loudly that only very weak laws could be passed. One law, or Factory Act, said that children could only work twelve hours per day! Another Factory Act said that a child had to be eight before going to work in a factory.

Now it was perfectly legal for an eight-year-old to work from sunrise to sunset in a factory. All over England—and soon, across Europe—children, women, and men worked long, cold, miserable hours, earning just enough money to buy food.

The Luddites

Not everyone objected to the spread of factories. Over in the United States, the politician Alexander Hamilton argued that factories were good for the country. In the old days, people who had never been trained to weave, farm, or work in some other craft became beggars or thieves. Now they could find work in the factories. Hamilton also thought that factory owners were doing a *good* thing when they hired children. "In general," he wrote, "women and children are rendered more useful, and the latter more early useful, by [factories], than they would otherwise be."

But weavers, spinners, and others who *were* trained in a craft had been pushed out of their jobs. Now, a skilled weaver who had once taken pride in making beautiful cloth had to go to a factory, work long hours in a badly-lit and noisy room, and perform one boring task over and over again.

In England, weavers and spinners began to attack factories and smash the machines that were changing their lives! They were joined by other workers—carpenters, blacksmiths, and tailors—who realized that factories might soon force *them* out of their livelihoods as well! An underground army formed. Their leader was a mysterious man who called himself "General Ned Ludd." No one knows who he was or why he chose this name. But all over England, workmen joined in General Ludd's Army. They became known as Luddites.

Luddites had their own regiments, weapons, and secret handshakes. They had a secret password: "Free Liberty!" They sang war songs as they marched up to factories, waving axes and hammers. "How gloomy and dark is the day, when men have to fight for their bread!" one song went. Another song warned:

> You tyrants of England,
> Your race may soon be run.
> You may be brought to account
> For what you've solely done.

Luddites broke hundreds of machines and shut down dozens of factories. To the poorest factory workers, Luddites were heroes! A popular song of the day began,

> Chant no more your old rhymes about bold Robin Hood
> His feats I but little admire.
> I will sing the Achievements of General Ludd
> Now the Hero of Nottinghamshire!

Today, people who are suspicious of new machines like computers are sometimes called Luddites. But the Luddites weren't just smashing the machines because they didn't like scientific discoveries and new advances. The Luddites were angry that their whole way of living was changing. They couldn't make a living at home any more. They *had* to work in the factories—or starve! And factory owners had the power to choose how much money the workers would make and how many hours they had to work. The workers themselves had no power at all. They couldn't demand to be paid a decent amount of money. They couldn't ask for shorter days or weekends off. They couldn't even ask for proper light and reasonable lunch breaks. They worked six days every week and sometimes a half day on Sunday too. England was so full of hungry people that factory owners could just fire anyone who complained and hire someone else!

The protests and the machine-breakings went on for years. But finally, the British government joined with the factory owners to stop the protests. New laws made breaking a factory machine a capital crime. Anyone who smashed a machine could be put to death! Soldiers were marched in to protect the factories. Workers were told that they were lucky to have work at all.

Many of them didn't feel lucky. "What with the heat and the hard work," one factory worker complained, "[it feels] as if the Devil was after us....We are told to be content in the station of Life to which the Lord has placed us. But I say the Lord never did place us there so we have no Right to be content."

Over in the United States, leaders such as Thomas Jefferson agreed. "While we have land to labor," Thomas Jefferson wrote back to Alexander Hamilton, "let us never wish to see our citizens occupied at a workbench....let our workshops remain in Europe." Jefferson thought that the United States would be a much better place to live if all of the cotton, wool, and wood were shipped over to Europe, to the factories there, and the finished goods were then shipped back. Factories, Jefferson complained, would "add just so much to the support of pure government, as sores do to the strength of the human body."

But businessmen in the United States couldn't resist the money that factories brought. Soon the factory system spread to the United States as well. Factories were built at the edges of the cities of Boston and New York. Factory workers lived near the factories, in tiny, shabby houses built just for them. Because they made so little money, two or three families might live together in a single house. So many people crowded to these "worker settlements," or *slums*, that cities couldn't keep up with building roads or laying down pipes for fresh water. Slums often had open sewers, where human waste mixed with the drinking water. Trash in the water decayed and gave off gases. The water became so foul and filled with gases that in hot weather it would actually catch on fire. Diseases like typhoid and cholera spread through the water and killed thousands of factory workers. In the city of Boston, an Irishman who had come from Britain to find factory work could expect to live only fourteen years before dying of overwork and disease. Thomas Jefferson was right. The factory slums had become "sores" on the body of the United States!

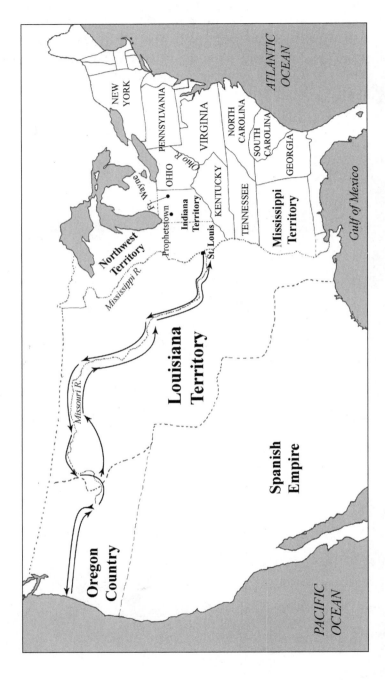

Lewis and Clark's Journey

Chapter Thirty-Two
The Opened West

Lewis and Clark Map the West

An American looking east might see slums around Boston and New York. But to the west lay a much more beautiful sight: vast fields, deep forests, and soaring mountains, just waiting for American settlers.

Directly west of the original thirteen states lay the midwestern territories. After the Revolution, Britain had given the United States all of the land east of the Mississippi. The thirteen colonies, now states, had agreed to divide this land into *territories*. When a territory had the same number of settlers as a state, it would be allowed to join the United States. So far, two states had been added: Tennessee and Kentucky. The rest of this land still lay in three territories: the Indiana Territory, the Northwest Territory, and the Mississippi Territory.

Then Thomas Jefferson, who had become President in 1801, bought the Louisiana Territory from Napoleon. Now, the United States had even more western land, stretching out far beyond the Mississippi! Jefferson wanted Americans to build towns and farms across all of this land. But before he could send settlers out into the West, he needed to know what was out there. No one was sure what the land on the other side of the Mississippi really looked like.

Jefferson hired two explorers to travel across the Louisiana Territory and map it out. Meriwether Lewis was an army captain who had become Jefferson's personal secretary. William Clark was a friend of Lewis's who had served with him in the army. Together, the two men built a boat and gathered together a group of about thirty other explorers. On May 14th, 1804, Lewis and Clark loaded their goods, their men, and Lewis's big, shaggy dog Scannon onto the boat and set off to sail up the Missouri River. They planned to travel up the

Missouri and then to head west, across the unknown land of the Louisiana Territory.

At first, the journey was all upstream. The men had to wade in the river, pulling their heavy boat with ropes against the swift Missouri current. Mosquitoes and gnats bit their heads and shoulders; river snakes swam by their knees. They labored on, far into the land that is now North Dakota. They traveled through lands where friendly Native American tribes lived, into unknown places where the fierce, hostile Teton Sioux prowled through the woods. They had been traveling now for six whole months! The weather began to grow cold. In the morning, an ice film covered the edges of the river. It was November, and soon snow would halt their journey.

Lewis and Clark decided that the expedition would stop and build a winter camp in the land where the Mandan tribe lived. The Mandan were a friendly people; they were accustomed to white men, because Canadian traders often traveled down from the north to swap furs and other goods with them. Lewis and Clark directed their men to begin building a fort. On Christmas Day, the fort was finished. Lewis and Clark hoisted a United States flag over the roof. Now the fort had become the most distant western outpost of the United States of America.

Clark wrote about the progress of the expedition in his journal, which was bound in elk-skin

As they waited for spring to come again, Lewis and Clark met a white Canadian trader named Charbonneau who had journeyed down to trade with the Mandan. He spoke little English, only French. But one of the explorers in the American expedition translated his words for the two leaders. Charbonneau could speak the language of several Native American tribes. His Native American wife, Sacagawea, could speak several more. Charbonneau offered to come along with the expedition in the spring. He and his wife could help to interpret the speech of the tribes Lewis and Clark would meet along the way.

Lewis and Clark agreed. By the time the expedition left again in April, though, Sacagawea was carrying a tiny baby: her first son, only two months old. His name was Jean-Baptiste, but the whole party had nicknamed him "Pompy"!

The whole party set off west. Soon they reached the *junction,* or joining, of the Missouri and the Yellowstone rivers. Lewis decided that the expedition should camp and hunt for meat. He took his gun and went off hunting. When he saw a bear, he aimed his gun and shot.

The bear, stung by the bullet, reared up and roared. But this wasn't a timid black bear, like the bears Lewis was accustomed to seeing back east. This was a grizzly. Instead of running, it turned and chased Lewis. He had to run for his life, reloading his gun as he went, and then turn and shoot again while still sprinting for his life. Lewis killed the bear just in time. The Americans had never seen such enormous bears— nine feet tall from nose to toe!

It wasn't the last time that the party would be in danger. Now they were drawing close to the Rocky Mountains. If they could cross the Rockies, they would finally be across the *Continental Divide.*

The Continental Divide is the ridge that runs down the middle of North America. Both sides of the continent slope up to the Divide. If a drop of rain falls on the east side of the Divide, it rolls down and down and down, heading east, until it finally reaches the Atlantic Ocean. But if a drop of rain falls just inches on the other side of the Divide, it rolls down and down and down, heading west, until it reaches the Pacific Ocean! If the party could get across the Continental Divide, they could find a river and sail down it all the way to the coast.

The party climbed and climbed and climbed toward the Rocky Mountains. Finally, Lewis and a few men went ahead. They were hoping to find Shoshone Indians who lived nearby. They had to buy horses from the Shoshone to ride across the mountains. Without horses, the expedition might not be able to cross the Continental Divide.

When Lewis finally did find Shoshone Indians, he managed to convince them to take him to their chief. The Shoshone were suspicious of these strange white men. What were they doing so near the mountains? Did they intend to lead an attack against the Shoshone people? Lewis was relieved to see Clark and the rest of the expedition finally catching up with him. Perhaps Sacagawea could help him assure the chief that they came in peace.

The Shoshone and the Americans all sat down together. The conversation went slowly! Sacagawea did not speak enough English to translate the chief's words into English. Instead, she translated the Shoshone words into one of the Native American languages her husband knew, Minnetaree. Then Charbonneau, who also spoke very poor English, would translate the Minnetaree into French. Then the French-speaking explorer translated the French into English for Lewis and Clark. When the two captains answered in English, their words then had to be put back into French, then into Minnetaree, then back into Shoshone. It took a very long time to say anything!

Suddenly, Sacagawea jumped to her feet, ran to the chief, and threw both of her arms around him. She had recognized him! Years before, Sacagawea had been kidnapped from this very Shoshone tribe and taken away. Now she had found her family again. The chief was her brother!

When Sacagawea explained to her brother that Lewis and Clark needed horses, the chief agreed to exchange thirty Shoshone horses for guns. The journey across the mountain could continue.

The crossing was the coldest, hardest part of the journey. Snow set in. The men were used to shooting deer or buffalo for their meals, and Sacagawea had taught them to eat wild vegetables like onions and prairie turnips. But now in the mountains, snow and ice covered bare rock or thin grass. Starvation loomed. "No fish," Clark wrote in his journal, "and the grass entirely eaten out by the horses. The mountains... much worse than yesterday.... steep and stony, our men and horses much fatigued.....I have been as wet and as cold in every part as I ever was in my life.....Encamped on a bold running creek passing to the left which I called Hungry Creek, as at that place we had nothing to eate." Finally, reluctantly, they decided to kill one of the horses. "A colt being the most useless part of our Stock," Clark wrote grimly, "he fell a Prey to our appetites."

The horsemeat kept them from starving. But if they killed too many horses, they wouldn't be able to move fast enough to survive. So they ate some of the hunting dogs as well. Clark thought the meat was disgusting, but Lewis wrote that it tasted quite good! (Of course, his dog Scannon was spared.)

Finally, the party came through the mountains and found themselves at a river flowing west. They had crossed the Continental Divide! A Native American village nearby gave them food and fish and told them that this river, the Clearwater, flowed into the Columbia River. The Columbia then flowed into the ocean! The party hollowed canoes out of huge logs and paddled down the rivers. On November 7th, 1805, Clark wrote, "Great joy in camp! We are in view of the ocean, this great Pacific ocean which we been so long anxious to see."

Once more, though, winter had come. They built another winter camp, waited until spring, and started back. Three years after leaving on their voyage, Lewis and Clark returned. In all that time, only one of the party had died—from appendicitis. Sacagawea had traveled the entire distance carrying little Pompy in a sling!

Lewis and Clark had met dozens of Native American tribes. They had discovered new plants and animals. They had written descriptions of everything they saw and had drawn detailed maps of their route west. Soon, settlers would begin to follow the path that Lewis and Clark had blazed into the distant lands of the West.

Tecumseh's Resistance

Thanks to Lewis and Clark's maps, white settlers were beginning to head west. Some were searching for a new home. Others hoped to trap rich mountain furs and sell them for money. Hardy trappers began to make homes on the rough sides of the Rocky Mountains. These "mountain men" lived on whatever game they could shoot. They set steel traps for beaver in high mountain streams, dried the furs, and traded them to Native American and Canadian traders. Many of these men married Native American women.

Other settlers began to push farther west, building houses and farms into the Ohio Valley and beyond. Some of the Native American tribes nearby welcomed the settlers. But others feared them—because these white explorers were claiming to own Native American land.

A Shawnee named Tecumseh had learned to fear the whites from his earliest days. His father had been killed by white settlers when Tecumseh was only six. The little boy had been adopted by the Shawnee chief Blackfish. Blackfish had also adopted several white boys who had been kidnapped from settler families. He taught all of the boys, white and Shawnee, to hate and fear the settlers.

When he was fifteen, Tecumseh went with Blackfish to attack settlers who were moving down the Ohio Valley. The Shawnees captured a white man, tied him to a stake, and burned him. Tecumseh was furious. "We do not torture our prisoners!" he shouted at the Shawnee warriors. "We do not use cruelty! We fight with honor!" Tecumseh was so angry that no prisoner was ever mistreated in front of him again.

But although Tecumseh did not want to see the whites tortured, he knew that his people were fighting a war against these invaders—and he was willing to attack and kill whites in battle. He led raids against white towns and forts all through the Northwest Territory. His brothers joined him. Two of them were killed in battle.

As time went on, Tecumseh saw that other tribes were willing to sign treaties with the whites, "selling" land in exchange for gifts. Again, Tecumseh grew angry. "We do not own the land!" he told his followers. "Land is like air and water. No one owns it. We all use it in common!" But Tecumseh saw that more and more Native Americans were beginning to think like white people—believing that they could own land and sell it to each other. He realized that although he could fight battles against the whites, he had a much bigger job: to keep the Native Americans from acting and thinking like the white people who were flooding into their land.

Tecumseh joined forces with his youngest brother, a strange and frightening preacher named Tenskwatawa. As a child, Tenskwatawa had stuck an arrow into his own eye by mistake. From then on, his right eye drooped and the right side of his face was pulled down. His twisted face made his message even more frightening. Tenskwatawa claimed that he had traveled to the Great Spirit's dwelling place and returned with a message for all Native Americans. The Great Spirit, he declared, was angry that his children were behaving like whites. Unless the Native Americans changed their ways, they would lose their land forever. "Do not drink the white man's alcohol!" he preached. "Don't wear their wool and cotton clothes; wear the furs and skins of our people. Do not sign treaties with them, for none of us own the land. Do not marry them!" Because of his preaching, the Native Americans called Tenskwatawa the "Prophet."

Tecumseh did not seem completely convinced that the Prophet had actually been to visit the Great Spirit. But his brother's preaching fit with his own ideas. Tecumseh wanted all of the Native American tribes to join together in a *confederacy,* or union, against the white settlers.

Together, the brothers settled in the Indiana Territory. The Prophet preached about the old ways. Tecumseh traveled around, visiting tribes all over the Midwest, trying to convince them to unite together. Many Native Americans came to the settlement, nicknamed "Prophetstown," to join them.

In 1809, the governor of the Indiana Territory, William Henry Harrison, invited tribal chiefs from all over the Northwest to his headquarters at Fort Wayne. He didn't invite Tecumseh, though. He wanted to convince the chiefs to sign another land treaty. He told them that the United States wanted to buy their land and then pointed to the hundreds of soldiers camped nearby. "We could take your land by force," he said. "But we'll pay you generously instead. You'd better accept our offer before we change our minds."

This was exactly the sort of offer that Tecumseh had warned his people about. But, frightened by the soldiers, the chiefs agreed to sell Harrison three million acres of land—for seven thousand dollars.

Angry Native Americans who heard about this deal began to flood to Prophetstown. When Harrison heard about the gathering of hostile warriors, he sent a message to the Prophet. "I will take you to Washington and show you the Great White Father!" the message said. Harrison hoped that if the Prophet saw the President, the White House, and all of Washington, he would be too frightened of the whites to resist them.

Instead, Tecumseh sent back word that *he* would come—not to Washington, but to the governor's own head-quarters. He took four hundred armed warriors and eighty war canoes with him! He left his army camped nearby and stalked to the governor's mansion with his bodyguards. An army officer who saw him wrote, "He was one of the finest looking men I ever saw....about six feet high, straight, with large fine features, and altogether a daring bold looking fellow."

Tecumseh refused to go into the mansion, insisting that the governor meet with him in a group of trees nearby. Harrison agreed and ordered chairs brought for everyone. Tecumseh waved the chairs away. "The Great Spirit is my father," he said.

"The earth is my mother, and on her bosom I will lie." With that, he sat on the grass.

Harrison and his officials sat on the chairs.

"You have stolen this land," Tecumseh began. "No one can sell it to you. It belongs to no tribe or leader, but to us all. I speak now for all Indians, for I am the head of them all. We do not accept this treaty. It was made by those who were afraid, and greedy."

"I cannot cancel the treaty," Harrison said. "And all of the tribes speak a different language. They are all separate. You cannot speak for them all!"

"We are like your United States," Tecumseh retorted. "Independent, but united together to defend ourselves. How can you object to this?"

Harrison was out-argued. But he still refused to cancel the treaty. When Tecumseh and his bodyguard stalked away, Harrison got ready for a fight. He sent a message to Washington, asking for more soldiers. Tecumseh also went searching for more warriors. He told his brother, the Prophet, to wait for his return and hurried down south, hoping that the Choctaws would join with him against the whites.

The Choctaws refused. And before Tecumseh could return, Harrison marched an army to Prophetstown and camped outside it, on the banks of the Tippecanoe River.

The Prophet didn't wait for Tecumseh to come back. Instead, he told the Native Americans that his magic had made the white man's bullets useless and that they could attack Harrison's army without fear of death! The warriors believed him. They attacked the army camp—but without Tecumseh, they fought wildly and without a plan. Harrison ordered his men to fire. The bullets killed dozens of warriors. The Prophet's magic had not worked!

The Prophet fled. Frightened, the Native Americans fled too. Harrison marched his army into Prophetstown and burned it to the ground. He even ordered his men to dig up the bodies in the Prophetstown graveyard and throw them on the ground, so that the settlement would be cursed!

When Tecumseh returned from the south, he found his town destroyed, his warriors scattered, and the word spreading to all of his allies that the Prophet was a fraud. Only a few loyal warriors remained. But they had captured the Prophet as he ran from the battlefield and tied him up. Tecumseh put his knife to his brother's throat but then pulled it away and shoved the Prophet out of his sight. He would not kill Tenskwatawa.

For the next twenty years, the Prophet would slink from village to village, a dishonored beggar. But Tecumseh's attempt to unite the Native Americans had failed. His confederation had been destroyed, along with Prophetstown.

Note to Parent: Historians sometimes disagree about the name of Clark's dog because Clark's handwriting is hard to read. Many books will say Scannon and others will say Seaman.

The World of Napoleon Bonaparte

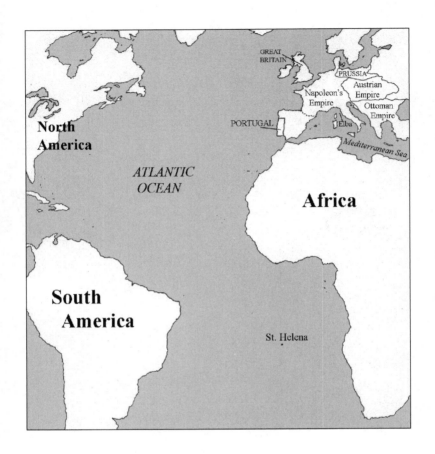

Chapter Thirty-Three
The End of Napoleon

Napoleon's Wars (and 1812 Too)

While settlers were beginning to trickle west, a different kind of invasion was taking place in Europe. The Emperor Napoleon was pushing the border of his empire further and further out—until most of Europe was forced to salute the French flag.

After Napoleon lost the Battle of Trafalgar to the British navy, the British asked Austria and Russia to join with Britain in defying Napoleon. The two countries agreed. Just a month after Trafalgar, the Austrian and Russian armies gathered together to fight Napoleon's great army. But Napoleon avenged his defeat at Trafalgar. His soldiers smashed through the combined lines of the Russians and Austrians. Austria was forced to give up all its land in Italy! Napoleon gave the city of Naples to his brother Joseph to rule. The Prussian army marched against Napoleon and was defeated. The Russians retreated and then attacked again—and lost.

The czar of Russia, Alexander I, was Catherine the Great's grandson. But he didn't have Catherine's stubborn will! He was tired of fighting Napoleon. He signed a treaty, promising to give Napoleon part of Poland in exchange for peace.

Now Napoleon had Europe under his thumb. But England still irritated him. Why couldn't he beat the British?

Napoleon knew better than to try to invade Britain again. So he decided to starve the British instead. He announced that no British ships could dock at any European port. No country in Europe would be permitted to buy English goods. Any ship from any country that went to Britain with food or supplies would be seized and its captain accused of treachery against France!

The little country of Portugal, on the coast of Spain, objected. Portugal made a lot of money trading with the English. If Britain starved, the Portuguese might starve too!

Napoleon wasn't going to let tiny Portugal defy him. But in order to attack Portugal by land, he had to go through Spain. So he marched into Spain, removed the Spanish king, gave Spain to his brother Joseph too, and headed toward Portugal with his army.

But Napoleon never managed to conquer Portugal. The Spanish, who hated Joseph, occupied his army with rebellions and revolts. And then Alexander I, the czar of Russia, changed his allegiance. He declared that he was no longer Napoleon's friend and ally.

Napoleon's huge empire was acting like a bucket of fish—all caught, but still trying to wiggle out over the edge of the bucket! Napoleon decided that the Russian fish needed to be caught and shoved back in! So he massed his army all together and, in June of 1812, marched over half a million men into Russia.

Instead of standing up and fighting, the Russians retreated. Napoleon's army marched further into Russia. The Russians retreated some more. By late summer, the French army was spread across seven hundred miles! Napoleon kept marching, ordering his troops to burn and destroy the countryside as they went.

In the second week of September, he arrived at Moscow. The beautiful city was mostly empty. Napoleon ordered his army to burn it to the ground! Then he sent word to Alexander I, offering to sign a treaty with him.

No answer came.

Alexander had planned all along to lure Napoleon into Russia. "We have vast spaces to retreat in," he had told his advisors. "We will leave it to winter to wage our war for us." Napoleon had been caught in the same trap as the Swedish army years before. While he waited in Moscow for word that Alexander would surrender, the air grew colder and colder. Far away, Alexander remarked, "Before I sign a peace treaty, I'll go eat potatoes in Siberia." And he let Napoleon wait some more.

Finally Napoleon ordered the French army home. But it was already October. The French were marching home through the country they had burned on the march in. There was no food anywhere in the shattered countryside. They were wearing summer uniforms. Snow started to flake gently down from the sky. The temperature fell—to thirty degrees below zero. Soldiers began to freeze in their tracks. "The road is covered with our men, frozen to death," one of Napoleon's generals wrote. "We have thrown away our guns; they are too cold to hold. We step over the dead as we walk." When the French army reached the Berezina River, the border between Russia and Poland, they discovered that the Russians had burned all of the bridges.

Finally, Napoleon's army struggled across the freezing water to the other side. Six hundred thousand men had died. Only forty thousand soldiers remained!

The conquered states of Europe took heart. The French-ruled countries of Prussia, Germany, Austria, and Italy began to chant, "Down with France!" Even in France itself, Napoleon's subjects were growing tired of war, blood, and destruction. In the streets of Paris, people grumbled about Napoleon. A few voices murmured, "Down with the emperor!"

The murmur grew louder. Napoleon, hearing of these mutterings, hurried the shattered remnants of his army back to Paris. Europe was about to slip from his grasp!

The Americans chose that exact moment to pick a fight with the British.

For several years, American sea captains had been complaining about the way they were treated by the English. British ships always needed more seamen to help fight the long war against Napoleon—so their captains had taken to stopping United States ships at sea, announcing that the American sailors were English deserters, and taking them on board to serve in the royal navy. Americans were also angry that British soldiers had come down from Canada to help Tecumseh and his Shawnee warriors attack American settlers. So on June 18th, 1812, the United States declared war on Britain.

Britain didn't want to turn around and fight the United States. It had its hands full with Napoleon! But while Napoleon rushed back to Paris to defend his power, the British sent part of their navy over to America. English ships sailed into Lake Erie and Lake Michigan and landed British soldiers on the shore, ready to invade Ohio.

At that, Tecumseh saw one more chance to fight against the United States. He declared that the Shawnee were allies with the British in the War of 1812. He and his warriors helped the British soldiers invade the Northwest Territory and capture the city of Detroit. For a full year, Tecumseh's Shawnee warriors fought alongside the British.

Then William Henry Harrison, now a general commanding part of the American army, marched against Tecumseh once more. In a huge battle, Harrison defeated the combined British–Native American army and drove them back out of the Northwest. Tecumseh was killed. His body disappeared from the battlefield; his warriors took it away and buried it in a secret spot.

The Americans had won in the Northwest, but the British were still fighting. The following summer, British ships landed on the shores of Washington, D.C. President James Madison fled, just ahead of soldiers who stormed into Washington and set fire to the Capitol Building. The Library of Congress and all its books went up in bright, hot flame. The soldiers looted the President's House, stole its treasures, piled up its red-velvet chairs, and lit them. Soon the whole house was wreathed in fire and smoke.

But the British didn't really want to occupy America; they had too much work to do fighting Napoleon. So finally the two countries signed a treaty. They agreed to behave as if the war had never happened. The War of 1812 had achieved absolutely nothing.

By 1814, France was demanding that Napoleon make peace! Austria, Russia, Prussia, and Great Britain swore together to stay united until Napoleon was defeated. Once more, Napoleon rallied his army. He marched out of France, toward the combined armies of Europe.

While he was gone, a French official announced that the emperor no longer ruled. Messengers had been sent to Louis XVIII, the brother of the guillotined king. Louis, who had been living in England, was a fat, slow-witted man, almost sixty years old. He agreed to come back to France as its king.

Facing a huge army, without the support of his own country, Napoleon finally admitted defeat. The British, Russian, Austrian, and Prussian allies met together and decided that Napoleon should be taken to the tiny, rocky island of Elba, in the Mediterranean Sea. Here, Napoleon was told, he could still have the title emperor—the Emperor of Elba. He could still have an army—with four hundred men in it. Napoleon would spend the rest of his life on an island seven miles wide, watching the sardine boats float by and the olives grow.

Waterloo!

Napoleon Bonaparte, the "monster of Europe," now spent his days in exile. He was made the ruler of Elba, which had a few people on it, and given a staff so that he could form a little island government. He had a small palace. His mother and sister came to live with him. And the French government had agreed to send him money every year so that he could run his island.

Napoleon bustled around his island, working in his garden and adding rooms onto his palace. He improved the roads, built bridges, and tried to make the fields bear better crops.

But the man who had once ruled Europe was bored. He was angry. He was humiliated; tourists sailed to Elba just to see the famous Napoleon in his prison. And as time went on, he got poorer. France never sent a single penny of the money it had promised.

Back in France, Louis XVIII was not making himself popular. He was determined that people would treat him with the same respect that the Bourbon kings of France had always been given, just as if the Revolution had never happened. In his first big public appearance, he fell down and was too fat to get up without help. He wouldn't allow anyone to help him up but the most important of all the palace officials, so he had to lie on the ground until the official could be found! The common people of France began to fear that the king would once again become a tyrant.

Napoleon watched his country from a distance. He wrote letters to the soldiers who remained in France. Many of them wrote back, telling him that he should return to France and chase the Bourbon king away.

Napoleon knew that the leaders of Europe were discussing sending him much further away, to some distant island in the Atlantic Ocean. Once that happened, he would never escape. On February 26th, 1815, Napoleon arranged for a ship with soldiers, gold, guns, and ammunition to dock at Elba. He told his mother that he was leaving to go fight again.

"Good," she said. "Go die with your sword in your hand, not sitting here in exile."

Napoleon boarded the ship and was away before anyone in Europe realized what was happening. He landed at Cannes, France, with his little guard. "I am the emperor of Elba!" he announced. "I've come with my six hundred men to attack the King of France and his army of six hundred thousand. But I'll conquer!"

He started toward Paris. The peasants, remembering the bad old days of the monarchy, flocked to welcome him. The nearest division of the French army was sent to arrest him. When Napoleon saw them approaching, he told his own men to play the French national song, the "Marseillaise." Then he walked forward, holding open his coat. "I am your emperor!" he shouted. "Do you recognize me? If any one of you would like to kill your own emperor, here I am! Forty-five of your own leaders have invited me back. Three European countries stand behind my return!"

The soldiers lowered their weapons. Someone cheered. Soon, the soldiers were shouting, "Long live the emperor!"

Hearing the terrible news, Louis XVIII sent his top general to stop Napoleon. But when this general met Napoleon, he found himself unable to arrest his former emperor. He had fought by Napoleon's side too many times. Instead, he joined in the parade.

Louis ran from Paris. Just three weeks after landing, Napoleon arrived in the city and took back his throne. Not a single shot had been fired! "I am here in the spirit of the Revolution!" Napoleon announced. "I have come to free the people of France from the slavery of the priests and nobles!"

Does this sound familiar? Napoleon used the same line twice before—once in Italy, and once in Egypt. But he didn't bring freedom either time—and he didn't bring freedom this time either. The excitement soon began to fade. Soon, everyone could see that the common people of France were no better off than they had been under Louis XVIII.

As soon as England, Austria, and Prussia heard about Napoleon's return, they moved their armies toward the French border. They were not going to let the "monster of Europe" eat their countries one more time!

Napoleon managed to raise an army of 72,000 soldiers. He marched to meet the English army at Waterloo, a village just south of the Belgian town of Brussels.

The English army, commanded by the Duke of Wellington, had almost as many men as Napoleon's army. The battle raged evenly for hours. Thousands of men died on both sides. The English fought bravely; so did the French surrounding Napoleon. Finally, Prussian soldiers arrived to reinforce the English. Napoleon was defeated and his soldiers scattered. The general who had joined him instead of arresting him was captured—and shot. Napoleon's "Hundred Days" of power were over.

Even from exile, with an unprepared army, Napoleon had come close to defeating Wellington's men. As he walked through the battlefield, the Duke of Wellington kept repeating, "A close thing. A very close thing." Many of his own friends lay dead.

Napoleon went back to Paris and wrote out a paper, giving up the throne of France again. Then he quietly left the city. For a few weeks, no one was quite sure where Napoleon was. He was actually hiding in the homes of old friends, deciding what to do next. He thought he would like to go to the United States and study botany. But the British shut down the ports of France to keep any ships from leaving until Napoleon was found.

Finally Napoleon gave up and surrendered to the British. Now, the British had to decide what do with him. They didn't want him in the United States, stirring up trouble, or back on Elba, where he might escape again. If they executed him, the French who had welcomed him back might revolt. The British would have been very happy for France to offer to execute him—but the French didn't suggest such a plan.

Finally the British announced that they were going to send Napoleon to Saint Helena, far off in the Atlantic—twelve hundred miles west of Africa. The little island was only ten miles long and six miles wide. It was even smaller and barer than Elba!

On October 15th, 1815, Napoleon arrived at his exile. Even on this tiny little island, he wasn't allowed to go anywhere without an English officer following him, so he spent most of his time in the study of his house. He wrote a book about his life, read books in French and English, played cards, and sometimes gave small parties. Even though he was far from Europe, tourists still came to look at him. One English writer, William Makepeace Thackeray, remembered seeing Napoleon. When Thackeray was five, his ship stopped at St. Helena and a servant took him to see a man walking in a garden. "There's Bonaparte!" the servant whispered. "He eats three sheep every day, and as many small children as he can get hold of!"

Two years after arriving on St. Helena, Napoleon began to complain about stomach aches. He became worse and worse. Doctors could do nothing to make him better. By 1821, Napoleon could no longer get out of his bed. He asked for paper to write his last will. At the end of it, he wrote, "I wish my ashes to rest on the banks of the Seine, in the midst of that

French people which I have loved so much." He also wrote, "I am not dying a natural death. I have been killed by the English and their hired assassins!" Napoleon thought he had been poisoned, but he was probably dying of stomach cancer.

A few hours later, Napoleon died. He was buried on the island, but his stone had no name. It merely read "Here Lies," as though the name of Napoleon were too frightening to be spoken out loud.

South America During the Time of Bolívar

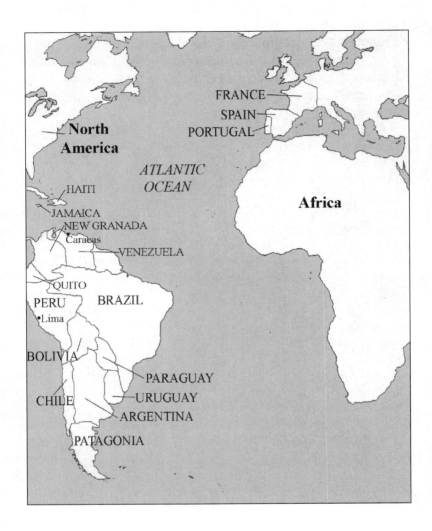

Chapter Thirty-Four
Freedom for South America

Simón Bolívar: The Liberator

Let's imagine now that we can leave Napoleon's grave in St. Helena and travel back in time—and in space. The cool spring air grows suddenly warmer. The rocks of St. Helena fade away. Look down at your feet; you're standing on thick green grass. Hot summer sun pours down on you. A few feet away, a servant on his hands and knees clips each blade of grass to the same length with a pair of shears.

You're standing on the tennis court of the Royal Palace in Madrid, Spain. Two young men with rackets are batting a tiny cork ball, bristling with goose feathers, back and forth. The queen of Spain sits beside the court beneath a gold and crimson canopy, fanned by her maid. The year is 1799. Over in France, Napoleon has just become First Consul. But here in Spain, the royal family has no idea that they will soon be driven from power.

The queen has invited a visiting guest from the Spanish colonies of South America to play tennis with her son, Prince Ferdinand. Prince Ferdinand isn't playing very hard. He hasn't even taken off his fancy cocked hat! He expects that his guest, sixteen-year-old Simón Bolívar, will let him win. But young Bolívar is doing his best to knock the ball past the prince's racket. He swings the racket high above his head and drives it toward Prince Ferdinand's head. The prince, startled, drops his racket and ducks. The ball knocks off his hat!

The queen lazily claps her hands. But Ferdinand stands up, his face red with fury.

"How dare you!" he hisses at Bolívar. "Apologize at once!"

"Why?" Bolívar answers. "It was a fair shot."

"You have no right to beat *me* at tennis," Ferdinand snaps. "You—you—you *creole!*" He grabs his hat and stalks away. The game is over.

Bolívar stands on the tennis court alone. His family owns a huge estate in South America, in the Spanish colony of Venezuela. He has been sent to Spain to see the land of his ancestors. He is well-educated, good at fighting and riding, strong and brave. But over here, in Spain, he will never be able to become an army general or a Spanish minister of state. He is a *creole,* a Spaniard born in the colonies, and those jobs are given only to *peninsulares*—natives of Spain itself.

The creoles of Bolívar's own colony, Venezuela, had been unhappy with Spain for many years. Not long after that tennis game in Madrid, a creole named Francisco de Miranda tried to convince the other creoles to join him in driving the Spanish governor and soldiers out of Venezuela. But the rebellion failed. Miranda had to flee to London!

By then, Simón Bolívar had spent several years traveling through Europe, reading the books of Enlightenment philosophers like John Locke, and learning about the revolutions in France and the United States. Bolívar knew that other colonies had thrown off the power of the countries that founded them. He made up his mind that Venezuela would join them! "I swear before the god of my fathers," he vowed, "I shall not rest until I have broken the chains that oppress us." And when he returned home to Venezuela, he soon made his plans clear. At a party held by the Spanish governor, he was asked to lift his glass and make a toast. Other guests had already toasted the king of Spain, wishing him long life and health. But Bolívar stood and lifted his glass for a different kind of toast. "I lift my glass to the honor of the king of Spain," he said. "But I lift it higher for the freedom of South America!"

Soon, Venezuela's chance came. Napoleon marched into Spain, took the throne away from Prince Ferdinand and his family, and declared that his brother Joseph would now rule. A little group of army officers called a *junta* gathered in Seville to fight against the French invaders. Portuguese and British soldiers came to Spain. Battles raged across Spain's villages and fields.

The creoles of South America believed that the junta was too busy with Napoleon to pay much attention to Venezuela. Encouraged by Bolívar, the creoles picked up weapons, drove the Spanish governor out of Venezuela's capital city of Caracas, and declared Venezuela free! Bolívar became a colonel in the new Patriot Army. Francisco de Miranda came back from London and became the Patriot Army's commander in chief. The South American war for independence had begun! Far south, the colony of Argentina had already declared its own independence. Not long afterward, Paraguay, just north of Argentina, announced that it too was free.

But the Spanish weren't willing to give up their empire just yet. A regiment of Spanish soldiers left the fight against Napoleon and sailed west, across the Atlantic. They arrived at Venezuela's most important port, ready to recapture the colony for Spain. Bolívar was in charge of defending the port. But one

Simón Bolívar

of his own Patriot officers decided that the rebellion had been a mistake and convinced other Patriot soldiers to join the Spanish invaders, rather than to fight with Bolívar! Bolívar had to retreat. He sent a message to Miranda, begging him to come help—but Miranda had already decided that the war for independence was doomed. He was making plans to board a ship and flee back to London.

Bolívar and the other Patriots were furious. They stormed into Miranda's house, took him prisoner, and locked him in his own fortress. When the Spanish arrived, they found the leader of the rebellion already in jail! They sent Miranda to Spain—where he spent the rest of his life in a Spanish dungeon.

Bolívar was forced to flee from Venezuela so that he too wouldn't end up in a Spanish jail! But he didn't go far away. He traveled to the neighboring colony of New Granada, which had also declared its independence, and pled with the creoles there to help Venezuela.

The New Granadans agreed. Bolívar became a colonel in *their* army. He had fewer than a hundred soldiers, but he led these soldiers into attacks on towns held by the Spanish along the border of Venezuela. His little army managed to drive some of the Spanish out. More soldiers came to join him. His army grew. After two years of war, Bolívar had fought his way all the way back to the capital city of Caracas. He marched into Caracas on August 6th, 1813, and declared that Venezuela was free—for the second time! The people of Venezuela welcomed him. "The liberator!" they cheered. From now on, Simón Bolívar would be known as "El Libertador."

But the war for independence wasn't over. Spanish soldiers still had control of many of Venezuela's cities. And the Spanish generals had a trick to play on Bolívar. El Libertador and his followers claimed that their rebellion would throw off the rule of Spanish aristocrats—just like the French Revolution, which had given the common men and women of France power. But all of the leaders of the Venezuelan rebellion were creoles. They owned huge estates and ranches. Bolívar himself had inherited farms, copper mines, and an enormous mansion!

Out in the open plains of southern Venezuela, much poorer men made their living herding cattle. These cowboys, called *llaneros*, hated the rich creoles. They agreed to join Spain in the fight against Bolívar!

Bolívar couldn't manage to drive off the combined army of Spanish soldiers and rough-riding llaneros. In less than a year, this army was marching into Caracas, once more claiming it for Spain. Bolívar had to flee to the nearby island of Jamaica, which was owned by Great Britain! Even worse, Spain had finally managed to drive Napoleon out. Ferdinand, the prince who had lost that tennis game so long ago, was now King Ferdinand VII of Spain. He sent eleven thousand soldiers to South America. The rebellious colonies were soon back under Spanish control! Napoleon was dead, and Europe was free—but El Libertador was in exile, and the Spanish colonies of South America had lost their brand-new independence.

Freedom, But Not Unity

Bolívar was not ready to give up the fight for Venezuela. He was convinced that he could lead his country to freedom. And after that, he wanted to lead the *rest* of South America to independence. He wrote out his plans for South America and published them in a magazine in Jamaica. The plans, called the "Letter from Jamaica," soon made their way down to South America. Creoles in every colony read Bolívar's letter. He wanted the South American colonies to become states, each with its own elected congress and a president. And then those states could join together, like the United States of America, into a huge, strong country—a new world power!

But Bolívar believed that the United States system was too weak. The President, he thought, didn't have enough power to run his country. *His* country would be more like Great Britain. It would have a constitution, but it would also have a king who ruled for life over all of the united South American states.

Bolívar wanted to be that king! But he had no army, and Venezuela was in the hands of Ferdinand VII, his old enemy.

Bolívar left Jamaica and traveled to Haiti instead. The emperor of Haiti was glad to help another colony rebel against its rulers! He gave Bolívar a handful of ships and soldiers. In return for this tiny army, Bolívar promised that he would free all of the Africans who were still kept as slaves in Venezuela. Together with a few Patriots who had joined him in exile, Bolívar prepared to take back his homeland.

Three years of war followed! Bolívar's little army fought and fought. Bolívar tried to make alliances with the leaders of rebel groups in other colonies, so that all of South America could stand together against the Spanish.

One of these other leaders, José de San Martín, finally helped Bolívar drive the Spanish out.

San Martín had been born in the colony of Argentina. He had joined the army of Spain and had sworn allegiance to the junta of Seville (the little group of officers fighting against Napoleon and his brother Joseph). But even though he fought bravely, San Martín couldn't rise all the way through the ranks of the army to become a commander—because he was a creole.

San Martín left Spain and went back home to join the rebellion. He knew that Spain would never be driven out of South America unless the rebels could conquer Lima. Lima was the most important city in Peru, the colony that stretched along the coast of South America. There were more Spanish soldiers in Lima than in any other South American city. If Spanish power over Lima could be broken, the rebellion might succeed!

The Spanish in Lima weren't worried about invasion. All of the roads to Lima were well guarded. Any rebel army would be destroyed long before it got to the city walls.

San Martín knew this too. So he decided to sail into Lima instead! He would put his rebel army on ships, land them on the shore near the city, and drive the Spanish out.

To get to the ocean, San Martín had to lead all of his men from the inside of South America to the coast—across the

Andes Mountains. The Andes Mountains were one of the biggest mountain ranges on the whole earth. The mountains soared high up into the sky and stretched all down the coast without a gap. Snow lay on their peaks all year long, and icy winds howled down their sides. No one had ever taken an army across the Andes!

But San Martín marched his men right over them. It took him a month to get his whole army across the slippery, treacherous slopes. When the commanders of other armies heard what San Martín had done, they shook their heads in amazement. "No one but Napoleon himself could do such a thing!" they exclaimed.

San Martín loaded his men onto leaky cargo ships—his new navy! He sailed up the coast, unloaded his soldiers, and marched to Lima. After months of siege, the Spanish soldiers in Lima finally gave up. They retreated back to the mountains of Peru. San Martín declared that Peru was free!

Now, Bolívar didn't need to worry about attacks from the south. He led his army into New Granada, between the colonies of Peru and Venezuela, and drove the Spanish out! Then he met with other rebel leaders to draw up a constitution for a new South American union. This union, La Republica de Colombia, would have three states in it: New Granada, Venezuela, and Quito (the small colony between Peru and New Granada, now called Ecuador).

Quito still belonged to Spain, but José de San Martín was willing to help out. He lent some of his soldiers to Bolívar for the fight. Soon Quito too was free. By 1822, most of South America had shaken off the armies of Spain. Bolívar ruled over La Republica de Colombia. San Martín was the Protector of Peru.

But Bolívar's dream of a united South America would never come true.

The new South American countries refused to join together under one president. Many of the rebel leaders who had fought hard for independence thought that Bolívar was too anxious to grab for power. Sometimes, Bolívar acted like another Napoleon, building himself an empire! Bolívar even seized a port that belonged to Peru and took it for his own.

José de San Martín objected. He was having trouble convincing the people of Peru to follow him. Many Peruvians were angry that San Martín had given important jobs to creoles from Argentina. Others complained that San Martín hadn't driven all of the Spanish soldiers out of Peru. Some were still hiding up in the mountains! San Martín wanted to prove that he was a strong, good leader. If he could get the port from Bolívar, everyone would see that he was just as powerful as El Libertador.

San Martín journeyed up to La Republica de Colombia to argue with Bolívar about this port. No one knows what Bolívar said to his old ally, because the two men met in secret. But San Martín went back to Peru without his port. When his officials asked him what had happened, he said only, "The Liberator is not the man we imagined him to be." A month later, San Martín resigned. He told his closest friends that the Spanish countries were not ready to be free. There was too much fighting going on inside each country. The creoles insisted on ruling over the "Indians," the descendents of the Native American tribes who had lived in South America before the conquistadores came. The Indians quarreled with the African descendents of slaves. South Americans who were "pure blooded" Spanish or Indian often fought with South Americans who were only *part* Indian, called *mestizos*, or part African, called *pardos*. And the landholders and army officers were too busy quarrelling with each other and grabbing for power to unite together under leaders who could make South America great. "I have tried for twenty-four years to promote liberty," San Martín complained, "and have produced only calamities. Liberty! It is like giving a two-year-old child a box of razors to play with and waiting to see what will happen!"

Soon Bolívar too was forced to give up his power. Many people loved Bolívar for helping to lead the fight for independence. The upper part of Peru was even renamed Bolivia, in his honor! But others hated him for taking so much power for himself. His supporters and his enemies began to fight together. Once, his enemies even broke into his house to kill him. Bolívar had to escape by jumping out of a window!

Finally Bolívar had to leave South America. He had been feeling ill, and he no longer had the energy to keep on working for a united South America. He hoped that, once he was gone, the countries of South America would stop quarrelling with each other. But not long after he left, Bolívar grew even sicker. When he died of *tuberculosis*, a disease of the lungs, his country was free of Spanish rule—but still divided.

New Spain

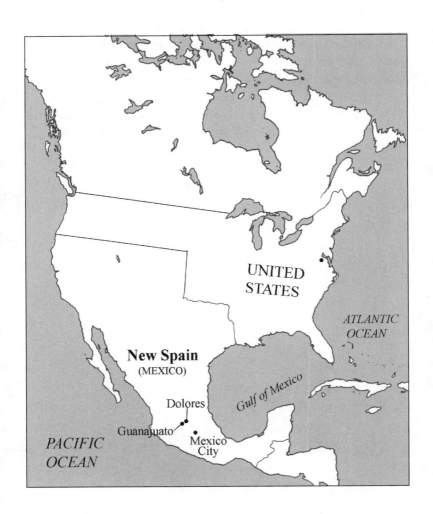

Chapter Thirty-Five
Mexican Independence

The Cry of Dolores

Don Miguel sat reading in front of his kitchen fire. His breakfast of bread and coffee stood untouched at his elbow, but occasionally he moved his hand to turn a page, or to scratch absently at the ears of the cat draped across his lap. Finally he reached the end of the chapter and closed the book. The cat, disturbed, rolled over and batted at the pages. Don Miguel lifted the book out of harm's way. "You and Fray Estrada both," he scolded the cat, "out to get my book!"

He stood up, dumping the indignant cat on the floor, and crossed the room to put his book in the pantry, beneath a basket of eggs. Curious eyes might notice that he was reading essays by the French philosopher Voltaire. Voltaire wrote about the equality of all men and their right to rule themselves. Here in New Spain, the Central American colony ruled by the Spanish, no priest should be seen reading the works of revolutionary Frenchmen!

Don Miguel picked up his cold coffee and drank it, staring out the window. The sun was rising, and the farmyard outside was growing lighter. Soon he would need to go and see that the horses had been fed, the eggs collected, and the cows put out to pasture. Then he would put on his cloak and walk to the church for Mass. Since his friend and fellow priest José Joaquin had died, Don Miguel was the only priest in the tiny town of Dolores, part of the Spanish colony of New Spain.

He missed José Joaquin, but he was lucky that he could still work as a priest at all. Not too many years ago, a priest named Fray Estrada had complained to the officials of the Roman Catholic Church that Don Miguel was a heretic. Fray Estrada claimed that Don Miguel taught strange, untrue beliefs, instead of true Catholic doctrine, and that he spent his days drinking and amusing himself rather than taking care of his church!

The officials had asked many questions of all of Don Miguel's friends. Finally they decided that Fray Estrada was lying. But Don Miguel knew that the officials had written down, "Don Miguel is innocent of the charges, but he does read forbidden books—especially books in French. And he has dangerous ideas about revolution!" Don Miguel had lost his job and had not been given another church to serve until José Joaquin's death left the church of Dolores empty.

The officials had been right. Don Miguel *did* read forbidden French books about liberty and equality. But here in New Spain, which lay in Central America between the continents of North and South America, men were *not* equal. New Spain was still ruled by the Spanish. Peninsulares born in Spain held all the power to govern the creoles, the Indians, and the half-Indian mestizos.

Don Miguel had done his best to help the Indians in Dolores. He himself was a creole who owned two farms, so he had used his own land and his own money to teach the Indians skills. He had built a factory where the Indians could make valuable pots and bricks for sale. He had raised mulberry trees on his land, hoping that the Indians could make silk from silkworms. He had taught them to make wine from the vineyard planted outside the farmhouse. Don Miguel loved his vineyard. At the end of the day, he would walk through it, examining each grape for any sign of disease. He even talked to the vineyards. "Grow the best grapes in all of New Spain," he would tell a spindly little plant. "We need you to help us make money, little vine!"

Don Miguel set his empty cup down and reached for his cloak. As he did, he felt a strange tremor under his feet. Horses were approaching; many horses, riding fast. He pulled the door open and ran out onto his doorstep. Spanish soldiers were riding through his vineyard, slashing at the vines with their swords, ripping them down and throwing them onto the ground. Their captain thrust a torch into the thickest tangle of leaves.

Smoke began to rise. At the far end, the vines were already blazing.

The captain reined his horse around to the house. "These grapes are forbidden by the king of Spain!" he shouted. "Only wine made in Spain can be drunk here in the colonies! You cannot make your own wine. You must buy ours. Never forget that you rely on Spain for everything!"

When the soldiers galloped away, the vines were in ashes. Don Miguel's face was white with anger. For years, he had hated the cruelty of the Spanish governors of his home. But the loss of his vines was the last straw. Don Miguel was ready for war.

On September 16th, 1810, Don Miguel rang the bells of his church for Mass. But after the celebration, he didn't dismiss them as usual. Instead, he said, "Listen to me! Listen to the truth about those who rule you!" And then he told them that their lives were hard because Spain refused to let them be free. "Now is the time for action!" he shouted.

The Indians and mestizos shouted back, "Long live independence! Long live our America! Death to bad government!"

The rebellion of New Spain had begun.

Everyone who had heard the speech, called *El Grito de Dolores,* or "The Cry of Dolores," repeated it to others. Unhappy colonists gathered around Don Miguel. They didn't have many guns or swords, but soon twenty thousand New Spanish were ready to march behind their new leader. Don Miguel the priest was now known as Captain-General Miguel Hidalgo of the New Spain Army!

The mob of mestizos and Indians captured the nearest small town and then marched toward the larger city of Guanajuato. The Spanish governor there refused to see them or take their rebellion seriously. But the mob overran the royal fort, taking over the city's government. And then, furious and disorganized, they killed everyone inside. Hidalgo was unable to stop them until over five hundred men and women were dead!

The capture of Guanajuato gave the New Spain rebels courage. They marched on, fighting their way toward Mexico

City. More men joined them. Hidalgo's army now had more than fifty thousand soldiers!

But when they reached the gates of Mexico City, Hidalgo stopped his army. "No," he said. "We will retreat."

The soldiers couldn't believe what they were hearing! But Hidalgo and his officers turned the army around and went back. Hidalgo, still a priest beneath his sword and helmet, was afraid that his army would charge through the capital city, burning and killing the innocent, just as they had in Guanajuato.

Once Hidalgo had retreated, Spanish soldiers marched out of Mexico City and attacked his army. The rebels fought back—but finally were forced to scatter. Hidalgo tried to escape across the northern desert into the United States. But he was caught and put into prison, along with the officers who had gone with him. The other men were shot for treason at once.

Don Miguel Hidalgo was a priest, so the Spanish army couldn't execute him. First, the church would have to give its permission. The Roman Catholic Church agreed to consider the case—but the Spanish governor of New Spain lost patience. "I'm not waiting any longer," he snapped. "Find a bishop who'll unpriest this priest!" So his aides found a bishop who agreed to *defrock* Hidalgo. (When a priest is *defrocked,* a church authority declares that he isn't a priest any longer.) Then Hidalgo was taken from his prison cell and beheaded.

Miguel Hidalgo hadn't made New Spain free. But he is still remembered today in Mexico, the country that was once New Spain. Every September 15th, the president of Mexico rings a bell and then repeats Don Miguel Hidalgo's speech, the "Cry of Dolores." On the next day, September 16th, Mexicans celebrate their Independence Day!

The Republic of Mexico

Miguel Hidalgo's army had failed. But south of New Spain, the South American colonies had declared independence from Spain. New Spain saw their fight for freedom—and rebelled again.

The second revolt against Spain was led by another priest, José María Morelos y Pavón. Morelos had commanded a group of soldiers in Hidalgo's army. After Hidalgo was executed, Morelos and his men formed a *junta*—a group of army officers who claimed to be the true rulers of New Spain. This junta wrote a constitution for New Spain, which they called simply "America." The constitution said that all men of New Spain, whether creole, peninsular, Indian, or mestizo, would be equal. They would all simply be "Americans," with the same rights to vote, own property, and earn money.

Morelos and his army fought against the Spanish soldiers, just like Hidalgo and *his* army had done just a few years before. But Morelos too was captured and put to death.

Leading a rebel army was a dangerous business! Hidalgo and Morelos had both died fighting for independence.

But the third rebel leader, Agustín de Iturbide, would be more successful.

Agustín de Iturbide was a creole, born in New Spain. But he had always been loyal to the king. As a matter of fact, during Hidalgo's rebellion, Iturbide had been fighting on the opposite side—for Spain. And he had helped the Spanish government chase Morelos too!

But then Iturbide asked to be awarded a special honor: the Order of San Fernando. This military *order* was a special medal given to soldiers who had been brave and loyal. Iturbide was certainly loyal. And although he was often accused of being a cruel and greedy man, he was certainly brave. But he was told that he couldn't have the medal. He was a creole. Only peninsulares could receive the Order!

Iturbide was angry—and humiliated. He realized that he would never fight his way to a position of power in the army, or be given an important job in the government. Peninsulares would be given these honors instead.

So while he went on serving in Spain's army, Iturbide started to write down ideas about how New Spain might become independent. In 1821, he gathered the army officers who served with him together, and explained his plan. New Spain should become a new, independent kingdom called Mexico, with its own king. All of its people would be equal, no matter where they were born or who they were. And Roman Catholicism would be the official religion of Mexico. These were called the Three Guarantees.

The officers liked Iturbide's plan. So did the Mexican revolutionaries. The most powerful rebel leader, Vicente Guerrero, agreed that he and his soldiers would fight for the plan. The combined armies of Iturbide and Guerrero marched to Mexico City and ordered the Spanish governor to step down!

The governor agreed. This time, the rebel army was too strong for the Spanish soldiers to defeat. On August 24th, 1821, Spain signed a treaty giving Mexico its independence. The third rebellion had succeeded, after only six months!

Now that Mexico was independent, Mexicans called a congress to write a new constitution. Some Mexicans wanted a republic, like the United States. Others wanted a king who would have to obey a constitution, like Great Britain. Some of the Mexicans who wanted a king thought that Ferdinand VII should be invited to be the king of Mexico—as long as he moved to Mexico and promised to obey the constitution. Others wanted Iturbide to be king.

Iturbide's supporters won. In 1822, the creole soldier became Emperor Agustín I of Mexico.

But although he was a good soldier, Agustín was a very bad king. He had his sister made a princess and his father made a prince. He set up a lavish household with lots of servants. When the Mexican congress refused to obey him, the new emperor threw its leaders into jail. The American ambassador who traveled down to Mexico to meet Emperor Agustín I wrote back to President James Monroe, "His exercise of power [is] arbitrary and tyrannical."

After Agustín I had ruled for only nine months, an army general named Antonio López de Santa Anna led a revolt against him. Santa Anna wanted Mexico ruled as a republic, with no king at all. After suffering through nine months of rule by Agustín, the army agreed. Agustín fled to Italy, afraid that he might be killed by angry soldiers! With Agustín out of the way, the Mexican congress met again and drew up a constitution for the United Mexican States. Mexico would have a president, a congress, and states, just like the United States of America. New Spain was now a republic!

Agustín Iturbide never had a chance to live in the republic of Mexico. His enemies, pretending to be friendly, told him that the new constitution wasn't very popular. "The people are restless and unhappy," they said. "If you return now, you'll be welcomed back and given your throne again!"

At those words, Agustín came running from Italy. But when he arrived in Mexico, he was arrested at once—and then put to death.

Europe, Africa, and the United States

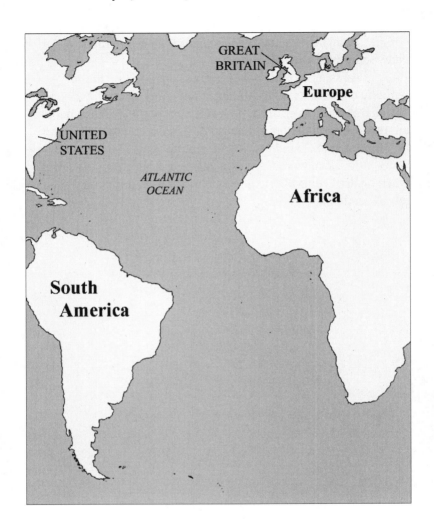

Chapter Thirty-Six
The Slave Trade Ends

The Work of the Abolitionists

All over Europe and both Americas and in the countries in between, men seemed to be talking and thinking and writing about equality.

And all over Europe and both Americas and in the countries in between, men owned slaves.

Why?

That's the question that *abolitionists*—men and women who wanted slavery *abolished*, or made illegal—asked. In his essays about natural law, John Locke had written that every human being has the right to "life, health, liberty, and possession." Weren't Africans human beings? And didn't an African slave have a natural right be free?

In England, the Quakers had been insisting for a long time that slavery was wrong. But now, more and more English began to agree the slavery should be made illegal. Anti-slavery associations sprang up. Their members wrote accounts of slavery and published them, so that no one in England could claim that they did not know about the plight of the slaves. John Wesley, the founder of the Methodist Church, wrote,

> Banished from their country, from their friends and relations for ever, from every comfort of life, they are reduced to a state scarce anyway preferable to that of beasts of burden. In general, a few roots…are their food; and two rags, that neither screen them from the heat of the day, nor the cold of the night, their covering. Their sleep is very short, their labour continual, and frequently above their strength; so that death sets many of them at liberty before they have lived out half their days….They are attended by overseers, who…whip them most unmercifully, so that you may see their bodies long after

wealed and scarred usually from the shoulders to the waist....Did the Creator intend that the noblest creatures in the visible world should live such a life as this?

Former slaves published stories of their lives. "I was abandoned to despair," wrote the freed slave Olaudah Equiano, describing his journey across the Atlantic Ocean on a slave ship:

I now saw myself deprived of all chance of returning to my native country or even the least glimpse of hope of gaining the shore....With the loathsomeness of the stench and the crying together, I became so sick and low that I was not able to eat, nor had I the least desire to taste anything. I now wished for the last friend, Death, to relieve me.

Stories like these turned more and more British against slavery. But Parliament still refused to make slavery illegal. English merchant ships made too much money selling slaves!

Abolitionists in the United States had an even harder job in front of them. The Constitution of the United States itself said that slaves weren't really people!

In 1776, the Declaration of Independence had announced, "All men are created equal...they are endowed by their Creator with certain inalienable rights...among these are Life, Liberty, and the pursuit of happiness." But when the United States Constitution was written less than ten years later, the delegates had decided that an African slave was not really a person. In fact, the delegates agreed that, when states counted their people, five slaves would count as three whole people. Each African slave was worth only three-fifths of a white person!

Why?

In the northern states, many people believed that slavery should be against the law. Few people in the North owned slaves—or needed them. But farmers in the South made their living selling cotton and tobacco. Both of those crops needed hundreds of workers to plant, tend, and harvest them. Southerners wanted slavery to stay legal so that their farms would survive!

338

But even though the North believed that slaves should be free, northern delegates suggested that a slave should be worth only three-fifths of a white person. You see, because there were so many slaves in the South, southern states had more people than northern states. If southern states got to elect one member to the House of Representatives for every thirty thousand people, the South would have many more members in the House of Representatives. The South would have more power than the North! If a slave were only three-fifths of a person, though, the South wouldn't have as many representatives.

So American abolitionists argued that Americans in both the South *and* the North were guilty of the evil of slavery. When the abolitionist Angela Grimke went to Philadelphia to give an anti-slavery speech, she began,

> As a Southerner, I feel that it is my duty to stand up here to-night and bear testimony against slavery. I have seen it…I know it has horrors that can never be described…. Nothing but the corrupting influence of slavery on the hearts of the Northern people can induce them to [make excuses] for it….I fled to the land of Penn; for here, thought I, sympathy for the slave will surely be found. But I found it not….We may talk of occupying neutral ground, but on this subject, in its present attitude, there is no such thing as neutral ground. He that is not for us is against us!

Abolitionists held rallies, describing the evils of slavery. Freed slaves told stories of their lives in bondage. Anti-slavery songs were sung to the tunes of familiar hymns. One song began,

> Come join the Abolitionists,
> Ye young men bold and strong,
> And with a warm and cheerful zeal,
> Come help the cause along.
> Come join the Abolitionists,
> Ye dames and maidens fair,
> And breathe around us in our path
> Affection's hallowed air;

O that will be joyful, joyful, joyful,
O that will be joyful, when all shall proudly say,
This, this is Freedom's day,
Oppression flee away!

Abolitionists in both countries knew that the slave trade—the buying and selling of slaves from Africa—had to be outlawed before slavery itself would become illegal. In England, a member of Parliament named William Wilberforce asked the rest of Parliament to outlaw the slave trade, no matter what the cost. "I mean not to accuse any one," Wilberforce told Parliament, "but to take the shame upon myself, in common, indeed, with the whole parliament of Great Britain, for having suffered this horrid trade to be carried on under their authority. We are all guilty….[But the opportunity to make money] can draw a film across the eyes, so thick, that total blindness could do no more….A trade founded in iniquity must be abolished…. let the consequences be what they will."

Wilberforce argued for nineteen years before Parliament agreed to make the slave trade illegal. The law, passed in 1807, didn't do away with slavery. But it said that no English ships could buy slaves in Africa and then sell them in other countries. In 1808, the United States passed the same law.

It took another twenty-six years for Great Britain to outlaw slavery. Finally, in 1833, Parliament made slavery illegal by passing the Emancipation Act. The law was voted on just three days before William Wilberforce died. When he heard the news, he exclaimed, "Thank God that I have lived to witness the day in which England is willing to give £20 million for the abolishment of slavery."

The abolition of slavery cost Britain at least twenty million pounds! As soon as the law went into effect, plantations began to break up. Without free hands to work the land, planters began to go bankrupt. They could no longer afford to grow sugar, coffee, cotton, and tobacco.

But the English could still buy these things from American plantations—because slavery would be legal in the United States for years to come.

340

Africa in the Early Nineteenth Century

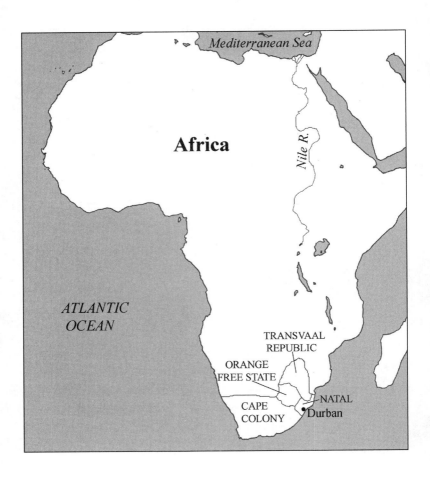

Chapter Thirty-Seven
Troubled Africa

The Zulu Kingdom

While the colonies of Central and South America fought against Spain, a much bigger war was going on somewhere else in the world. In this war, two million people died during ten years of fighting. But except for two Englishmen, we might not know anything about this war or the people who died in it.

This war took place in Africa. Few Europeans had trekked into the mysterious center of Africa. They called this huge land the "dark continent" because when Europeans peered into Africa's history, they felt as though they were peering into a dark room. For thousands of years, African tribes had lived through feasts, harvests, wars, kings, catastrophes, victories, births, weddings, deaths, and everything else that people in Europe lived through. But because African tribes did not use writing to record their history, much of this history is lost to the West. We know the most about the African tribes and rulers who fought with Western countries, traded with Western merchants, or spoke to Western travelers—because sometimes the soldiers, travelers, and explorers wrote their experiences down.

In 1824, two English merchants landed on the coast of South Africa and met hunters from an African tribe. When they asked the hunters for permission to build a trading post, the hunters took them to see their ruler: Shaka, King of the Zulus. Shaka thought the two Englishmen were harmless enough, so he granted them enough land to build their little settlement. The English merchants named their trading post Durban. They were fascinated by the Zulu people and the Zulu language. They learned enough Zulu to speak with Shaka and his warriors. They discovered that the tribe was called Zulu after their word for the sky; the Zulu believed that they were the descendants of a young man who had once lived in the sky but had been sent to earth because he caused trouble for the sky-god once too often.

They also learned that Shaka, the Zulu king, had caused trouble for all of South Africa.

Shaka's mother, a princess named Nandi, had married the son of a nearby Zulu chieftain. Soon, she and her new husband, Sezangakhon, were expecting a baby.

But Sezangakhon's family muttered about his new wife. Her clan was too closely related to her husband's! It was against the custom of the Zulus for two people from related clans to marry each other. Sezangakhon's family and people refused to welcome Nandi. By the time her baby was born, Nandi was too unhappy to stay with her husband any longer. She took the little boy and went back to live with her own family.

But her family was angry as well. They treated Nandi like a disgrace. The other little boys taunted Shaka. As he grew, the older men criticized him and laughed at him. Finally, Nandi's family told her to take her son and leave. Nandi and Shaka traveled away from the angry Zulus, to live in another kingdom called Mtetwa.

In Mtetwa, Shaka grew taller and stronger. He learned to fight, and served the king of Mtetwa as a soldier. When Shaka's father Sezangakhon died, the Mtetwa king sent Shaka to go and take over his father's kingdom.

Shaka, hardened by war, arrived at the Zulu village where Sezangakhon had once ruled. With the power of the Mtetwa army behind him, Shaka seized command without opposition. Now he set out to build his own army—an army that would obey him without question. One day, Shaka would prove that he was not the child of a despised woman but a king who should be feared!

First, Shaka changed the weapons that his father's soldiers used. The Zulu army had always fought with spears, which they hurled from a distance. Using throwing spears, the soldiers could only attack once; then their spears were gone, so they had to run away! Shaka ordered them to fight with short stabbing spears instead, so that they would have to grapple with the enemy face to face. He sent them to walk on thorns with their bare feet, so that their soles would be tough enough to run over any rough land. He gave them uniforms to wear. He divided them into four sections and taught them to attack in the same order during each battle: the first group would attack the enemy from the front and fight up close; the second and third groups would run around both sides of the enemy and attack from the back; the fourth group would wait nearby to strengthen whichever group seemed to be losing strength. They were ordered to sit with their backs to the battle, so that they wouldn't become so excited that they joined in before they were needed!

When his new, disciplined army was ready, Shaka sent them against their first target: the men from his mother's family who had thrown Nandi out. He found all of the men who had laughed at him when he was a child and killed them first! Then he turned his army, marched back to Mtetwa, and murdered the king.

Now Shaka was ready to spread his rule across all of south Africa.

He began his campaigns in 1818. For the next ten years, Shaka's warriors terrified the tribes throughout the south and center of Africa! The Africans called this the *mfecane,* which in Zulu means "The Crushing." Today, it is sometimes called the Time of Troubles. Villages were destroyed. Tribes were shattered. The traditional structure of Africa's tribal kingdoms was no more. Tribes packed up and fled away from the advancing Zulu warriors. As they fled, they searched for new land, attacking and driving away other tribes to claim their villages. During the mfecane, the African tribes were like falling dominos: each tribe, driven out of its land, attacked and destroyed another tribe. Two million Africans died in the mfecane.

In 1827, Shaka's mother Nandi died. Shaka had always been violent and uncontrollable, but now he went mad. He raged through his country, killing his own subjects. He ordered that no crops be planted for a whole year, even though his people would go hungry. He forbade anyone to drink milk, because milk reminded him of a mother's love and care. He ordered that all cows with calves be killed, so that even the calves would know what it was like to lose a mother.

His warriors put up with all of this. But then Shaka began to send them out on raid after raid, farther and farther away. Each time they returned, he sent them out again without a rest. At last, the warriors, exhausted and fed up, turned against him. Two of his own half-brothers murdered Shaka. The rule of the greatest Zulu king had ended; now his half-brother Dingane would rule in his place.

The Boers and the British

Dingane did not share Shaka's anger or his desire to conquer as much of Africa as possible. But Dingane too was a warrior king. His turn to fight would come soon.

Down at the bottom of south Africa, almost a thousand miles away from the Zulu villages where Dingane reigned, lay the European settlement called Cape Colony. A hundred and fifty years before, the Dutch had built a little trading post here, so that Dutch ships heading around the African coast toward the East could stop and restock with food and water. The Dutch governor of the trading post built a fort, plowed himself a garden, and then planted an almond hedge around its edge. The almond hedge showed the edge of the Dutch land in Africa!

As the years went on, more Dutch settlers came to Cape Colony. They were given farms behind the fort, close to the coast. They grew vegetables and pastured sheep on the slopes of the African hills. These Dutch called themselves *Boers*— Dutch for "farmers." Their farms extended further and further into Africa. The nearby African tribes, the Khoikhoi and the San, tried to fight back when Boers invaded their lands. But the Dutch had guns and horses, and the Africans were forced to retreat.

Like other European colonists, the Boers used slaves to help run their farms. The sheep needed plenty of feeding, watering, shearing, and herding. The cows needed to be milked and pastured. Butter and wool had to be carried down into Cape Colony to trade for sugar, coffee, tobacco, and gunpowder. By the time that Shaka started on his conquests, there were fifteen thousand slaves in Cape Colony!

The British had always wanted to own Cape Colony. After years of skirmishing with the Dutch, occupying Cape Colony, giving it back, and then taking it again, the British finally claimed the colony for good in 1820. English settlers began to arrive. An English governor now ruled over the colony.

The Boers hated British rule, and they weren't fond of the English colonists who were settling down nearby. But when Britain declared slavery illegal in all of its islands and colonies, that was the last straw. The Dutch didn't think that they could manage without their slaves.

Between 1835 and 1843, ten thousand Boers left Cape Colony. They put their furniture, their goods, their families, and their slaves into wagons pulled by oxen and set off into the unknown depths of Africa, looking for another place to settle down. This journey was called the Great Trek of the Boers. It was a hard and perilous trip, but the Boers had been toughened by life on their sheep farms. The British writer Sir Arthur Conan Doyle, who invented Sherlock Holmes, lived in the days when the Boers were settling south Africa. He called these Boers the "most rugged...unconquerable" people on earth. "Take a community of Dutchmen," he wrote, "...who defended themselves for fifty years against all the power of Spain.... Intermix with them a strain of those inflexible French....Train them for seven generations in constant warfare against savage men and ferocious beasts, in circumstances under which no weakling could survive, place them so that they acquire exceptional skill with weapons and in horsemanship.... Combine all these qualities...in one individual, and you have the modern Boer....Napoleon and all his veterans have never treated us so roughly as these hard-bitten farmers!"

The hard-bitten Boers traveled into Africa through the wasteland left by Shaka's soldiers. When they reached

Dingane's territory, they were pleased with what they saw. This could be their new homeland!

Dingane didn't want them there on the edge of his kingdom, but he was wary of their horses and guns. The Boers settled down, unpacked their wagons, and started to build new farms. A small party of them struck out toward the village where Dingane lived, hoping to make friends with the Zulu.

Dingane ordered them all put to death.

That was a mistake! The Boers gathered themselves together for the attack. But they didn't rely on their guns alone. Boer leaders found out that one of Dingane's half-brothers, Mpande, hoped to be king. They promised Mpande that they would make him king of the Zulu if he would fight on their side!

With Mpande's help, the Boers fought several bloody battles with the Zulu. The most famous took place on the banks of the Ncome River. Later, the Boers claimed that the blood of fallen Zulu warriors turned the river red! The battle became known as the Battle of Blood River.

This defeat settled Dingane's fate. He fled from the Boers and disappeared into the heart of Africa. The Zulu hostility was broken. The Boers settled down near Durban, where the two English merchants had established their trading post. They called their new home Natal.

Four years later, the British claimed Natal from the Boers too. The Boers traveled back toward the center of the continent. When their journeys were over, they had established two more nations in Africa: the Orange Free State and the Transvaal Republic. South Africa was slowly becoming a land filled with white settlers—and their slaves.

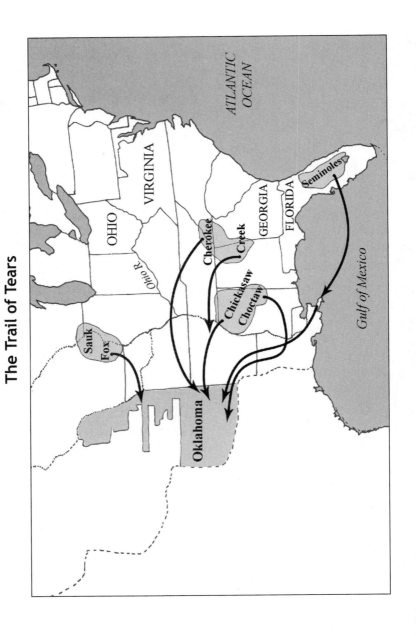

The Trail of Tears

Chapter Thirty-Eight
American Tragedies

The Trail of Tears

When the Boers settled in the southern African plains, they drove away the native tribes who lived there. But over in the United States, the American government had a different way of doing things. If American settlers wanted to build their houses on land where Native American tribes lived, they were supposed to pay for the land and sign a treaty explaining that the Native Americans had agreed to sell it.

Often, the Native Americans weren't given much choice. And they were hardly ever paid enough money for their land. White settlers bought entire forests and farms with handfuls of cheap jewelry and a few pounds of tobacco. But at least the settler who handed over the jewelry had to admit that the Native American tribe had "owned" the land first!

By 1830, more and more Americans wanted to "buy" land from the Native Americans who lived in the Ohio Valley and in the southeast states. The United States was growing. Settlers coming from Europe, called *immigrants,* didn't want to go all the way out to the empty western lands of the Louisiana Purchase, where there were no roads or stores or doctors. They wanted to settle near cities and rivers.

But the Native American tribes who lived on the valuable land in the Southeast and Midwest were too slow to hand those lands over. Many tribes refused to sell any of their land at all!

So the President of the United States, Andrew Jackson, signed a law called the Indian Removal Act. The Indian Removal Act said that the President could now take Native American land without asking for it or paying for it, as long as he gave the Native Americans who lived there an equal amount of land in the unsettled prairies of the west.

351

The Indian Removal Act seemed like a good idea to Congress and President Jackson. For over a hundred years, whites and Native Americans had quarreled, fought, and killed each other. Now, white settlers could live near each other, and the Native Americans could have their own part of the country, further away.

But to the Native American tribes, the Indian Removal Act meant that they would lose their homes—without any way of getting them back. Many Native Americans had begun to follow white customs. For years, they had lived in log houses, growing fruit trees and planting gardens. Their children went to schools run by white missionaries. Many Native Americans wore European clothes and had taken English names. In the Southeast, five Indian tribes—the Chickasaw, Choctaw, Seminole, Cherokee, and Creek—had been nicknamed the "Five Civilized Tribes," because so many of them lived just like white settlers. Cherokee Indians had their own towns, with stores and churches. They published a newspaper written in both Cherokee and English. Cherokee Indians married white men and women and had children. Cherokee chiefs had adopted English names, like John Ross and David Vann. Some Cherokee even owned plantations and kept African slaves to work the land. They were no longer the same people who had once roamed through the forests, moving their tents and carrying their belongings with them.

But the Indian Removal Act decreed that all must go!

Some of the Five Civilized Tribes decided that they could not fight the United States government. The Chickasaw loaded wagons, preparing to leave. The Choctaw Indians began their journey west in the middle of the winter, the year after the Act was passed. The government had promised to give them money to buy food and clothes during the journey, but the money never arrived. The Choctaw ran out of blankets and coats. Many trudged toward their new homes barefoot, in the snow.

The Creek Indians refused to go. So United States soldiers came to their homes, chained them together, and marched them toward the west. Hungry, cold, and loaded down with chains, thirty-five hundred Creek Indians died before reaching the new Indian territory.

The Cherokee and the Seminole tribes fought the hardest to keep their homes. Down in Florida, the Seminole picked up weapons and went to war. It took the United States seven years to defeat the Seminole and drive them out of Florida. The seven-year fight is now known as the Second Seminole War.

The Cherokee Indians tried fighting in a different way. They went to court to keep their homes. Judges heard them argue that they deserved to live on their own farms. The court hearings dragged on for almost eight years. But the governor of Georgia, where many Cherokee lived, didn't bother to wait for the judges' decisions. He divided up the Cherokee land and started to give it out to settlers who had won a lottery.

Finally, seven hundred soldiers invaded the Cherokee lands in Georgia, broke down the doors of Cherokee cabins and plantation houses, and chased the families who lived there outside. "They were dragged from their houses," wrote a Baptist minister who had watched the invasion, "...allowed no time to take anything with them except the clothes they had on....It is the work of war in the time of peace." They were herded into camps where they were organized into bands for the long walk west. Meanwhile, white settlers—and their own neighbors—looted their

A Cherokee Indian

houses and farms, stealing their furniture, clothes, jewelry, books, dishes, and silverware! Even the soldiers who guarded them felt sick with anger over their actions. "When I went into the army," one of them muttered, "nobody told me I'd have to herd people like cattle." "I [have seen] men shot to pieces [in war] by the thousands," another soldier wrote later, "but the Cherokee Removal was the cruelest work I ever knew."

In June of 1838, the Cherokee were marched toward the new Indian Territory in Oklahoma, eight hundred miles away. On this long, wretched journey, they marched through drought, dying of thirst. Measles and other diseases began to spread along the long line. "Almost every child and many grown persons…are sick with the whooping cough," a soldier wrote, two weeks into the journey.

They marched until winter came and snow howled down on them. At night, they camped in the open, with nothing but blankets and campfires to keep them warm: no tents, no shelter. A white traveler passing by wrote, "We found the poor Cherokee Indians camped for the night by a road side, under a severe fall of rain, with…the cold wet ground for a resting place after the fatigue of the day….We learned from the inhabitants on the road where the Indians passed, that they buried fourteen or fifteen at every stopping place." More weak and sick Cherokee lay down to rest and never got up. Every morning, the Cherokee had to bury their own dead before marching on.

It took the Cherokee nation a year to walk to Oklahoma. One out of every four Cherokee died on the journey. The Cherokee called their journey *nunna-da-ul-tsun-yi,* or "The road where we cried." Today, this journey is called the Trail of Tears.

Nat Turner's Revolt

The Seminole Indians weren't the only Americans to rebel against their own countrymen. In the southern states of America, slaves worked from early until late on plantations.

They had little food, no beds, no rest. They were whipped if they disobeyed their overseers. Their brothers, sisters, fathers and mothers might be sold at any time and taken away, never to be seen again. Slaves in the American south had even less freedom than the Cherokee Indians!

When the slaves on the island of Saint Domingue revolted and killed their masters, plantation owners in the south shuddered with fear. What if their own slaves got ideas about freedom—and banded together in rebellion? Planters who heard stories of Toussaint L'Ouverture and his victories checked their ammunition and kept their guns nearby. They watched their slaves carefully for any sign of rebellion. Every Sunday, they sent all their slaves to church, where a white preacher told them that God wanted all slaves to obey their masters without question.

But on Sunday evenings, the slaves held their own church services. They sang songs about freedom and about God's judgment on cruel wrongdoers. Black ministers preached about a coming time of freedom when God would heal all the suffering of the slaves!

One of these black ministers was a slave named Nat Turner. For as long as he could remember, Nat Turner had worked on a Virginia plantation. But he also believed that he had been called by God to lead other slaves to freedom. His owner, Thomas Moore, let Nat Turner travel around to nearby villages and preach to other slaves. Nat preached about the visions God had given him. "I saw white spirits and black spirits engaged in battle!" he preached. "The blood flowed in streams….The great day of judgment is at hand!"

Thomas Moore thought that Nat was probably preaching about the end of the world, described in the book of Revelation. He didn't really listen all that closely anyway. Why shouldn't slaves get together and worship? Religion would make them better slaves. They'd work harder and be more obedient!

But Nat Turner's preaching was preparing the slaves to rise up and fight. Turner told them that he had heard a voice like thunder, telling him to lead them into battle against their masters.

In February of 1831, Nat Turner was mending a fence. The pale February sun shone down on his hands as he bent and twisted wire back into place. Nat squinted. It wasn't even near sunset, but the light seemed to be fading. He could barely see the wire.

He looked over his shoulder. The sun was fading from sight. A little at a time, a black circle moved across it. Soon, the whole farm was plunged into an eerie greenish darkness.

The moon had moved between the sun and the earth in a *solar eclipse*. But to Nat Turner, the eclipse was a sign. It was time to break free—just like the slaves of Haiti had done, not long before. Nat Turner could read a little bit. He knew about Toussaint and about Napoleon's armies. Now he would form his own army, with lieutenants and soldiers who would fight for the freedom of the slaves.

Nat began to make his plans. One by one, he told other slaves that he was forming an army. They met in secret in barns, in cellars, and out in the woods. The word spread to slaves on other plantations. They drew maps of all of the nearby houses and farms. Nat chose a slave nicknamed "Hercules" to be his second in command. Hercules was huge—a giant among the slaves, taller than any white man nearby!

Late on the night of Sunday, August 21st, 1831, Nat Turner met Hercules and five other slave leaders at a pond. Later, Nat Turner's friends said that he made a speech. "It is necessary that all the whites we meet die," he told his lieutenants. "Ours is not a war for robbery. It is a struggle for freedom. Spare no one."

Then the seven men picked up axes and knives and started out.

First they went to the house where the family of Nat Turner's master lived. They killed everyone in the house. Then they walked in silence down the road to the next house and killed the farmer who lived there. And to the next house. And the next.

The group of rebels grew. Now there were fifteen armed men. They split into two groups and attacked more houses.

By ten o'clock the next morning, Nat Turner's army had forty men in it, all waving axes or guns. By noon, the whole county was in a panic. More than fifty whites lay dead! White men were yelling for their guns. Church bells rang. Riders thundered along the roads, headed to find reinforcements. And in the middle of the noise, the slaves were cheering, dancing, and shouting for joy!

Nat Turner, now called "General Turner" by his men, hoped to ride into the nearby town of Jerusalem, Virginia. There, he could establish headquarters and hold off white soldiers who might arrive. But his men had been drinking brandy all morning. They were moving slower and slower. Before Turner could get them into the town, an armed band of slaveholders came riding up behind him. In the gunfire, Turner and his men fled into the woods and hid.

Turner hoped that the next morning he would be able to reassemble his army. But his men were too scattered. One by one, they were captured. Nat Turner slipped deeper and deeper into the woods. Soon, he had disappeared.

Panic ruled in Virginia. Where was Nat Turner? Was he going to come back in the middle of the night with an even larger army? Whites, frightened and angry, began to kill their slaves. Over a hundred and twenty black men and women who had nothing to do with Nat's attack were murdered. His captured men were convicted and hung.

For two months, Nat Turner remained free. He was living in the swamps nearby, finding food in the woods, hoping that somehow he could again raise an army and fight for freedom. But a white farmer out hunting stumbled across Turner one morning as he crawled out of the ditch where he had been sleeping. Nat Turner was captured and taken back into the nearest town.

Before he was tried, convicted, and executed, Turner told his side of the story to his lawyer, Thomas Gray. Gray wrote Turner's story down and published it as *The Confessions of Nat Turner, Leader of the late Insurrection in Southhampton, Virginia.*

"My mother and grandmother always told me I was intended for some great purpose," Nat Turner told Gray. "The Lord had shown me things that had happened before my birth. Knowing the influence I had obtained over the minds of my fellow servants...I now began to prepare them for my purpose, by telling them something was about to happen that would terminate in fulfilling the great promise that had been made to me....I should arise and prepare myself and slay my enemies with their own weapons."

Two weeks later, Nat Turner was hanged. His rebellion hadn't freed the slaves. Instead, they were worse off than ever! Their owners were terrified of another revolt. Laws were passed keeping slaves from meeting together in groups of more than three. Black ministers were told that they couldn't preach to their congregations. Anyone who taught a slave to read or write would be punished by a year in jail. Free African-Americans suffered too. They were not allowed to own guns or to meet together at night unless at least three white men were present at all times.

All of these laws were meant to keep slaves from plotting rebellion. But many Americans realized that unless slavery were brought to an end, more bloodshed would happen. "I foresee," one of them mourned, "that this land must one day or another become a field of blood."

China During the First Opium War

Chapter Thirty-Nine
China Adrift

The First Opium War

, George Macartney, the English ambassador to the court of Chi'en-lung, had called China an old ship drifting toward shore, ready to be broken to pieces. In the last years of Chi'en-lung's reign, China began to drift closer to destruction.

The old emperor gave more and more power to his favorite army officer, Ho-Shen. He arranged a marriage between Ho-shen's son and his own daughter. He let Ho-Shen be responsible for carrying out all of his orders. Ho-shen spent those years taking bribes and forcing government officials to pay him money. Everyone at the Chinese court knew that Ho-Shen was a corrupt liar. But Chi'en-lung wouldn't let anyone complain about his Ho-Shen.

At the end of his sixtieth year on the throne of China, the emperor announced that he would give the throne over to his fifth son, Pinyin Jiqing. His ancestor, K'ang-hsi, had ruled for sixty-one years; Chi'en-lung believed that it would be disrespectful to rule longer than the greatest Manchu ruler.

Pinyin Jiqing was crowned emperor and took the royal name Chia-ch'ing. But he didn't actually get to rule the country. Even though Chi'en-lung was eighty-four years old, he held on to the real power in China.

Finally, Chi'en-lung died at the age of eighty-seven. Immediately, Chia-ch'ing arrested Ho-Shen and took away all of his property. "I'm not going to execute you," he told Ho-Shen, "out of respect for my father, who loved you. I'll allow you to commit honorable suicide instead." Ho-Shen, trapped, agreed to kill himself.

Even though Ho-Shen was gone, the government he left behind him was almost bankrupt and full of corruption. Chinese officials were used to taking bribes. The royal treasury was almost empty. The peasants were paying high taxes so that China's government officials could spend money on themselves.

Chia-ch'ing tried to clean up the mess Ho-Shen had left. But the government of China was so huge and there were so many dishonest officials all over the country that Chia-ch'ing didn't get very far. When he died, he was the most hated emperor of his dynasty. And the government was still full of corruption and bribe-takers!

His heir, Tao-kung, inherited an empty treasury. The dikes along the Yellow River needed repair—but all the money for repairs had been embezzled! Tao-kung had to spend less of his own money on meals and clothes for the royal court, so that China would have enough money to repair the dikes.

But Tao-kung faced an even bigger problem: Opium.

Opium had been illegal for years. But more Chinese were addicted to opium than ever. Eighteen thousand chests of opium came into China every year! Because it was illegal, it had to be brought into the country by pirates—or by British merchants who were smuggling it in while pretending to sell other goods. In 1832, a British merchant named William Jardine bought a whole fleet just to smuggle opium. His "opium clippers" didn't just sail into Canton. He sent them into other ports as well. This was doubly illegal: the British weren't supposed to trade at other Chinese ports!

The Chinese poured silver into the pockets of opium merchants from Britain and pirates from other countries. They spent so much money on opium that China started to run short of silver coins!

One of Tao-kung's officials suggested, "Why don't we just make opium legal? Then we could grow it ourselves. All that silver would come to us and stay in China."

But Tao-kung hated opium. Instead, he turned to one of his trusted officials, a man named Lin Zexu. Lin Zexu's nickname was "Blue Sky" because he was as honest and pure as a cloudless summer sky! Tao-kung gave Lin Zexu the job of finding and arresting opium dealers and stopping the trade in opium. "Sever the trunk from the roots," Tao-kung told Lin Zexu.

Lin Zexu knew that meant he had the power to take whatever action he wanted. He could have opium dealers arrested; and at once, he sent out orders for sixty Chinese opium merchants to be thrown in jail. But he knew that in order to wipe out opium, he had to stop the British from bringing it into the country.

Lin Zexu went to the port of Canton and sent a message to the British whose ships sat at anchor. Unless all the opium on every ship in Canton was handed over, no trade would be allowed at all at any Chinese port—ever. And any British merchant found trading in opium afterward would be arrested and put to death at once.

The merchants in Canton didn't want to risk losing their right to sail into China's only harbor. As night fell, they argued among themselves over what to do.

When morning came and the sun rose over Canton's harbor, the merchants came out onto the decks of their ships—to see giant posters on every wall, each one repeating Lin Zexu's command. Chinese soldiers, thousands of them, stood on every roof, aiming ancient firearms into the harbor, directly at the merchants down below.

The merchants agreed to hand over their opium—twenty thousand chests full! Lin Zexu ordered three enormous holes dug near the water. The opium was dumped into the holes and dissolved in water. Then the holes were flooded, washing the opium soup away. It took three weeks to dissolve all the opium and wash it out into the ocean!

Back in London, the British government decided that the time had come for war. British warships would *force* China to open *all* of its ports—to whatever Britain wanted to sell.

The Chinese had no warships (and not much of a navy). But the British had spent the last hundred years fighting at sea. They sailed enormous battleships, powered by steam, into Canton. Until the Chinese surrendered, no ships would come in or out of this port!

In 1842, the Chinese finally gave in. They signed the Treaty of Nanjing, which they called the "unequal treaty." It gave Great Britain everything the British wanted and gave China nothing! China had to pay Great Britain twenty-one million dollars for the opium that had been destroyed. They had to agree to open up five more ports for British ships to trade in. The Chinese had to allow English merchants to build settlements and live in China year round. The whole island of Hong Kong, off China's southern coast, had to be given to the British. And China had to agree to make the same treaty with France and the United States.

The Kingdom at the Center of the World no longer had the freedom to turn its back on other nations. Now, like India, it would follow Britain's orders.

North America During the Mexican-American War

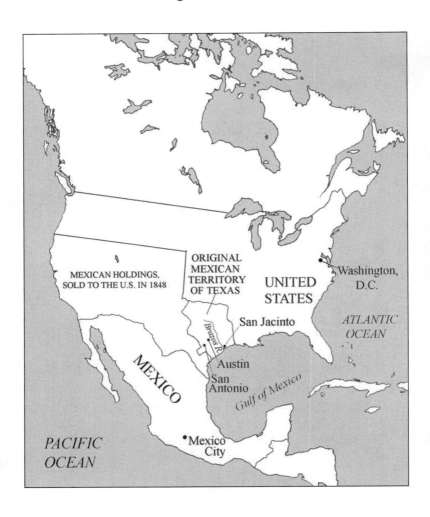

Chapter Forty
Mexico and Her Neighbor

Remember the Alamo

The brand new republic of Mexico had a problem. It had barely been free from Spain for ten years. And already, one of its states was rebelling against *Mexico*!

Texas, the Mexican state farthest to the north, was home to Mexicans—but it was home to even more people of English descent, called *Anglos*. Back when New Spain still belonged to the Spanish empire, an American banker named Moses Austin and his son made an agreement with Spain that would allow American settlers to live in the northern part of the Spanish colony. These American settlements in the Spanish land were called *empresarios*.

Now that Mexico was free, the congress made another agreement with the United States so that American settlement could continue. The empresarios were good for Mexico. Few people lived in the dry, hot plains; American settlers would build prosperous new towns in this empty part of Mexico and pay plenty of taxes to the Mexican government. The United States agreed that any Americans settling in Mexico would become citizens of Mexico, convert to Catholicism (the official religion of Mexico), and obey Mexican law.

But as time went on, Mexicans began to be annoyed with the empresarios. So many Americans had settled in Texas that now more Texans spoke English than Spanish. The Americans did pay their taxes—but many of them refused to be Catholic or follow Mexican laws. Worst of all, Americans insisted on bringing their slaves to Texas, even though slavery was illegal in Mexico! When Congress objected, most of the Americans just ignored them.

In 1830, Mexico announced that no more Americans could come into Texas to live. The Americans in Texas didn't like this order. It seemed that the congress of Mexico was behaving like that old English parliament again, telling them what to do without asking them for their opinion!

Back in Mexico City, the Mexican president was defeated in an election by the popular general Antonio López de Santa Anna. Just a year later, Santa Anna made himself the dictator of Mexico! Santa Anna wanted all of Mexico to obey him without question. And he thought that the Anglos up in Texas were too independent. He ordered a new law passed: No one in Texas could have a gun unless the Mexican government gave them permission. Any Texan who owned an illegal gun would be convicted of piracy and hung!

The Texans were furious. Everyone in Texas had guns! They hunted for game and protected themselves from wild animals with their guns. Texans refused to follow Santa Anna's new gun law. All over Texas, settlers began to talk about fighting for their freedom against Santa Anna. They started to collect weapons together and to form little *garrisons* (gatherings of armed men) all over Texans.

One of these garrisons remembered that, years before, a nearby settlement had been given a cannon to defend itself from attack by Native Americans. The settlement hadn't needed the cannon for years. As a matter of fact, they'd buried it in a big pit! Now, they dug it back up again and cleaned it out. No cannonballs were left, so the Texans stuffed chains and pieces of iron into it instead!

The nearest Mexican army outpost demanded that the Texans give up the cannon. The Texans refused. Mexican soldiers marched to the garrison to take it away. When they arrived, they found the Texans ready for a fight, waving a flag that said, "Come and Take It!"

The Mexicans backed away. But as far as the Texans were concerned, the war with Mexico had begun. Signs went up all through the empresarios. "Freemen of Texas! To arms! To arms!" the signs read. "Now's the day and now's the hour!"

Texans armed with guns and cannons took over the southern towns of San Antonio and Gonzales. Meanwhile, fifty-nine delegates from all over Texas met together in a settlement on the northern Brazos river. They called this settlement, their new capital city, Washington-on-the-Brazos, after the capital city of the United States. Together, the delegates wrote a constitution for Texas. They voted to make a huge, quick-tempered frontiersman named Sam Houston the general of the new Texas army.

It took Sam Houston weeks to gather an army. Meanwhile, Santa Anna had ordered his army to march north into Texas. Sam Houston sent a message to the Texans of the south. "Hold out as best you can!" Houston ordered them. "We'll come as soon as we're able."

The Texans at San Antonio, closest to the border, prepared for war. Some of the best fighters in Texas had gathered here. Jim Bowie was so famous for his bravery and daring that a hunting knife, the Bowie knife, had been named after him; he had ridden alligators in Louisiana, sailed with pirates in the ocean nearby, and mined for gold in Texas. Davy Crockett, a Tennessee frontiersman who had fought against the Creek Indians, came down to help out too.

By early February, the little group of soldiers in San Antonio had grown to 189. They thought that Santa Anna's army was still weeks away. But Santa Anna was just over the river, a few miles away! When the commander of the San Antonio fighters, William Travis, realized that Mexican soldiers would arrive in just a few hours, he ordered all of his soldiers into the nearby fort. This fort, built years before by Catholic priests as a *mission* (a center for Catholic worship), had a wall around it. The Texans called it the Alamo.

On February 23rd, 1836, the Mexican army reached the Alamo. Four thousand Mexican soldiers surrounded the 189 Texan rebels. Santa Anna ran up a red flag over his men. This was a military code that meant, "Surrender without conditions!"

The Texans refused. William Travis sent a rider from the fort, carrying a letter that appealed for help. "To the people of Texas," he wrote, "...the enemy has demanded a surrender...I have answered the demand with a cannon shot, and our flag still waves proudly from the walls. I shall never surrender or retreat....I call upon you in the name of Liberty...to come to our aid....If this call is neglected, I am determined to sustain myself as long as possible and die like a soldier who never forgets what is due his own honor and that of his country. VICTORY OR DEATH."

But no one was close enough to come. For twelve days and nights, the Texans fired at the Mexican army while the Mexicans shot cannonballs into the Alamo. On the thirteenth day of the siege, the Mexican soldiers made a final attack. They climbed the walls and poured into the fort. Texans and Mexicans fought with swords and knives up and down the stairs of the fort, in its dark hallways and tunnels. In less than half an hour, all of the Texans were dead. The 189 men had killed 600 Mexican soldiers and wounded hundreds more.

The Alamo had fallen. But all across Texas, Texans rose up to fight against Santa Anna. "Remember the Alamo!" they shouted as they gathered together, with Sam Houston in their lead. Santa Anna had captured San Antonio, but his plan to capture Texas was doomed.

The Mexican-American War

Santa Anna was angry. The Mexican state of Texas was filled with American settlers who refused to obey him. His army had captured San Antonio, but towns all over the north of Texas were filled with Sam Houston's men. "If they fight against me," Santa Anna snarled, "I will cut them to pieces! I will march all the way to Washington and plant the flag of Mexico there!"

Santa Anna never marched an army to Washington. But the fight with Texas would soon turn into a much bigger fight: a war with the whole United States.

Santa Anna's army marched from San Antonio further into Texas, where Sam Houston waited at the town of San Jacinto with nine hundred men. Less than a month after the Alamo fell, Santa Anna camped less than a mile away from Sam Houston's army. He didn't think that the ragged Texas soldiers were much of a threat. He didn't even post watchmen at the edge of his camp! Instead, the Mexican soldiers lay down for their usual afternoon nap, called a *siesta.*

Houston's soldiers burst from the trees nearby! Mounted Texas soldiers thundered into the camp, firing their guns. Sleepy, startled Mexicans scrambled for their weapons—but it was too late. In eighteen minutes, the Texans had killed seven hundred Mexican soldiers and had captured seven hundred more. Santa Anna himself, surprised in his tent, was under guard. The Mexicans surrendered. Most of them repeated over and over, "No Alamo! No Alamo!" They didn't want the Texans to think that they had taken part in the siege of the Alamo—they might be killed at once!

Sam Houston ordered the prisoners spared. Santa Anna was forced to sign a treaty recognizing Texas as an independent republic. Then he was sent, under guard, to Washington, where President Andrew Jackson met him. "What if the United States were to buy Texas from Mexico?" Andrew Jackson suggested. "Then the fighting between Texans and Mexico could stop."

Santa Anna agreed that this might be a good plan. But the rest of Mexico didn't agree. Mexicans claimed that Santa Anna didn't have permission to sell Texas. He didn't even have permission to sign a treaty giving Texas its independence. Texas still belonged to Mexico!

The Americans politely sent Santa Anna back to Mexico and ignored these objections. The citizens of the new Republic of Texas went on behaving like an independent nation. They voted to approve their constitution and elected Sam Houston president.

For his new government, Sam Houston had a single wooden building in Austin. Texas didn't even have enough money to buy firewood to heat his office! He didn't have enough money to pay a regular army. And he knew that if Mexico attacked again, Texas might well lose.

The solution was simple: Join the United States. If Texas became a state, all of the U.S. Army would march to its defense.

Many Texans weren't anxious to give up any of their brand-new independence. And not everyone in Washington wanted Texas to join the United States. Americans who opposed slavery pointed out that Texas would be a slave-owning state. Texas was so huge that, once it became a state, the slave-holding areas of the United States would more than double! Others objected that Texans were rough, crude, violent trouble-makers.

But after ten years of arguing, the people of the Republic of Texas finally voted to join the United States—and the United States Congress agreed to accept them. "Be it resolved," Congress wrote on March 1st, 1845, "that a state, to be formed out of the present Republic of Texas…with two representatives in Congress…shall be admitted into the Union…on an equal footing with the existing states."

At once, Mexicans protested that the United States had stolen their land! Bands of Mexican and American soldiers roamed along the border between Texas and Mexico, shooting at each other. Finally, the United States declared war on Mexico. This war would do more than claim Texas. The United States planned to drive Mexico out of North America all together! Mexico still claimed to own land to the north and west of the old Texas republic; the United States would capture this territory too! "We must march from Texas straight to the Pacific Ocean!" one Congressman exclaimed.

One young congressman from Illinois disagreed. Abraham Lincoln had not served in Congress for very long. But when the United States Army marched over the Mexican border, headed toward Mexico City, Abraham Lincoln objected. It was wrong, he said, to send an army into Mexico itself, "into the midst of a peaceful Mexican settlement, frightening the inhabitants away, leaving their growing crops and other property to destruction."

Lincoln and other protestors were outvoted. United States soldiers fought their way toward Mexico City.

Santa Anna had been living quietly on a country farm in Cuba, disgraced by his defeat in Texas. But now he decided to return to Mexico. He rode through the country, begging Mexicans to follow him once more. "Once, you called me

Soldier of the People!" he shouted. "Allow me to take that title again, and I will devote myself til death to the defense of our liberty and independence!"

The Mexican army poured out to meet Santa Anna and acclaimed him as their leader. As the Americans drew close to Mexico City, Santa Anna prepared to meet them at a village nearby. He ordered his soldiers to dig trenches and build barriers around three sides of the Mexican camp. But he decided that no army could manage to cross the high hills behind the army, so he left those hills undefended.

The general commanding the United States soldiers at once sent a young captain named Robert E. Lee to climb those hills! Lee built a system of posts and ropes that the Americans could use to haul their cannons and ammunition up to the hilltops. The next morning, the Americans attacked Santa Anna's army from all sides at once! Santa Anna was forced to call a retreat.

With American soldiers pouring through the streets of Mexico City, the Mexican Congress agreed to sign a peace treaty—as long as the United States paid the Mexican government for the land it was losing. In 1848, the United States paid Mexico fifteen million dollars. In return, Mexico gave up Texas and another piece of land where California, Nevada, Utah, Arizona, Colorado, Wyoming, and part of New Mexico now lie.

A few years later, the United States paid Mexico another ten million dollars for the rest of New Mexico. The Mexican-American War was finally over. And the United States of America now held most of the land it owns today.

The Two Islands of New Zealand

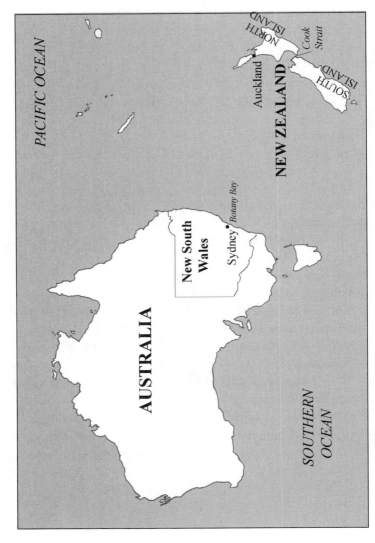

Chapter Forty-One
New Zealand and Her Rulers

The Treaty of Waitangi

The United States had *annexed* (taken for itself) land that had once belonged to France, Spain, and Mexico. While Mexican and United States soldiers were fighting over this land, another annexation was taking place on the other side of the world.

The two islands of New Zealand are about as far away from the United States as you can get. Even today, it takes over twenty hours of flying time to take a plane from Washington D.C. to New Zealand.

Not too many Americans had ever seen New Zealand. But more and more British citizens had settled on these two little islands. Whaling ships from Australia fished in the waters off New Zealand's coasts. English convicts who had finished serving their prison terms and now wanted to leave Australia came to New Zealand and built houses there.

The natives of New Zealand were friendly to the newcomers. "They are a friendly humane people," wrote one English visitor to the islands. "For fine turned Limbs & well made persons I think they cannot be excelled. The Children are in general exceeding beautiful….I have slept all Night in their houses 8 miles up the Country, without any attempt being made on me." As English colonists began to settle on their shores, the natives traded with them. They called the English *pakeha,* "white strangers," and called themselves *maori,* "ordinary people."

The settlers thought that *maori* was the proper name for the natives. But the "Maori" weren't just one people. They were a whole collection of different tribes, each with its own name and its own customs. Often, these Maori tribes fought with each other, using spears and stone axes. But now the tribes could trade game, sweet potatoes, and other food to the pakehas in exchange for guns. The tribal battlefields rang with the sound of musket fire. The smell of powder and smoke filled the air. More Maori warriors died in the battles than ever before. Wounded warriors suffered from infections caused by the musket balls—infections that traditional Maori medicine could do nothing to heal.

And the Maori also caught new diseases from the pakehas: smallpox, measles, influenza. Thousands died. In less than forty years, half the Maori were dead.

The Maori fought with each other—but so did the English settlers. New Zealand had no laws. Farmers quarreled over the boundaries of their land and over the right to use water. Missionaries who came to New Zealand to teach the Maori about Christianity saw that more and more Maori land was being stolen. And they worried about the Maori trade with the settlers. The Maori were handing over food in exchange for English alcohol and drinking themselves into illness.

Missionaries and English settlers both begged the British to come to New Zealand and make it a law-abiding place. Great Britain refused to come and lay down the law. New Zealand wasn't a British colony. The British had no right to make rules for all of its people, Maori and pakeha, to follow.

But the British suggested a solution. If the Maori would *give* New Zealand to the British, the British could make laws that would protect them from white invasion. The British promised that the Maori could keep all of their land and that British soldiers would make sure that no settlers took it away.

On February 6th, 1840, a British navy captain named Captain William Hobson met with a group of Maori leaders. Together, Hobson and the Maori signed a treaty between the Maori and Great Britain. This "Treaty of Waitangi" said that Britain would protect the property and the rights of the Maori against the British settlers. In return, the Maori would recognize England as their ruler. Hobson became the governor of New Zealand and declared it to be a British colony!

As soon as New Zealand was declared British, more settlers arrived. Most of them decided to live on the South

Island of the colony, which had plenty of grazing land for animals and good farmland for crops. In 1844, a ship brought two flocks of sheep to New Zealand from Australia. No sheep had ever been seen on the islands before. But they liked to eat the rough grass on the hillsides. Soon the two flocks had grown to hundreds of sheep. Settlers sent the wool to European ports. Many grew rich from the wool. Farmers who had claimed huge amounts of South Island land sold some of their pastures for high sums of money to newcomers—and grew even richer.

Some of the Maori decided that they too would sell their land for money. But the British governor called them to his headquarters and told them, "The treaty says that you can only sell land to the British government itself—to me. Then I can resell it to settlers."

The Maori were puzzled. They didn't know that the treaty said any such thing! The governor was offering them a low price for their land, and they could see that Britain would make a great deal of money buying Maori land for a small amount and then reselling it to settlers for much more. But the governor showed them his copy of the treaty. "There," he said. "You agreed to this condition!"

Soon the Maori realized that the Treaty of Waitangi had set many conditions that they were not aware of. There had been two versions of the treaty: an English version and a Maori one. The Maori version of the treaty had used different words from the English version. In Maori, the treaty only gave the British the right to *govern* the lands—to rule them as long as the Maori agreed with their actions. But in English the treaty said that the British had *sovereignty*, or complete control over the Maori lands. The British had annexed New Zealand—and the Maori hadn't even known!

The New Zealand Wars

On the North Island of New Zealand, a Maori chief named Hone Heke decided to take his country back.

By this time, British settlement had spread across the South Island. Most of the Maori had retreated to the North Island to live. But now the English wanted to buy land on the North Island too.

The Maori people were afraid that they wouldn't be able to keep any of the land for themselves. Many complained that the Treaty of Waitangi should be thrown out altogether. They argued that the chiefs who had signed it didn't have the authority to make decisions for all of the Maori people.

Hone Heke himself had been the first chief to sign the treaty. But now, as he looked toward the settlement of Kororareka, where the governor's house stood, he saw only one flag flying: the Union Jack of Great Britain.

Hone Heke sent men to cut down the flagpole at Kororareka. The British put the flagpole back up. The Maori cut it down again. The British put it back up. The Maori cut it down a third time. This time, when the British put the flag back up, they stationed soldiers in front of it.

So Hone Heke sent one of his men to make a fuss on the outskirts of the town. The soldiers, hearing shouts and confusion, went to see what was happening. Another one of Hone Heke's warriors ran and chopped the pole down again!

Now the governor began to worry. Would the Maori attack? He decided that, to be on the safe side, the town's British settlers should leave until he could be sure that the town was safe. So he packed the settlers onto ships anchored off New Zealand's coast.

When the Maori saw that the town lay nearly empty, they ran through it, setting it on fire. The British capital of New Zealand had been sacked! The ships pulled up anchor and sailed to another settlement, Auckland, further down the island. Some of the settlers armed themselves and waited for Auckland to be attacked. Others decided to head for Australia and wait until the conflict was over!

British soldiers armed themselves and marched toward Hone Heke's tribal grounds. But Hone Heke had been joined by another Maori chief named Kawiti. Kawiti was seventy years old. He had seen many battles fought in his day! Together, the two chiefs planned out a defense for their lands. They dug trenches so that the Maori could shoot at the British from safety. At the first big battle between the Maori and the British, 114 British soldiers were killed!

The British governor, George Grey, tried to make peace with Hone Heke. At first Heke refused. "God made this country for us," he wrote to Governor Grey. "If it were a whale, we might slice it in half. But it cannot be sliced. We will have to fight for the land that lies between us."

Governor Grey brought in more troops from Australia. The British kept on fighting. The Maori fought back. The battles raged back and forth with no clear winners. At last, Grey persuaded Hone Heke to make peace. The first Maori war, the Flagstaff War, had ended, but nothing had been settled. The Maori still resented the British presence; the British still insisted that the Treaty of Waitangi bound the Maori to obey the British governor.

Great Britain had annexed New Zealand, but their new colony wasn't firmly in their hands yet. In the next thirty years, the Maori and the British would fight a whole series of wars. Eventually, the Maori would have to give up most of their land to the British.

But they would never give up protesting. Today, the country of New Zealand is still a member of the British Commonwealth, a group of nations that once belonged to Great Britain and are still friends and allies of the British. And even today, descendents of the Maori people gather at the flagpole that Hone Heke once cut down to protest the loss of their lands.

The World in 1850

Chapter Forty-Two
The World of Forty-Nine

The Gold Rush

Jim Marshall had spent years in the wild places of the United States. He'd been born in New Jersey, but he'd struck out for the west while still a young man. Jim Marshall had marched south with the army to fight against Mexico. He'd wandered north to work as a carpenter. He'd farmed in Kansas, drifted through Missouri, and raised cattle on a California ranch. Now he had a new job. A businessman named John Sutter had hired him to build a sawmill on the American River, in the Sacramento Valley.

Jim Marshall took his tools with him and went to work. John Sutter had given him enough money to buy supplies and hire help; he'd promised that Marshall would get one-quarter of all the money the sawmill earned. Marshall hired Native American workers, a couple of white foremen, and a cook and then set up a camp on the banks of the American River. In eight months, the sawmill was up and running. River water rushed past its wheel, turning the saw blades. Marshall tested the sluice gates, watching water run beneath them. He figured that the sawmill would make a lot of money for Sutter—and for him. There were plenty of trees around to cut, and the lumber could be floated down the river and sold.

He walked over to the river's edge and stood looking around. A glint from the river's bed caught his eye. The afternoon sun bounced off the water, making it hard to see the sand and rock beneath. Marshall bent down and tried to touch the glint. His fingers closed around a pebble, "half the size and shape of a pea." He lifted it and let the water run off.

The pebble was the color of gold.

Marshall and his men sifted through the gravel and sand, looking for more yellow pebbles. Soon they had a whole handful of yellow chips and flakes. Marshall knew that the "gold" might be "fool's gold" — a worthless yellow mineral called *iron pyrite* that shone like real gold. If the yellow metal hammered out smooth, it was probably gold. If it shattered when struck, it was more likely to be iron pyrite.

Marshall put the largest pebble on a rock and smashed it with another rock. It flattened out into a thin, soft sheet.

The pebbles were pure gold.

The mill workers collected the gold bits and took them down to the local trading post to use for money. The owner of the trading post, a man named Sam Brannan, was amazed. How much gold was up there at Sutter's Mill? He went up to the mill himself to look. Sure enough, he collected a whole bottleful of gold!

Gold miners of California

Sam Brannan bought all the mining picks and gold pans he could find, went right back to his trading post, and put the tools on sale. And then he saddled up his horse and started on the hundred-mile trip to San Francisco. There, he rode through the streets, waving his bottle of gold. "There's gold at Sutter's Mill," Sam Brannan shouted to everyone who would listen. "You can get rich mighty fast! And make sure you come buy your picks and pans at Brannan's trading post, in nearby Sutterville!"

A few miners went up to the American River to find gold—and returned to San Francisco with bags of treasure. A few hundred more arrived. Then a few thousand followed them. By 1849, everyone in the United States knew about the gold at Sutter's Mill.

Because California was a new territory, anyone who was willing to travel to California could drive a stake into the ground and claim empty land as their own. This was called "staking a claim." Thousands of people raced to California to stake their claims up and down the American River. They sang songs as they traveled:

Oh, Susannah, don't you cry for me,
I've gone to California with my tin pan on my knee.

And:

Then blow, ye winds, hi-ho,
For Califor-ni-o
There's plenty of gold, so I've been told,
On the banks of the Sacramento!

In less than two years, the population of California grew from fifteen thousand people to over a hundred thousand. Most of these newcomers, or *Forty-niners*, were miners. They lived in camps on the river banks and bought supplies at the trading posts nearby. Whole towns called *boom towns* grew up around the trading posts. Miners who found gold, or "struck it rich," spent wildly in these towns. Sam Brannan's trading post sold so many supplies that Brannan became a millionaire! He owned a fifth of the land in both Sacramento and San Francisco and opened his own bank.

Thousands of miners didn't do so well. To keep hold of a claim, a miner had to stay on it. If he left for more than a week, other miners could claim his land. So miners camped in tents near their stakes, working all day to pan gold in the freezing water or chip it out of the rocky shore. Many barely found enough gold to buy food and supplies. Miners who lost their claims and their savings sometimes turned into bandits, stealing gold and claims from other miners, robbing the brand-new banks of San Francisco and Sacramento. Gangs of thieves roamed the countryside. Farmers and ranchers armed themselves to protect their land and their cattle—and to drive off miners who hoped to stake a claim in their pastures!

But the possibility of finding a huge gold deposit drew miners from all over the world. They came from China, England, France, Germany, Spain, Italy, Portugal, and Sweden. All along the California rivers, men whose countries had been at war for centuries rubbed elbows with each other in the mining camps. Over five hundred camps, with names like Dead Mule Canyon, Ground Hog Glory, Liar's Flat, Squabbletown, and Coffee Gulch, dotted California's rivers. The miners spent their days laboring on their claims and their evenings in the towns, where they drank, argued, sang, and danced. There were hardly any women in the boom towns, so when the miners danced, they danced with each other! Sometimes they finished off the evening by shooting each other.

In 1850, California and all its lawless mining camps became part of the United States of America. California was the thirty-first state to join the Union. And in 1850, it was the richest state in America!

A World of Unrest

Two hundred and fifty years earlier, the Spanish had been digging gold out of South American mines. Now, Americans dug gold from California rivers.

In the years in between, the whole world had changed. All over the world, factories were churning out goods. Cities grew up around those factories—cities with beautiful buildings and wide roads at their centers, but slums around their edges. Railroads lay from the factories through the cities, out into the country. Tracks led from the gold mines of California all through the American West. Tracks ran from one English coast to the other. Tracks even ran from Europe up into the cold icy lands of Russia!

The new republics of South America struggled with themselves, as dictators and generals tried to seize power and throw away the brand-new constitutions. In the United States, Americans who owned slaves quarreled with those who refused to believe in slavery. Englishmen in Australia and New Zealand kept a careful watch over the Aborigines and Maori, who plotted war to take their lands back. Indian soldiers in Calcutta whispered to each other about a day when they could throw off their British captains and generals. The Chinese emperor watched English merchants unload opium and longed for the day when he could drive the English out once more. In Europe, still scarred from years of war, young revolutionaries walked the streets, shouting out against the power of the old kings and noblemen who still ruled over Spain and Italy. In Russia, millions of hungry peasants cast wretched eyes on the lavish palaces of the czar and wished for food.

Soon, war would divide the United States. War would sweep over Russia and India and China. War would break Europe into fragments.

Between 1600 and 1850, the modern nations of the world—the United States, Mexico, Brazil, China, India, France, Spain, Russia, England—took shape. But over the next 150 years, the greatest conflicts the world had ever seen would shake those nations to their foundations.

Dates

1368	The first Ming dynasty emperor rules in China
1498	John Cabot disappears in the northern Atlantic
1524	Giovanni da Verrazano first sails across the Atlantic for France
1534	Jacques Cartier's first arrival in Canada
1553	Sebastian Cabot's expedition sets off on the northeast route
1555	The Peace of Augsburg allows each German state to follow its own religion
	Charles V relinquishes the title Holy Roman Empire
	Philip II inherits the throne of Spain from his father, Charles V
1556	Ferdinand I, Charles's brother, inherits Charles's lands and title
1567	Mary, Queen of Scots, is imprisoned in England
1576	Englishman Martin Frobisher sails into Frobisher's Strait
1583	Nzinga of Angola born
1587	John Davis leads an expedition to find the Northwest Passage
	Mary, Queen of Scots, is beheaded
1588	Abbas I becomes shah of Persia
1592	Hideyoshi directs Japan's first invasion of Korea
1598	Philip II of Spain dies
1603	Samuel Champlain's first arrival in Canada
	Elizabeth I dies and James I (James VI of Scotland) comes to the throne
	Ieyasu becomes shogun of Japan
1605	Jahangir (World Seizer) becomes emperor of India
1605	Ieyasu appoints his son Hidetada as shogun
1607	Jamestown colony founded in Virginia
	Henry Hudson makes his first voyage to the northeast
1608	Quebec colony founded in Canada
1611	Henry Hudson is set adrift in Hudson Bay
1614	Pocahontas marries John Rolfe

1616	Ieyasu Tokugawa dies
1618	The Thirty Years' War begins with the Bohemian revolt
1620	The *Mayflower* sets sail for the New World
1623	Sultan Murad IV comes to the throne of the Ottoman Empire
1623	Iemitsu becomes the third Tokugawa shogun
1625	Charles I becomes king of England
1627	Jahangir of India dies
1628	Shah Jahan (King of the World) becomes emperor of India
1629	Shah Abbas I of Persia dies
1633	Iemitsu closes the ports of Japan
1637	The Holy Roman Emperor Ferdinand II dies
1638	Samuel Champlain dies
1641	European traders are forbidden to enter Japan
1642	Cardinal Richelieu dies
1644	Li Tzu-ch'eng enters Peking with his army
1648	The Treaty of Westphalia ends the Thirty Years' War
1649	Charles I of England is executed
1653	Oliver Cromwell becomes Lord Protector of England
1658	Aurangzeb (Conqueror of the World) becomes emperor of India
	Oliver Cromwell dies
1660	Charles II is invited to return to England from exile in France
1661	K'ang-hsi takes the throne of Manchu China
1663	Queen Nzinga of Angola dies
1665	The Plague decimates London
1666	Shah Jahan of India dies
	The Great Fire of London
1672	Peter the Great is born
1675	King Philip's War begins on June 20
1678	The fighting ends in King Philip's War
1681	The city of Philadelphia is founded in the colony of Pennsylvania
1682	Peter the Great becomes the czar of Russia
1683	The Ottoman Turks are defeated at Vienna
	K'ang-hsi adds Taiwan to the Chinese empire

1687	Isaac Newton publishes *Principia Mathematica*
1688	Mary and William come to the English throne in the Glorious Revolution
1689	Peter the Great takes control of his throne away from Sophia
	King William's War begins
1690	Aurangzeb gives the British permission to build Calcutta
	John Locke publishes Two Treatises of Government
1696	K'ang-hsi adds Mongolia to the Chinese empire
	King William's War ends
1700	Beginning of the Great Northern War between Russia and Sweden
1701	Jethro Tull invents the seed drill
	Queen Anne's War begins
1702	Peter the Great founds St. Petersburg
1703	The Tulip Period begins in the Ottoman Empire
1707	Aurangzeb of India dies and Bahadur Shah I takes the throne
1710	Crop rotation becomes widespread, thanks to Charles Townshend
1712	Bahadur Shah I of India dies
1713	Queen Anne's War ends
1714	George Louis becomes George I of England
1715	Louis XIV dies and Louis XV becomes king of France
1719	Mohammad Shah of India comes to the throne
1722	K'ang-hsi dies
1725	Peter the Great dies
1726	Tibet becomes part of the Chinese empire
1727	George I dies and George II becomes king of England
1730	The Tulip Period ends in the Ottoman Empire
1735	Chi'en-lung becomes emperor of China
1739	The War of Jenkins' Ear begins
1744	King George's War begins
1748	Mohammad Shah of India dies
	King George's War ends
1754	The French-Indian War begins
1756	The British capture Bengal in the Battle of Plassey

1756	The Seven-Year War begins
1762	Catherine the Great is proclaimed empress of Russia
1763	The French-Indian and Seven-Year Wars end
1769	Chi'en-lung adds Burma to the Chinese empire
	James Watt receives a patent for the steam engine
1771	James Cook maps the coast of Australia
1776	James Cook starts out on his last voyage
	The North American colonies declare their independence from Great Britain
1787	The Constitutional Convention meets in Philadelphia
1789	The Estates General (representatives of France) meets in May at Versailles
	The Bastille falls on July 14
1791	The Bill of Rights is added to the American Constitution

The slaves of Saint Domingue rebel

1793	Louis XVI and Marie Antoinette are executed in France
	Eli Whitney invents the cotton gin
	George Macartney visits China
1794	The Reign of Terror in France ends with Robespierre's death
1796	Chi'en-lung of China abdicates in favor of his son
	Catherine the Great of Russia dies
	An imperial edict forbids importing opium to China
1797	Eli Whitney popularizes the ideas of standardization and interchangeable parts
1799	Napoleon becomes consul
1802	Napoleon becomes consul for life
1804	Napoleon is crowned emperor
	Lewis and Clark begin their expedition
1805	Napoleon is defeated at the Battle of Trafalgar
1806	Lewis and Clark return from the west
1807	Britain outlaws the slave trade
1808	Charles IV is deposed by Napoleon
	The United States outlaws the slave trade
1810	Argentina declares independence
	Don Miguel gives the speech, "The Cry of Dolores"
1811	Venezuela declares independence
1812	Napoleon marches into Russia

1812	The United States declares war on Britain (The War of 1812)
1814	The War of 1812 ends Napoleon is exiled to Elba
1815	Napoleon tries to regain power and is exiled to St. Helena
1818	The Time of Troubles (mfecane) begins in South Africa
1820	The British claim the South African Cape Colony
1821	Napoleon dies Mexico becomes independent
1824	Mexico becomes a republic Durban is founded on the South African coast
1828	Shaka, king of the Zulu, dies
1830	The United States passes the Indian Removal Act
1831	Nat Turner's Revolt
1833	Great Britain passes the Act of Emancipation Santa Anna declares himself dictator of Mexico
1835	The Great Trek of the Boers begins The Second Seminole War begins in Florida Texas declares its independence
1836	The Battle of the Alamo
1839	The Cherokee set off on the Trail of Tears The First Opium War begins
1842	The First Opium War ends with the Treaty of Nanjing
1845	Texas joins the United States
1846	The Mexican-American War begins
1848	The Mexican-American War ends
1849	California Gold Rush
1850	California becomes the 31st state of the United States of America

Index

C

398

F

H

M

O

P